Straight Talk about Professional Ethics

Straight Talk about Professional Ethics

THIRD EDITION

BY KIMBERLY STROM
University of North Carolina, Chapel Hill
Oxford University Press

OXFORD
UNIVERSITY PRESS

OXFORD
UNIVERSITY PRESS

Oxford University Press is a department of the University of Oxford.
It furthers the University's objective of excellence in research, scholarship,
and education by publishing worldwide. Oxford is a registered trade mark
of Oxford University Press in the UK and in certain other countries.

Published in the United States of America by Oxford University Press
198 Madison Avenue, New York, NY 10016, United States of America.

For titles covered by Section 112 of the US Higher Education Opportunity
Act, please visit www.oup.com/us/he for the latest information about
pricing and alternate formats.

Library of Congress Cataloging-in-Publication Data

Names: Strom-Gottfried, Kim, author.
Title: Straight talk about professional ethics / by Kim Strom, University
    of North Carolina, Chapel Hill.
Description: Third edition. | New York : Oxford University Press, 2022. |
    Includes bibliographical references and index. | Summary: "Social
    service professionals use a unique set of principles to guide their
    decisions within a broad and complex array of situations. Straight Talk
    about Professional Ethics provides readers with the guidelines that will
    help them make decisions in a manner that is clinically and ethically
    effective. This book explains the seven core concepts that guide ethical
    practice in the helping professions: self-determination, informed
    consent, competence, confidentiality and privacy, attention to conflicts
    of interest, maintenance of professional boundaries, and professionalism
    and integrity. Developing a commitment to the ethics of a profession and
    an understanding of how those ethics apply to commonly occurring
    workplace situations is a major element of professional preparation"—
    Provided by publisher.
Identifiers: LCCN 2022018901 (print) | LCCN 2022018902 (ebook) | ISBN
    9780197534533 (paperback) | ISBN 9780197534557 (epub) | ISBN
    9780197534540 (pdf)
Classification: LCC BJ1725 .S83 2022 (print) | LCC BJ1725 (ebook) | DDC
    174—dc23/eng/20220711
LC record available at https://lccn.loc.gov/2022018901
LC ebook record available at https://lccn.loc.gov/2022018902

Printed by Integrated Books International, United States of America

To George M. Gottfried and Smith P. Theimann, Jr.
Both lived the values of service, humility, kindness, and integrity.

CONTENTS

PREFACE

My agency has a policy against accepting gifts. Does this mean I shouldn't accept a jar of pickles when I visit my home-bound client?

The older adult male I counsel via telehealth visits is often on the video without a shirt. Is it ethical to ask him to put one on?

My client is fascinated by disturbing video games involving workplace violence. Do I have a duty to warn someone?

Is it ethical for my employer to prohibit me from attending a Black Lives Matter protest?

My teenage daughter is dating a former resident of the psych ward where I used to work. What should I do?

My client is asking me not to keep records of his treatment because he is in the military. Isn't it in his best interest if I agree with him?

I used to see a fellow professional in my mediation practice. Is it unethical for us now to refer clients to each other?

If these examples are any indication, ethics is a peculiar, complex, and high-stakes area of professional practice. Too often, though, when practitioners think of ethics, they think of high-minded philosophical discussion far removed from the challenges of their daily lives. Or they become overwhelmed considering so many options that they simply throw up their hands and say, "I'll trust my gut." Or they become so preoccupied with avoiding risk that they make their decisions guided by the question "Whom would I rather be sued by?" None of these is a recipe for sound ethical decision making. None accounts for the fact that ethical excellence and clinical excellence are intertwined. None of these gives credence to the standards of professional practice exemplified in our codes of ethics.

This book discusses risk but is not driven by it. It examines the ethical standards governing social work practice as they might be applied in a variety of situations. It offers a nimble, useful framework for considering ethical dilemmas to help you develop your capacity for critical thinking in arriving at ethically sound decisions. It equips you, the reader, with well-grounded tools to use in preventing ethical difficulties or in weighing options if ethical challenges do arise. It acknowledges and addresses the fact that often the challenge of ethics lies in having the courage to do the right thing, and not simply the ability to discern the right thing. It is written in a lively and conversational manner intended to make ethics accessible to students and experienced practitioners alike. It employs practical guidance, sound resources, and authentic cases featuring an array of roles, settings, and issues. It doesn't just present dilemmas, but also guides you through the critical thinking needed to resolve them. It doesn't just stick to the easy right–wrong dilemmas, either. Together, we'll address the spectrum of ethical challenges, including the challenges in choosing between competing "goods" and competing "bads." While many of the dilemmas are drawn from direct practice examples, the book covers a variety of ethical dilemmas that arise for supervisors, managers, and planners, and for those in other roles and settings.

How is it organized? The book begins with a discussion of what ethics means and what it means to be ethical. This section lays an important foundation for all that follows, and it contains useful case material as well. The second chapter offers a framework for examining ethical dilemmas and weighing your options for addressing them, and it gives you examples that apply that framework.

Each of the remaining chapters focuses on a particular area of ethics—confidentiality, self-determination, informed consent, and so forth. Each of these chapters uses a consistent format that provides an overview of the ethical concept and the related standards, a case example in which the standard is violated, and another where the standard is upheld. The rest of the chapter is devoted to ethical decision making in a more complex dilemma utilizing the decision making framework introduced in the second chapter. Sometimes there will be one right answer, and sometimes the analysis will reveal several right answers. Sometimes (maybe often) you'll dispute my view of the case or disagree with the outcome. Wonderful! To take a differing perspective, you must be engaged with the question, striving to find a path that fits with your understanding of ethical practice. Such engagement with ethics can only make us stronger as we consider the views of others and articulate and advance our own. I hope to hear from you as you use this book. Let me know the insights it raised, the dilemmas it brought to mind, and the ideas you have for improving ethical practice in our professions and in our daily lives. I am certain we'll all be better for it.

As you read the cases, you may feel you recognize the characters involved. Each case is a composite of a commonly occurring dilemma, a case that has been created from an actual dilemma, or a case that has been made up. No case in the book is, in and of itself, a real case, though I hope you find them all realistic and useful. In addition to sending your feedback, please send me your dilemmas so that others can benefit in the future from novel, real-life examples.

As I write this on Valentine's Day 2022, my heart of full of gratitude for the many people who shaped my interest in ethics and created opportunities for me to learn and study this fascinating topic. Special thanks to Ana Sobočan, Sarah Banks, Teresa Bertotti, Ed DeJong, and other global partners who have broadened my vision and deepened my understanding about social work ethics around the world. I'm also appreciative of my students, now colleagues, who helped with previous editions of the book, and I thank Jonathan Bell, Melissa Mcgovern, Brent Eisenbarth, and Jordan Wingate for their research and technical assistance on this edition. All my respect to the practitioners who reveal their ethical wisdom and struggles at workshops, classes, and consultations so that we all can learn and grow stronger from their examples.

Thank you to the following reviewers for their contributions to this volume: Kevin McDowell, Northern Michigan University; Barbara Gordon, University of Louisville; Mary Mastria, New York University; Elissa Madden, Baylor University; James Smalley, Southwest Minnesota State University; Mary E. Garrison, Millikin University; Bibiana Koh, Augsburg University; James Coleman, Central Michigan University; Elizabeth Peffer Talbot, Concordia University; Ann Obermann, MSU Denver; Clifton F. Guthrie, Husson University.

New to the Third Edition

The third edition of this text has increased the amount of global content, concepts, and sources. Increased attention has been paid to issues of racism, oppression, and inequality, such as examples of the abuse of and experimentation on Indigenous children in Canadian residential schools, and there is an expanded discussion on decolonializing approaches to ethical theories. Content on client rights and respect for Indigenous and consumer resources in decision making has been included. The impact of the COVID-19 pandemic on service user needs, dilemmas, and practitioner responses is discussed. There is also increased content on electronic service delivery, supervision, and the effects of social media.

Citations and content have been updated throughout. The text has been updated to include the 2017 and 2021 changes to the NASW *Code of Ethics*, as well as the NASW 2015 standards on cultural competence. In keeping with this edition's more global approach, standards from the Canadian provinces have also been incorporated.

ABOUT THE AUTHOR

Kimberly Strom, Ph.D., LISW, is the Smith P. Theimann Jr. Distinguished Professor of Ethics and Professional Practice at the University of North Carolina School of Social Work and director of the university's Office of Ethics and Policy. Professor Strom has been an educator for over 30 years and has written over 90 articles, monographs, and chapters. She is the author of *The Ethics of Practice with Minors: High Stakes and Hard Choices* and coauthor of *The Best of Boards, Direct Social Work Practice* and *Teaching Social Work Values and Ethics: A Curriculum Resource*. An internationally recognized scholar on moral courage, ethics, leadership, and social work education, Dr. Strom represents North America on the Ethics Commission of the International Federation of Social Work.

PART I

The Groundwork for Ethical Practice

CHAPTER 1

On Ethics and Ethical Behavior

Introduction

"It's an interesting time to be in the ethics business," a fellow trainer said to me at the outset of a recent workshop. The study of **ethics** goes back thousands of years: Socrates pondered the meaning of morality more than 2,400 years ago (Rachels, 2003). But the twenty-first century has brought a resurgence of interest in **normative ethics**—the application of ethical theories to our lives as individual citizens and as professionals in various disciplines (Reamer, 2019b). Some of this interest comes from the increasing complexity of our daily lives, from the ascendance of technology that speeds up communication but erodes protections of privacy, to climate change and the SARS-Cov2 pandemic that call attention to long-standing issues of environmental injustice and disparities in health and wealth.

The interest in ethics also comes from recent notorious lapses in ethical standards, such as harassment and violence by respected athletes and actors, misuses of power by police and politicians, or fraudulent behavior by too-big-to-fail banks. Revered institutions are not immune to disgrace, as the state-sponsored cultural genocide of Indigenous children in British Columbia starkly illustrates (Voce et al., 2021). The persistence of ethical failures should spur us all to seek guidance about the **ethical dilemmas** we confront in our own lives (R. Cohen, 2002, 2012).

My particular interest is in the ethical dilemmas that helping professionals experience and the guidance and support they need to do the right thing, often in difficult circumstances. This book is intended to be such a guide, delivering information on ethics and ethical decision making, as well as abundant examples through which you, the reader, can hone your skills. While the concepts in the book may be novel to students and new social workers, all professionals will probably be challenged by the cases presented and the complications imbedded in them.

Elements of Ethics

The journey must begin with an understanding of ethics.

- What are ethics?
- What does it mean to be ethical?
- Is being ethical in one's personal life the same as being ethical in one's chosen profession?
- What is an ethical dilemma?
- How can one choose the right course of action when faced with such a dilemma?

At its core, ethics involves doing the right thing in a given circumstance—behaving ethically. The challenge comes, of course, in defining the "right" thing. The determination of what is ethical is shaped by many forces, some of which conflict with each other. Consider a sixty-five-year-old man who lives in his car and uses his veterans' benefit payments to purchase diapers for himself and food for his dog. He refuses pleas to move to a shelter because he would have to part with his pet. (Shelters commonly refuse dogs because they pose a violation to health regulations.) Fiscal conservatives object to his misuse of veterans' funds. He maintains that he has as much right to use those funds for his needs as other veterans do to use theirs for cigarettes or golf games. Advocates worry about his safety. He maintains he is safer alone with his dog than he would be in congregate housing with other, often desperate, individuals.

What is right in this case? All of the positions are reasonable, well founded, and well intentioned. When all perspectives are valid, which constitutes the best choice? Who decides?

Ethical dilemmas come in all shapes and sizes. They can be interpersonal quandaries such as the etiquette of condemning a racially offensive joke or they can involve life-and-death questions that invoke multiple viewpoints, laws, faiths, morals, and values.

For instance, a patient in a hospital refuses to undergo a life-saving medical procedure because of religious beliefs.

- Should their beliefs and personal autonomy be honored even if they may ultimately result in death?
- Should the beliefs of the medical team, the patient's family, or the opinions of the courts that hear the case carry more weight than the patient's own convictions?
- What if the decision to forgo treatment is based on religious beliefs rather than the patient's philosophy about quality of life? Would that change the ethics of the patient's position?

Vexing or dramatic ethical dilemmas occasionally rise to the level of national attention and debate. More often, though, dilemmas are pondered and resolved by individuals, families, and work teams. Consider this: You see a parent in line at the grocery store viciously strike her child across the face for reaching out to the candy display. Should you intervene and try to minimize harm to the child? Perhaps doing so would make the mother think twice and break a cycle of escalating harsh discipline. Or should you mind your own business, reasoning that your intrusion might shame the mother or infuriate her more, leading to more punishment for the child? If you are simply a fellow citizen and have no obligation to put yourself on the line, should you still act? If you are a social worker with mandated reporting requirements, does this situation demand a report? Perhaps you wish someone in authority would speak up! Why doesn't the clerk or security officer say something?

What about ethics in the workplace? You're a teacher whose student has broken the school honor code by submitting a paper plagiarized from an Internet site. The honor standards are clear, as are the consequences. Enforcing them would result in the student's expulsion and probably lead to some uproar from parents, friends, and others. Perhaps the student is a star athlete or performer, or is an at-risk student for whom this might be the last straw to drop out for good. Maybe you should give the student a second chance. Maybe you should search for a reasonable explanation. But failing to follow the honor code's stipulations is unfair to other students who follow the code as well as to those who have been properly disciplined for not following it. And why have a code if there is always an exception, always a rationale or reason not to uphold it?

These examples illustrate several important points about ethics: dilemmas crop up throughout our daily lives, often without warning. They demand that we weigh numerous factors in choosing a course of action, and they don't usually give us much time to do so. Sometimes, we don't realize we have chosen poorly until after the fact, but even that remorse provides the opportunity to grow and do better the next time. When I faced the grocery store incident, I ruminated about what to do until the opportunity to act had passed. Then I rationalized, "Oh well, too late." Had I been better prepared to act, quicker to know what was right, and more courageous, I would have taken a better course of action—for the child and for my conscience. When I ask myself today, "Did I do the right thing?" the answer, unfortunately, is "No."

Some contend that ethical decision making involves not a choice between right and wrong, but one between competing goods or competing rights—that the choice between a good and a bad action does not constitute an ethical dilemma (Kidder, 1995). For example, the decision whether or not to steal a neighbor's furniture is not an ethical dilemma: every society clearly defines right and wrong, and considers doing wrong to be both unethical and illegal. But what if the neighbor left a bureau by the curb, ostensibly for trash pickup? Would it be ethical to take it under those circumstances? The decision and the rationale used to discern the right thing in this case involve ethical decision making. Some who subscribe to rule ethics (Rachels, 2003) would maintain that the circumstances do not matter. If it is unethical to take your neighbor's goods, it doesn't matter where they are or why they are there when you decide to take them.

Others would evaluate the appropriateness of the action based on the consequences—using the circumstances of the case to determine the correctness of an action (Reamer, 2018). They would appraise the situation, weigh the intent of the neighbor, consider the impact on others, and determine what harm or good might come of their actions. This, of course, requires one to be an accurate evaluator of the surrounding circumstances—to be certain that the bureau on the curb *is* trash and not awaiting pickup by a moving company or refinishing service, for example.

Perhaps you would decide what to do based on your own character and sense of integrity. The concept of virtue ethics emphasizes the personal traits and habits that form the path to ethical action. Your positive motivations and the alignment of your emotions, thoughts, and actions would lead to an automatic decision, congruent with past actions. Perhaps you would consult with the neighbor first, or leave the furniture for someone who may have greater need for it.

Some would evaluate the dilemma by deferring to the law—theft is illegal, but picking up someone else's discarded junk probably is not. The problem with deferring to the law is that there are many actions in personal and professional life that are not covered by the law. Is it ethical for a social worker to accept a gift from a client? The law is silent on the matter. And even where laws exist, they may not always provide an appropriate guide to just action. It is legal for politicians to accept large campaign contributions from the very industries over which they will be drafting regulations, but is it right for them to do so?

Even when laws are clear, following them may not always be the correct course of action. Some laws are simply unjust. Slavery was once legal in both the United States and Canada. Similarly, both countries forcibly relegated citizens of Japanese heritage to internment camps in World War II (Decoste, 2013; Park, 2020). Otherwise valid laws may be overridden for ethical or contextual reasons. For example, the law says vehicles must stop at a red light. But if you are a volunteer disaster responder in your car rushing to a call in the middle of the night on an empty road, should you sit there through the entirety of the light? Do the ends (responding efficiently to an emergency) warrant the means (breaking traffic laws)?

The rich tradition of civil disobedience is built on the notion that there must be some recourse for action when laws themselves are unjust. Rosa Parks, a heroine of the U.S. civil rights movement, was breaking the law when she refused to move to the "colored" section of an Alabama bus, but few would have suggested even then that her choice was unethical. Laws require people who are apprehended by police to follow officers' orders, yet mistrust borne of exploitation may cause citizens to challenge those commands. During the COVID-19 pandemic, laws and policies mandated that the public, including social workers, quarantine at home. This frequently gave rise to ethical dilemmas as concerns for public safety collided with acute, unmet client needs and the social work values of service and social justice (Banks et al., 2020). When people of good conscience perceive that the laws themselves are flawed, what is the right course of action? The easy answer is "change the flawed laws," but change is often a long time in coming or is blocked by powerful, entrenched interests.

So, the law is of limited help in ethical decision making. Doing something because the law says to do it (or not to do it) is a fairly narrow basis for behavior. These motivations correspond to the most basic stage in Lawrence Kohlberg's schema of moral development (Hutchison, 2015). And laws, at their essence, provide only a minimal guide for acceptable behavior—following them is not the same as being an ethical person (E. Cohen & Cohen, 1999). In fact, in acknowledging the shortcoming of law as guidance for action, Moulton (1924) defined ethics as "obedience to the unenforceable" (p. 4)—that is, our ethics are those considerations that mediate our free will. Ethics are guidance for the situations in which we enforce laws on ourselves (Moulton, 1924). The concept of **supereroga-tion** is germane to this discussion because it conveys the sense that individuals can go beyond the call of duty and beyond their obligations to behave altruistically for the good of others (Heyd, 2012).

Usually, the complexity of an ethical dilemma emerges in the details. Decisions that on their face may be simple become difficult when other factual elements are introduced. Assuring client safety is an ethical imperative, but clients may want to make their own decisions about the end of life.

- What about client autonomy and self-determination?
- What if the client is gravely ill with a terminal illness?
- What if the client is in excruciating pain that is not diminished by medication?
- What if the client lives in a jurisdiction where assisted suicide is legal and they have pursued their rights under that statute?
- What if family members support the decision even though they grieve the prospect of the client's death?
- Is it still ethical for the clinician to intercede to keep the client from carrying out the wish to die with more dignity than the client foresees if they let nature take its course?

The devil is in the details.

Some people, faced with all this equivocating on ethics, throw up their hands, demanding a clear answer—"Is it right or not? Just tell me what to do, and I'll do it!" Or they conclude that ethics are situational—that if everything is relative, then any action can be justified. In fact, neither position is valid. Core ethical standards provide us the guideposts for action. Knowing what they are and what they mean is an essential first step in ethical practice.

The challenges occur in those situations when standards collide, or when the standard fails to offer clear guidance for action. In these situations, doing the right thing involves examining the array of options available in upholding the ethical standard and considering, within that specific context, the most ethical course of action (Banks, 2021). This doesn't mean that anything goes. It means that, although there are many things to consider in sorting out the proper choice, some choices will be more ethically sound, or ethically defensible, than others. We discuss this notion of contextual ethical decision making further in Chapter 2 as you learn the elements to consider in ethical practice.

Ethical Development

On what basis do we as individuals develop our sense of right and wrong, or our preference for certain decision making schemata over others? When we are faced with a difficult decision, how do we select one option over another? The consideration of such questions extends as far back as Plato. Throughout history, a range of theories from fields such as philosophy, psychology, economics, religion, and anthropology have endeavored to explain ethical choices (Barsky, 2019). The following brief overview of these perspectives should help you better understand the ethical outlooks reflected in your own approach to ethics.

Philosophy

Although there are many types and subtypes of philosophical approaches to ethics (Chan, 2009), we briefly address six here: utilitarianism or consequentialism, deontology, contractualism, justice, virtue, and decolonization (see table in Box 1.1).

A fundamental concept in ethical thinking is whether an action is right objectively, meaning that it is the best action in an absolute sense, or whether it is right subjectively, in which case any decision could be considered right depending on the circumstances (Graham, 2004). This discussion is a major feature of Plato's dialogues, where Socrates argues that ethics are absolute, while the Sophists generally argue that ethics are subjective. The fact that rule-based ethical frameworks appeal to some and outcome-based frameworks to others is apparent in these early musings. The philosophical traditions of utilitarian and deontological ethics thus compare duty versus consequence in their consideration of right and wrong.

Utilitarianism or consequentialism. **Utilitarianism**, typically associated with the philosophers John Stuart Mill (1806–1873) and Jeremy Bentham (1748–1832), evaluates the rightness of a decision based on the outcomes or consequences of that decision. In the wake of the social upheavals of the late eighteenth and early nineteenth centuries in both Europe and the United States, Bentham found a climate ripe for the development of the utilitarian model (Rachels, 2003). Challenging the traditional beliefs that a right decision was one that pleased God or followed a set of rules, Bentham expanded on the French Revolution's mantra of "liberty, equality, fraternity" to posit a morality based on the greatest good or happiness. Using Bentham and Mill's classical utilitarian model, morality can be judged based on its consequences, the happiness elicited by those consequences, and the equality of the happiness brought to every individual involved (Rachels, 2003).

The question "Which choice creates the greatest good for the greatest number?" is frequently associated with utilitarianism. In Mill's words (1861/1967), "The creed which accepts as the foundation of morals 'utility' or the 'greatest happiness principle' holds that actions are right in proportion as they tend to promote happiness; wrong as they tend to produce the reverse of happiness. By happiness is intended pleasure and the absence of pain; by unhappiness, pain and the privation of pleasure" (p. 10).

In this model, and its more recent iteration, **consequentialism**, there are no absolute directives about what is right and wrong; rather, the outcome of a decision and the relative benefits determine the preferred course of action. Applying utilitarian concepts to practical dilemmas can be challenging in that what is good for the majority may not be right or fair for the minority or for certain individuals involved. And the specification of what is good or preferable can be difficult in that outcomes can be good in different ways. Critics argue that happiness and our beliefs about what is good or bad are inextricably intertwined. For example, Rachels (2003) gives the example that we may seek out a friend because we recognize that friendship is good in its own right, and not just because it is a means for our happiness. Other critics argue that utilitarianism conflicts with **justice**—or that, in some instances, the greater good may not allow for everyone to be treated fairly, and at times that good might hinder individual rights (Rachels, 2003). Also, many note the difficulty of estimating with any certainty the consequences of a particular action (Knapp & VandeCreek, 2006). Still, utilitarian thinking is hailed for its ability to challenge matters of moral common sense, which often involve individual biases and prejudices. The advantage, then, of viewing our choices through an outcome-based lens is that it forces us to examine the various potential results of our decisions.

Deontology. A contrasting theory to utilitarianism is the deontological perspective. Typically linked to the work of Immanuel Kant, the **deontological** model determines rightness by rules rather than outcomes. Unlike utilitarian theory, this duty-based model judges morality based on the motivating principles of an action without consideration of consequences. Happiness may occur as a result of moral action, but it is not the goal. Kant contrasted hypothetical or conditional imperatives, where a person acts a certain way in order to achieve a specific result, against categorical imperatives, where the person acts simply based on duty (Knapp & VandeCreek, 2006). You may recognize Kant's categorical imperative, which essentially says, "Follow only the principle that you want everyone else to follow" (Kidder, 1995, p. 24). Under deontology, ethical decisions are right because they comply with such an imperative, or because the principle that supports the decision is sound. Take, for example, two individuals who give clothes to a homeless shelter. If the first is motivated by a genuine desire to help the poor, and the other is motivated by an opportunity for a tax deduction, under the deontological view only the first person's actions are moral.

As in utilitarianism, there are challenges in using a deontological perspective in practice. One problem involves the difficulty in achieving consensus about a rule or policy that would hold for all conditions or contexts. Even valued concepts like honesty or loyalty have outer limits where they cease to be useful or where they lead to bad outcomes. Critics also argue that this view does not consider varying ethnic or cultural backgrounds where obligation for moral action may be understood in a different way (Linzer, 1999). Although the contextual nature of social work practice makes rule-based thinking tricky, it is still useful in weighing our choices in that it requires us to ask, "Would I want my reasoning to apply to all others' decisions?" and "Is there a rule or principle that would guide my choice in this matter?"

Contractualism. A somewhat different take on ethical behavior is **contractualism**, which posits that decisions and actions are ethical when they are congruent with the rules that citizens have agreed to live by (Blumenthal-Barby, 2015). This agreement, or social contract, as it is sometimes known, "forms the basis of law and morality and can be appealed to as the ground of our social obligation to recognize and accommodate the needs of others" (Graham, 2004, p. 164). Thus, the reasoning behind an ethical act is that it holds society together and prevents what Thomas Hobbes called "a war of all against all" (as cited in Graham, 2004, p. 170). The qualifications on the legitimacy of these contracts are the basis on which they were made. Whose voices matter? Are a handful of powerful interests allowed to make decisions affecting many, or are stakeholders reflective of all people affected by the particular social contract? Are the choices fairly and rationally made? Sound and defensible contracts must be democratically, inclusively, and pluralistically formulated.

Justice. John Rawls' **theory of justice** (1999) also reflects on the role of social contracts in the distribution of societal rights and goods. He offers a hypothetical scenario where anyone in society could be situated in "the original position" (Rawls, 1999, p. 11). Decisions are made from a **veil of ignorance**, where the individual would not know if or how they would be affected by the decision. The presumption is that these conditions promote justice. Individuals make fair and rational decisions (and avoid selfish or self-sacrificing decisions) because anyone could be subject to the given outcome.

Virtue. Yet another perspective on ethics moves the focus away from behavior or decisions and instead emphasizes character. Commonly referred to as **virtue ethics**, and emerging from the writings of Aristotle, Thomas Aquinas, and others, this approach rests on the traits of the individual—not "how we act, but who we are" (Barsky, 2010, p. 244). Thus, individuals' moral development, culture, integrity, and past decisions culminate in the approach that they will take in a current decision. **Virtues** are positive, "stable and firm dispositions" to do good, resting on qualities such as prudence, courage, temperance and justice (Adams, 2009, p. 87), all of which are needed for humans to flourish. Virtues have resonance across time, cultures, disciplines, and faiths. Social work and other helping or healing fields may be considered virtue-guided disciplines, in that members of those professions use education and practice to develop and sustain the habits required to help those in need.

Decolonization. Theories such as deontology or utilitarianism can provide clarity and promote communication about ethics and the search for right action. Theories can also be tools of oppression as some voices (typically white, Western, well-to-do, and male) gain hegemony while constraining or diminishing other perspectives. In the field of ethics, concerned with determining what is right, just, and preferable in given situations, we can imagine the power that certain social constructions have to define other theories as wrong, unfair, or undesirable. A **decolonizing** approach reexamines the Eurocentric authority of theory and calls out "the ways in which colonial knowledge and power structures are embedded in professional standards, language, and basic assumptions" (Finn, 2021, p. 13). In contrast, Indigenous, feminist, global, critical theory, and other movements offer valuable premises by which to understand ethics and resist dominant paradigms (Allen & Mendieta, 2021; Gray et al., 2008; Rossiter et al., 1998).

This overview does not do justice to the depth and breadth of the philosophy of ethics, but an example from social work practice may demonstrate how these traditions would inform an ethical decision. See Box 1.1, as these concepts are applied to the case of the Allen family.

BOX 1.1

The Allen Family

The Allen family lives on a fixed income and the parents are doing the best they can to provide for their two children, but with outdoor plumbing and food scarcity, hunger and cleanliness are constant concerns. They live in a cramped space and heat the main room with their oven, with all family members sleeping on the floor nearby. The parents each work two jobs and sometimes the mother will take the children to work. They play or sleep in the waiting area while she cleans offices. Occasionally the parents admit to locking them in the house alone, which they say is for safety, if both parents have to be out due to overlapping work shifts or another short-term need. The early-childhood social worker is aware of all of these issues. As a mandatory reporter, she must report any suspicion of child abuse or neglect to child protective services (CPS). However, the social worker is also aware of CPS caseloads and priorities and believes filing a report would not result in any action or change in the family's economic condition. She also worries that a report will be one more burden on a family that already has too many, and it may permanently ruin her relationship with, and thus her ability to help, them.

Philosophical Approaches to the Allen Case

Utilitarianism	The possible consequences of the decision include the following: If the social worker reports:

- Distress for the family
- Breach of trust with the worker
- Extra work for CPS
- Waste of time for the worker
- Possible assistance for the neglected children

If she does not report:

- Liability for the worker in not following the law
- Children continue to be neglected
- Possible harm to the children when they are left alone

Deontology	The rule on mandatory reporting is clear. CPS assesses the validity and severity of abuse or neglect. It is the worker's job simply to make the report whenever suspicion of neglect or abuse exists.
Contractualism	Part of our social contract is that citizens should take steps to protect vulnerable persons, especially children. In some regions this is codified into laws that apply to all residents. In all regions, social workers are expected to abide by mandatory reporting requirements. However, the voices of parents struggling to meet the needs of vulnerable children are not typically represented in the policies for child welfare.
Justice	What would the worker want in any of the roles in this case (children, parents, CPS, society, the worker)? What is the best outcome for anyone residing in the original position?
Virtue	The worker considers herself to be a compassionate, responsible professional and wants to fulfill her duties and meet the desperate needs of the clients.

| Decolonization | Structural systems that endanger or exploit the parents' labor, housing, and food security create and profit from the system within which the parents are trying to subsist. Ethics of resistance would advocate for systemic changes to protect the parents from harms while providing support for living wages and safe, stable child care. |

Psychology

Kurtines and Gewirtz (1995) outline four major psychological perspectives of moral development: **cognitive development**, **social constructivism**, **personality or psychodynamic theories**, and **behaviorism**.

The first and predominant perspective is the cognitive developmental perspective. Jean Piaget and Lawrence Kohlberg are the primary figures associated with this perspective. Piaget (1932) argued that individuals' moral development follows a linear progression beginning with egocentrism in young children and gradually advancing to higher forms of decision making where the individual increasingly considers the needs of others. Kohlberg (1984) built on this work but went one step farther. Where Piaget had used the term developmental "phases," Kohlberg selected the more rigid term "stages." Still, the basic premise remained that of progressively advanced ethical decision making.

Kohlberg's ideas continue to be influential, though theorists within the social constructivist perspective have described his methods and theories as gendered and culturally bound. Gilligan (2016) argues that the female voice has been ignored in the traditional understanding of morality, contrasting the traditional preoccupation of moral development with rights and rules with a **morality of care** that is more concerned with responsibility and relationships. The **ethics of care** place greater emphasis on the role of emotions in decision making, on the interdependence among people, and on honoring fundamental social units, such as the family.

A personality or psychodynamic perspective is typified by the ideas of Freud and later Erikson. This perspective is not concerned specifically with behavior or cognition, but rather with attempts to understand the whole of a person. Hogan and Emler (1995) state that moral conduct in adulthood "can be largely understood in terms of the concepts of identity and reputation-management" (p. 210). Individuals seek to establish an identity as an ethical person while simultaneously cultivating a similar reputation. Thus, people intent on identifying as a rebel may choose corresponding ethical behaviors (testing rules, speaking out, etc.) to bolster these reputations. This process may be deliberate, though it may also be instinctual.

The fourth and final psychological perspective, behaviorism, was to some degree a response to the Freudian ideas of instinctual choices. Burton and Kunce (1995) state, "Reasoning about moral issues results from early behavioral training and these judgments may eventually become guides to subsequent action as part of a feedback system" (p. 143). Ethical behavior would thus be perceived primarily as the result of preparation that occurs in homes, schools, places of worship, and other institutions.

Economics

The concept of rational choice grew out of the field of economics and posits that individuals make choices based on the perceived amount of personal benefit (Zsolnai, 1998). One always considers others' goals, desires, and needs secondary to one's own. The rational choice theorist might argue that choices that appear to be altruistic are ultimately guided by personal benefit. For example, even when people perform selfless acts, they might have been motivated to perform that act by the desire to feel good or to improve their social standing. Under this model, ethical decisions are not altruistic but rather are a risk–benefit calculation that takes into account the decision maker's well-being.

Religion

While it is likely that religion influences ethical decision making, the extent and form of influence is probably dependent on one's particular faith orientation and reading of the particular tenets of the faith. The Ten Commandments are considered the moral cornerstone of Christianity, Islam, and Judaism. Muslims further hold to the concept of *taqwa*, which refers both to the human ethical conscience and to the moral grounding that influences behavior, to measure the morality of an individual or community (Badawi, 2005). In Hinduism, the ten *yamas* refer to provisions such as truthfulness, nonharm, and nonstealing, and the five precepts of Buddhism address refraining from actions such as stealing, killing, and lying (Howard & Korver, 2008). Sikh ethics emphasize harmony between spiritual development and everyday moral conduct—doing good works for the sake of others in the honor of unity, justice, and equality (Singh, 2021).

The tenets and traditions of faith, internalized through family, culture, and formal institutions form moral and ethical dispositions. Religious or spiritual figures such as Abraham, Isaac, Jesus, Mohammed, Confucius, and Ghandi can serve as role models and inspire virtue (Barsky, 2019). Psychological and religious explanations of moral development highlight the role that social learning and ritual play in ethical action (Spohn, 2000). As such, ethical development emerges from a set of determined practices such as friendship, service, and worship. Religious practice does not supplant the psychological theories that explain internal mechanisms of ethical behavior, but religious habits and actions refine ethical decision making.

Culture

The extent to which one's culture shapes their ethical stance is the subject of lively debate in the field. Some take the stance of **ethical relativism**, which contends that there are no norms of right and wrong; decisions can only be made in the context of one's culture (cultural relativism) or lived experience (personal relativism or historic relativism). This can easily lead to **ethical skepticism**, wherein moral judgments are considered arbitrary and without moral authority (Ford, 2006).

Brannigan (2005) urges us to avoid two fundamental tyrannies: the false notions "that only the local is real . . . and that only the moment matters" (p. 7). Other rejoinders to the relativists urge us not to confuse cultural or regional differences in beliefs or behaviors with differences in values (Ford, 2006; Kidder, 1995). "The point is that many factors work together to produce the customs of a society. The society's values are only one of them. Other matters such as the religious and factual beliefs held by its members and the physical circumstances in which they must live, are also important. We cannot conclude, then, merely because customs differ, that there is a disagreement about values. The difference in customs may be attributable to some other aspect of social life. Thus, there may be less disagreement about values than there appears to be" (Rachels, 2003, pp. 23–24).

The issue of bartering in professional transactions serves as a useful example of Rachels' statement and of Brannigan's recommendation that "we ought not to confuse specific behaviors and practices with moral principles" (2005, p. 6). In the late 1980s efforts to prohibit bartering (exchanging goods or services for social work care) in the National Association of Social Workers (NASW) *Code of Ethics* were met with strong resistance from rural practitioners who argued that the practice was culturally appropriate, particularly in cash- and credit-poor regions. The core concern driving the move to ban bartering was the risk of exploitation of clients in the pricing and process of transactions. The social workers who engaged in bartering did not believe in exploiting clients either. On the basis of the shared value, the *Code* was amended to incorporate both positions: "Social workers should explore and may participate in bartering only in very limited circumstances when it can be demonstrated that such arrangements are an accepted practice among professionals in the local community, considered to be essential for the provision of services, negotiated without coercion, and entered into at the client's initiative and with the client's informed consent." (NASW, 2021, 1.13b)

Despite its problems, relativism does remind us to avoid the dangers of dogma, "of assuming all our preferences are based on some absolute rational standard" (Rachels, 2003, p. 30). It also encourages professionals to be curious, to seek to understand others' customs and practices, to keep an open mind, to engage in dialogue, and to avoid divisive conclusions. Oversimplifying a dilemma by assuming that one's culture or worldview prohibits consensus flies in the face of effective moral reasoning (Brannigan, 2005). Nevertheless, the process of developing cross-cultural understanding may also be challenging. Fortunately, a number of texts promote reflection and help readers examine cultural bias (Brannigan, 2005; Ermine et al., 2005; Healy & Link, 2011; Hugman, 2012; Velasquez et al., 2014) and consider various perspectives on issues such as reporting cheating, deceptive marketing, female genital circumcision, capital punishment and animal rights (Hooker, 2018; Kahn & Mastroianni, 2009).

What about You?

How, then, do you make ethical decisions? How do you determine right from wrong? Which of these theories (individually or bundled with others) resonates with you as you think of yourself as an ethical being? While this text examines dilemmas and applies standards from the helping professions, the insights, impressions, and growth that result will be built on your existing moral framework. This moral core on which the scaffolding of professional decision making is constructed may be explicitly drawn from a faith tradition or personal philosophy, or it may be the result of an unexamined set of preferences and ideals.

Each of us brings to our practice a personal tradition of ethical thinking that will shape and be shaped by the dilemmas we encounter in practice. This tradition will take an active role in shaping our responses and manifest itself in the personal values we weigh. It may be congruent with the ethical mandates and roles of social work, or it may be at odds with them. Regardless of the harmony between our personal and professional selves, we can be certain that in a lifetime of decision making the two will be in constant transformation as each influences the other.

Professional Ethics

The examples of removing a bureau from your neighbor's curb or confronting an angry parent in the checkout line exemplify questions of personal ethics—that category of ethics that governs how we conduct ourselves in our daily lives, in our interactions in the workplace, with our friends and family, and in larger society. The guidelines for personal ethics and their application are a compelling topic and are addressed nicely in other sources, from etiquette and advice columns to novels, films and historic texts. The focus of this book, however, is on professional ethics, and particularly the ethics of social work and similar fields. Our professions present us with unique principles to guide our choices, and a broad and complex array of situations in which we must make ethical choices. As such, it is quite different from deciding the fate of our neighbor's trash.

Professional ethics involve those dilemmas that occur in the course of our discipline or field of practice. Because of this, different considerations come to bear than in the dilemmas we face in our personal lives. Developing a commitment to the ethics of a profession and an understanding of how those ethics apply to commonly occurring workplace situations are core elements of professional preparation. Integrating our professional ethics with our personal ethics is another important part of the process. For example, if a person generally embraces philosophies such as "live and let live" or "to each their own," how will these be reconciled with a professional role that requires confronting a client about parenting practices, maintaining household hygiene, or living in their car? When we accept membership in a profession, we also accept the values and standards of that profession as they are put forth through codes of ethics and our professional organizations' credos. It involves "acquiring certain virtues . . . in the development of an ethical use of self" (Adams, 2009, p. 100). The process of professional acculturation helps people decide if they can embrace the values and standards of their chosen field. The Canadian Association of Social Workers (CASW) *Code of Ethics* (2005a) provides accountability for the upholding of these standards by stipulating that "behaviour or conduct that does not meet social work standard of care requirements is . . . subject to discipline" (p. 10). Those who find themselves in persistent conflict with the core beliefs of the discipline must reflect seriously on their suitability for the field they have chosen.

Even individuals who have great compatibility with their profession's standards still experience situations where their personal beliefs and professional ethics collide, requiring constant attention to the intersection of the two. If you personally believe that it is wrong for a fourteen-year-old to have a baby, how will you be effective in service of a young client who is sexually active yet refuses to take birth control or who chooses to carry an unplanned pregnancy to term? Social workers support client self-determination in all but the most exceptional of circumstances. Clearly it would be unethical to trick the client into taking birth control. But it is also unethical to say, "I can't work with you because you are making life decisions I don't agree with—decisions that violate my moral standards." We may say, "I'm concerned about your choice, and here's why," but that shouldn't rise to the level of threats or coercion, and our concerns should be based on the clinical indications or legitimate dangers involved, and not simply an argument of what behavior is right or wrong based on our personal values. We impose such judgments at the risk of foreclosing our own growth and of damaging our relationship with the client, within which conversations of morality may rightly take place (Doherty, 1995).

The principles of acceptance and nonjudgmental practice require us to separate what we would personally choose or how we would want to live from the choices others make. Our service to clients is not contingent on our approval of their choices. "Aha!," you say. What about programs that refuse to serve clients who arrive intoxicated or who harass other residents or staff? When those exclusionary criteria exist they must be grounded in program policies and sound clinical practice in order to serve other goods or rights (the safety of the client or other residents). Setting such organizational standards isn't the same as imposing our individual values on clients or selectively applying only those professional ethical principles we agree with. Ethical practice requires a high degree of self-knowledge, reflection and comfort engaging in dialogue with other professionals to ensure that we're acting on the norms of the field, and not on our idiosyncratic views.

Doing the right thing as a professional sometimes feels not like making a choice between good and bad, or between competing goods, but like making a choice between competing bads. A client discloses to their counselor that they committed a crime. To report it to the authorities, the professional would be breaking trust and the covenant of confidentiality—both bad outcomes. Being complicit in the client's crime by remaining silent is also a bad outcome. Which bad is better? Which undesirable choice is the right one?

Professional ethics guide us to ask the questions and weigh the factors that help us to arrive at the best possible decision. They also help us to carry out that decision in a way that is both clinically and ethically effective. Standards of confidentiality indicate that we breach a client's privacy confidence only for compelling professional reasons and to prevent serious future harm. Standards on informed consent require us to talk with the client at the outset of service about the circumstances under which we might have to break confidentiality, so that if the client reveals reportable information after that point, they understand what the consequences will be. Laws and principles place a high premium on professional discretion.

What is a compelling professional reason for revealing a client's past crime if the client has not been apprehended for it? Some would argue that absent some threat of a continued crime spree, there is none, even if someone innocent is being punished unjustly for the crime. Most would suggest that if the crime is serious or violent, it is important for the worker to encourage the client to turn themselves in—that doing so is important for their conscience and successful achievement of other treatment and life goals. They would argue that reporting the crime for the client undermines fundamental premise of trust on which the helping relationship, and in fact the entire profession, is based. We owe our clients a greater debt of trust than we owe people in our personal lives. If I know my brother committed a crime, I might be violating a family norm or sibling bond in reporting him, but I am not breaking the covenant of trust on which the helping professions are built.

Still, it's not easy. Most of us have sympathy for how difficult it was for David Kaczynski (2005) to come forward and identify his brother Ted as the Unabomber, even after his actions had caused three deaths and twenty-three injuries. It's not easy for professionals, either, to sit with information that makes us uncomfortable and vulnerable. Often those feelings are predicable results of work in fields where employees are entrusted with the pain and secrets of those they serve. Another troubling phenomenon, moral distress, arises when the worker's ethical or clinical actions are thwarted by external forces, such as administrative edicts or structural barriers. First arising in nursing field, moral distress is an all-too-familiar experience in social work: staffing shortages, funding constraints, burdensome procedures reduce the time and attention to provide quality care, reflect on moral concerns, or resolve ethical conundrums. The effects of moral distress range from physical and emotional reactions, to job withdrawal and apathy and staff infighting and burnout (Oliver, 2013; Strom-Gottfried, 2019).

Social workers must cultivate ethical awareness, motivation, character, and reasoning to remedy the corrosive effects of moral distress, the burdens of ethical dilemmas, and the imperative of professional integrity. This requires the foundation of sound knowledge, logic, and reasoning, including self-knowledge and awareness of biases and vulnerabilities (Banks, 2021). Building on this foundation, social workers need the support of regular, confidential consultation with peers and supervisors to sustain competence and their ethical compasses. Similarly, self-care, health, and balance are crucial for competence in managing the ethical, clinical, and managerial challenges of the workplace. These acts and abilities can seem like a tall order, and they are. But with attention and reflection, they can be internalized to become the core of your professional identity and mobilized to arrive at ethical conclusions throughout your practice.

Acting on Ethics

Identifying an ethical dilemma and deciding what to do are only two parts of the ethics puzzle. The third part involves action. As described above, the process by which we enact an ethical decision is critical to the success of that decision. Chapter 2 and each of the application chapters will provide you with guidance on that aspect of ethical action.

Sometimes, however, the challenge for the clinician isn't in knowing what to do or how to do it, but rather in having the courage to do it under adverse circumstances. Our earlier discussion of virtue ethics comes into play here as we consider courage as one of the traits that contributes to integrity and strength of character.

Imagine that you are a student, and your internship supervisor suggests you meet at a coffeehouse for your supervision session. You know this is inappropriate, as it puts clients' confidentiality at risk, even if names are never mentioned. It also reflects poorly on your professionalism and your organization if people at neighboring tables come to believe this is how you conduct sensitive business. Yet why don't you feel comfortable saying so to your supervisor? Is it because of the power differential? Is it because you believe it's not your place to contradict your supervisor, who after all is supposed to be socializing you to the norms of the profession, and not the other way around? Maybe you don't want to make waves, so you agree to the location but vow not to say anything substantive about your clients. The disadvantage in that choice is that you've protected confidentiality at the price of receiving meaningful supervisory feedback. And you've failed to improve the ethical climate at your agency by calling attention to what is probably an unintentional but common ethical failing.

The quality that helps us in actually doing the right thing is known as moral courage (Kidder, 2005). It is "the capacity to overcome the fear of shame and humiliation in order to admit one's mistakes, to confess a wrong, to reject evil conformity, to renounce injustice, and also to defy immoral or imprudent orders" (Miller, 2000, p. 254). J. K. Rowling (1997) captures it perfectly in the Harry Potter series when Dumbledore says to Nevell, "It takes a great deal of bravery to stand up to our enemies, but just as much to stand up to our friends" (p. 306).

Moral courage means accepting challenges that put one's "reputation, emotional well-being, self-esteem or other characteristics" in jeopardy (Kidder & Bracy, 2001, p. 4). It means having the courage to act on your convictions—having "the quality of mind and spirit that enables one to face up to ethical dilemmas and moral wrongdoings firmly and confidently, without flinching or retreating" (Kidder & Bracy, 2001, p. 5). It is unlike physical courage in that it involves standing up "against the unfair, the disrespectful, the irresponsible, the dishonest, and the uncompassionate" (Kidder & Bracy, 2001, p. 11) instead of standing up to the threat of bodily harm.

The willingness to act on ethical principles is essential to ethical practice. If you are unwilling to stand up for honesty, what good is embracing honesty as an important value? For some, the notion of moral courage conjures up images of whistleblowers from the movies or news such as Erin Brockovich, Daniel Ellsberg, or Edward Snowden, and in fact each could serve as an example of a person of virtue. We also picture the very steep personal price they often must pay in defending their principles. Yet acting with moral courage need not put one's life or livelihood at risk. Sometimes it puts a friendship at risk or jeopardizes a possible promotion. People display everyday courage in speaking up, despite these risks, when a colleague is demeaning a client, when patient information is being discussed in the elevator, when a bigoted cartoon is shared on the listserv, or when an able friend parks in a handicapped-reserved space.

Moral courage is not an excuse to be a whiner or a pedant (Miller, 2000). It is not a reason to find fault with every action, large or small. Not every adverse decision in an organization rises to the level of ethical failing, and complaining about each of them does not make one morally courageous. Similarly, speaking out about misconduct without an appreciation of the forces and risks at play is reckless and unwise. Courage is evoked when individuals are cognizant of the risks yet take action anyway. Moral courage also has to be used with care, as many atrocities have been committed in the name of one person's individual convictions. If you are taking on the status quo, it's important for you to understand how it became the status quo, and to explore the basis for your judgment that it is wrongheaded before embarking on a campaign for change.

This last point is important because it speaks to the process by which one acts on one's courage to become an effective agent of change. The steps you should take to bring about change depends, to some extent, on the nature of the difficulty you are confronting and on who you are in relation to the problem. For example, if you are the new head of human resources for an organization and you discover widespread discriminatory hiring practices and an organizational culture that rejects diversity, you are in a different position relative to the problems than if you are a student intern at the agency or an employee who has just quit because of the prejudiced work environment. In the language of organizational change, this problem has both depth and distance: it is pervasive throughout levels of the organization and affects an array of functions (Frey, 1990). As such, it will be more complex to address, even for someone in a position of power. Practicing moral courage requires a skillful application of organizational change strategies as well as the will to act.

If you are a guidance counselor attending a meeting concerning a student enrolled in special education and discover that the professionals are seated at adult-sized chairs while the student's parents are seated in two child-sized chairs, voicing your discomfort and suggesting another arrangement should be relatively simple. Even if you fail to notice this offensive arrangement or don't speak up about it at the time, raising it at a later date, apologizing to the parents, and ensuring it doesn't happen to another family is still better than taking no action at all. That doesn't mean it will be easy, or that others may not chafe at your suggestion: it only means that it requires less tactical skill than a large-scale change might.

Social work authors Brager and Holloway (1983) discuss strategies for internal organizational change that can be effectively applied to reversing unethical practices in systems of any size:

1. Extensive initial assessment involves understanding where the proposed change fits with existing organizational values, whether it addresses a generally recognized problem, whether it can be implemented incrementally or reversed if it does not work, what it requires in terms of resources, and how widespread its impact will be.
2. Preinitiation involves change agents positioning themselves as a force for change, building social capital, developing legitimacy on the issue, increasing the tensions so that others recognize the problem, and sharing leadership on the change effort.
3. Initiation involves developing a coalition publicly committed to the change, moving from allies who already care about the issue to key decision makers, and developing communications on the change that reduce others' resistance to its adoption.
4. During the implementation stage, the honeymoon period is followed by resistance to the change as others experience the pain of transformation and long for the familiarity of old patterns. The goals at this stage include acting when support is at its peak,

anticipating and addressing obstacles, achieving interim goals, being open and informative, and reducing tensions surrounding the
change and the problem it was designed to address.

5. Institutionalization involves standardizing procedures and linking
them to already established organizational elements so that the
chances of change being undone are lessened.

Some of the suggestions for enacting ethical decision making (discussed in Chapter 2) will also apply to acting with moral courage. The key
at this point is to have the will and the intent to uphold the ethical principles you'll be learning. The effort is important regardless of the outcome.

In its annual Person of the Year issue at the end of 2002, *Time* magazine selected three women it called "The Whistleblowers" (Lacayo &
Ripley, 2002). That year, Cynthia Cooper had exposed accounting fraud
at WorldCom, Colleen Rowley had been identified as the FBI bureau chief
whose warnings prior to 9/11 about terrorists in aircraft pilot training had
gone unheeded, and Sherron Watkins had written a confidential memo to
Enron chairman Ken Lay to warn him about the fiscal house of cards the
company had created with its subsidiaries. In his explanation of the selection of these women, *Time*'s editor spoke of them as "ordinary people who
in extraordinary ways tried to restore confidence to business and government" (Kelly, 2002, p. 8). While some may argue that there was more that
they might have done, the prevailing message was that they were honored
not for what they accomplished, but rather for their efforts. In the end,
terrorists flew planes into the Pentagon and World Trade Center, Enron
collapsed, and WorldCom filed for bankruptcy. *Time* decided to laud the
whistleblowers for having done the right thing, irrespective of the ultimate success or failure of their actions.

After all this talk about risk and reward, you may wonder why anyone
should be the giraffe and stick their neck out while others are being tur-
tles, especially if the giraffe's success is not guaranteed. There are several
reasons, from the personal to the global. On the personal level, you have to
live with yourself. Consider your personal integrity and self-concept if you
let an injustice stand. Second, there's the rust problem: sometimes a small
spot of rust on the car, if it's not rubbed out, will over time take out the
whole undercarriage. People sometimes refer to this as the boiled frog phenomenon: a (metaphorical) frog in a pot of water on the stove will make
incremental adjustments as the temperature of the water is increased in

order to adapt to its environment. Unfortunately, this accommodation will be the frog's undoing because the adjustments will obscure the warning system that it's too hot and it's time to jump out. It's easy to be a frog and look the other way or rationalize inaction so many times that we fail to see the toxic climate in which we reside. So often, when someone reports ethical scandals, outsiders shake their heads and say, "What on earth were they thinking!?" The transgressions are so clear. But that's viewing the tub of hot water from the outside, not from inside where gradual accommodations disrupt the moral thermometer.

Acts of courage help to ensure that an individual's own moral compass does not become clouded by repeated adjustments in an unethical environment. The individual's decision to do the right thing is also important for the organization. In R. Cohen's (2002) view, we judge the appropriateness of our behavior by those around us. Their behavior is a yardstick by which we evaluate our own. In what he calls "the ecology of ethics" (R. Cohen, 2002, p. 9), individual acts of courage diminish a corrosive organizational environment and reinforce an exemplary ethical culture. Multiply this across the web of interactions and systems that make up our daily lives, and hopefully the result of multiple acts of ethical behavior is a better, more-just world.

The Issue of Risk

Social workers must consider other risks beyond those that come from speaking out about injustice. Often they are concerned with the risk of doing the wrong thing or failing to do the right thing. They worry about a disaffected client or family filing a grievance with their employer, a complaint with their licensure board, an inquiry with their professional association, or a lawsuit for malpractice. They fear damage to their reputation and their livelihood, even if such complaints are unfounded. They fear the cost of defending themselves against such actions, even with the benefit of malpractice insurance. And they worry about the toll such a defense will take on their energy, their reputation, their personal relationships, and their work performance.

These are not unreasonable concerns. Litigation and other charges of professional misconduct exact an incredible toll. To some extent, though, they are the price of doing this business. Professions in which people intervene to address physical and psychic pain, to mend relationships, and to improve others' quality of life are not risk free. Even good practitioners may make mistakes. They may fail to act when they should to protect a client from harm, or they may act when they should not—for example, in speaking to the media about a deceased client's illness, thus violating her confidentiality. And because we live in a litigious society, it is true that anybody can complain about anything, and a good professional may be blamed for something for which she bears no fault. Yet practicing so conservatively and carefully that one takes no risks is almost impossible in social work, counseling, and similar fields.

Making ethical and professional decisions based on risk avoidance is akin to using the law as a standard for ethical practice. It is defensive practice, not practice that reaches for the highest standards of the discipline (Koocher & Keith-Spiegel, 2008). What does that leave for the rest of us who want to be skilled, ethical practitioners but don't want to be the target of client complaints? Good practice is the best policy.

What does good practice mean? In part it means knowing where your competencies lie and where they do not, building your capacity, seeking advice, and avoiding situations where you are practicing outside your scope of expertise. It means being conversant with the practice standards for your field so that you know what the norms are, what tests and assessment protocols are appropriate, and what interventions are empirically supported. It also means being familiar with social work's ethical standards, because they not only will guide practice, but also will support you when you can say, "My actions in this case were in keeping with the standards of my profession."

Beyond these steps, you want to be careful not to practice in a vacuum. Even those licensed to practice independently need ongoing consultation and continuing education to think through clinical and ethical dilemmas and to keep abreast of changes in the field. Consultation helps you discover new perspectives and unconsidered options and is a way to check your perceptions against those of other professionals. Colleagues also provide a sounding board in cases where you may be losing your objectivity or straying onto the slippery slope toward ethical transgressions (Gabbard, 1996).

Beyond ethical awareness and consultation, risk management demands that you keep good records. The saying "If it isn't written down, it didn't happen" captures the thinking behind this principle. Documenting your consultation in a record of supervision, recording your decision-making process in your business files, or noting in the client's chart the options and choices discussed will help substantiate the process you went through when faced with an ethical dilemma and the way that you made and enacted your decision (Reamer, 2018; Wilkins, 2017).

Where is the balance between a person who is reckless in their professional practice and one who is so timid that they can scarcely act autonomously with the baseline confidence needed to encourage clients? In all probability, we all practice on a continuum between those extremes where bold practitioners practice successfully alongside those who are more risk averse.

But to succeed amid the perils in the helping professions, a dose of professional humility is required. It takes a confident, thoughtful, self-aware social worker to say, "I don't know" or "I need help sorting out my options here." I'm reminded of a family practice physician I saw many years ago who called me on a Monday morning; she was scheduled to remove a mole from my face later that day. She said, "I've been thinking about you over the weekend, and I'd be more comfortable if we put this in the hands of a specialist." She went on to refer me to a dermatologist, and I continued to see her for all my other health care. I also recommended her to everyone I knew. She had thought about my case! She was comfortable enough with herself to call and cancel a previously arranged procedure! I could imagine an insecure doctor desperate for business who might not think twice about her suitability for the procedure, or who might believe that calling would undermine my confidence in her. To the contrary, my trust in the doctor's competence and in her integrity increased, and after all, aren't those two qualities all clients want in their caregivers? Knowing our limits, practicing within them, and seeking help from others are all part of competent, ethical, risk-managing practice.

How This Text Will (and Won't) Help You with Ethics

Now that we have a baseline notion of what it means to be ethical, we'll examine in Chapter 2 a process for addressing ethical dilemmas and the considerations that will help us unravel complex cases. Chapters 3 through 9 describe seven core concepts that guide ethical practice in the helping professions:

- Self-determination
- Informed consent
- Conflicts of interest
- Professional boundaries
- Confidentiality
- Competence
- Professionalism and integrity

In each chapter you will find excerpts of standards from social work codes of ethics that demonstrate how the concept is operationalized for practice. Each chapter contains examples of cases where the principle is upheld and cases where it is violated, as well as dilemmas to which we can apply the ethical problem-solving process. The cases are drawn from a variety of practice settings and locales such as schools, health-care facilities, and rural areas, and professional roles such as that of researcher, clinician, community organizer, instructor, and supervisor. We will examine the unique characteristics and demands of the role or setting because those features are important parts of the context in resolving dilemmas.

You will surely find that dilemmas you've encountered are not addressed in the book. No book, especially one short enough to be desirable reading, can address the variety of permutations that evolve in ethics cases. In fact, one of my joys in doing workshops on ethics is hearing all the different issues that participants bring up and working through them to an ethically sound conclusion. If you hope to find a final answer, this book will be a disappointment. I hope that, instead of expecting it to be a cookbook or a repair manual, you'll see it as a mental barbell—a tool to strengthen your critical thinking, with the goal of improving what Kidder (1995) calls our "ethical fitness" (p. 57). As his notion suggests, ethical fitness™ involves exercising our minds to be prepared so that we can adroitly respond when ethical dilemmas arise. The more exercise we get in addressing ethical dilemmas, the more likely it is that future dilemmas will be variations on a theme, rather than novel experiences. Thus, the purpose of this book is to help you

- build the competencies needed to identify elements of ethical dilemmas,

- decide what to do, and then
- have the courage to carry out that decision.

This book is not a resource to address conflicting values or broad moral questions. It will not fully acquaint you with the philosophical underpinnings of ethical thought, or take on vexing bioethical questions of the day, such as when life begins or the wisdom of artificial intelligence. These are all substantial, compelling areas of study, but they are just not the focus of this book. This text is situated in the area of applied ethics. It is grounded in the ways that ethics guide our practice as helping professionals. I use the term "practice" to mean not only direct practice or clinical practice, but also the execution of other tasks such as supervision, administration, case management, and the like. I hope to share with you the tools for arriving at ethically sound decisions and the strategies for enacting them effectively. You'll get a chance to try those tools out on the scenarios and cases I provide and, I hope, will gain a greater comfort, and fitness, in employing those tools wherever your professional journey leads.

For Continuing Conversation

1. What philosophies and people shape your ideas about right and wrong?
2. What was the most difficult ethical dilemma you ever encountered? Are you satisfied with the way it was resolved?
3. What situations have you encountered where you took a stand on behalf of principle?
4. How can professionals keep up their ethical fitness™?

Key Concepts

Consequentialism. The ethical doctrine that the moral rightness of an act depends only on the consequences of that act or of something related to that act, such as the motive behind the act or a general rule requiring acts of the same kind.

Contractualism. The view that morality is based on abstract contracts or agreements that are unquestioned. If an individual breaks the contract then the other persons involved no longer needs to respect their part in the contract.

Deontology. The study of what is morally obligatory, permissible, right, or wrong.

Decolonize. The practice of identifying, challenging, and decentering dominant Eurocentric paradigms, replacing them with heretofore marginalized ways of being, knowing, and doing.

Ethical dilemma. A situation that often involves an apparent conflict between moral imperatives, in which to select one would result in transgressing another.

Ethical relativism. The belief that nothing is objectively right or wrong and that the definition of right or wrong depends on the prevailing view of a particular individual, culture, or historical period.

Ethical skepticism. A diverse collection of views that deny or raise doubts about the roles of reason in morality. Different versions of moral skepticism deny or doubt moral knowledge, justified moral belief, moral truth, moral facts or properties, and reasons to be moral.

Ethics. A system of moral standards or principles that direct a person's or group's behavior.

Ethics of care. A normative ethical theory emphasizing the importance of response. The basic tenets are (1) all individuals are interdependent for achieving their interests, (2) vulnerable individuals deserve extra consideration if affected by our choices, and (3) it is necessary to examine the contextual details of a situation to promote the best interest of those involved.

Justice. The quality of being fair and reasonable; behavior or treatment that is fair and reasonable.

Morality of care. An ethical framework that seeks to acknowledge gendered differences in the understanding of morality. The traditional morality of justice is based on a Western moral philosophy and empirical research produced by male scholars. In contrast, the morality of care examines females' moral orientation, taking into account ideas of care, needs, interdependence, and human trust, and highlighting the gaps in traditional moral philosophy.

Normative ethics. The application of ethical theories to practical situations. Attempts "to give answers to moral questions and problems" (Banks, 2021, p. 40).

Supererogation. The performance of more work than duty requires.

Theory of justice. A work of philosophy and ethics by John Rawls, addressing the problem of socially just distribution of good in a society. Rawls' first principle of justice states that all persons have an equal right to liberty; his second principle states that social and economic inequalities ought to be distributed so that the greatest benefit goes to the most disadvantaged members of society.

Utilitarianism. The doctrine that an action is right if it is useful or for the benefit of the greatest number. *See* consequentialism.

Veil of ignorance. A method of determining the morality of a certain issue based on a scenario in which an individual is ignorant of her particular position within the social order of society, such that her decisions on principles for the distribution of rights, positions, and resources in society is unbiased.

Virtue. Behavior showing high moral standards; a quality considered morally good or desirable in a person.

Virtue ethics. An approach to normative ethics that evaluates the morality of an action or behavior by emphasizing the role of one's character and the virtues one's character embodies. Thus, we evaluate a particular action ethically based on what it reveals about the individual's character.

CHAPTER 2

Ethical Decision Making

Introduction

In the early 1980s I took one of the multiple-choice exams new social workers are required to pass for licensure. One of the questions was something along the lines of "A client takes off her necklace and throws it at you. What do you do?" One of the answers was "Keep the necklace" and another was "Throw it back." I don't recall the other two options, though I assume one of them was the right answer. What I do recall is sitting there with my Number 2 pencil and my bubble sheet (old school) and thinking, "It depends!" (This was *not* one of the choices offered by the exam.) And in fact, social work is an "it depends" profession. What we decide to do in any situation depends on a variety of factors, including the settings in which we work, our professional role, our knowledge of the client, the goals on which we are working, and our own competency. Ethical decision making requires that we take the same considerations into account.

There are very few clear proscriptions in professional codes beyond the sanction against having sexual relations with a current client. Our standards often include imprecise terms such as "when it is *feasible*," "*appropriate* physical contact," and "deal with them *responsibly*." In fact, even straightforward guidelines such as "Do no harm" turn out not to be all that clear in application. For example, a supervisor in a residential program finds that the one of the staff members has declined to be vaccinated for COVID-19 yet frequently has symptoms of the infection and is struggling to fulfil the job responsibilities. What should residents and fellow employees be told about the employee's condition—not only to explain the worker's failure to carry their share of the team's workload but also to ensure their own safety? Doing no harm would involve protecting the workforce, but what about the harm to the employee if their condition and vaccination status is exposed? What of the harm to the culture of (and laws on) workplace privacy if individuals' health conditions and supervisory conversations are not held in confidence?

As we discussed in the previous chapter, the lack of clear imperatives in professional ethics does not mean that anything goes, that every decision is relative. It doesn't mean that any action is acceptable as long as you can find a rationale for it. It does mean that disciplined, critical thinking is required to uphold ethical principles amidst the complexities of professional practice. It means that professionals must engage in a deeper examination, because the context or factors at play will shape the wisdom, the alternatives, and the impact of a particular course of action. Gallagher (2020) refers to this consideration as "slow ethics" and contrasts it with the pressure for efficiency and callous reliance on metrics, gut instinct, and snap judgements. Banks (2021) uses the term "ethics work" to describe the processes that social worker engage in intuitively before formal decision making: "Doing 'ethics work' involves practitioners being constantly alert to their roles in a situation and critically aware of the political context in which they are working; attending to the particular needs, desires, emotions, rights and responsibilities of the people involved and the ethically salient features of the situation; and being caring, compassionate, reliable and trustworthy" (p. 338). Ethical preparation and skills in decision making help us decide what it means to practice within professional standards in any given situation.

Take, for example, the question "Is it ethical to accept a gift from a client?" The answer is clearly "It depends." On the one hand, accepting a gift can lead to a **conflict of interest** if it impedes the worker from carrying out professional responsibilities such as holding the client accountable for a particular action. It can also lead to perceived conflicts of interest if other clients believe that it has led to favoritism for the gift giver. Sometimes gifts can lead to **boundary** confusion, such as if the client believes the gift signifies a friendship with the worker, or expects reciprocation as friends would do.

In defense of accepting gifts, we should note that in some cultures, the giving of gifts symbolizes the client's willingness to proceed in a therapeutic partnership with the worker (Spandler et al., 2000). At other times, it is simply an act of regard, or gratitude, as when clients share vegetables from their garden or bake the worker a cake, or a child offers some artwork they created. The timing of the gift can matter, too. Is the gift given around a holiday or life event when gifts may be given to others with whom we have relationships? Perhaps your client's gift to you is the same one given to the manicurist, mail deliverer, mechanic, or babysitter to mark the end of the calendar year. Sometimes clients present gifts to mark an important occasion in the worker's life, such as a baby gift when the worker returns from maternity leave. Is it unethical to accept gifts on such occasions? Is it facilitative of the clinical process? Is it culturally sensitive?

Organizational policies attempt to address the ambiguity involved in the considerations about gifts. The policies may set a limit on the monetary value of a gift, restrict gifts to only handmade items, or forbid gifts altogether. Such rules often prove unsatisfactory or imprecise. A handmade quilt may fit the cost limit and still be of great value. The unilateral prohibition on gifts seems neither ethically nor clinically sensible. In fact, most of the very agencies that hold these policies will solicit and accept large donations from clients or their families, suggesting disingenuously that corporate conflicts of interest are not problematic in the same way gifts to workers are.

Codes of ethics in the helping professions are silent on the issue of gifts but do caution against conflicts of interest. Thus, some clinicians resolve the ethical dilemma of gift acceptance by determining that homemade or inexpensive gifts don't cause them difficulties in carrying out their responsibilities. When possible, some clinicians share their gifts with the office—for example, by putting a cake in the break room, a baby gift in the play area, or a painting on the office wall. Because the gift is then shared with the staff, the possibility of a conflict arising because the individual worker profited from the gift is diminished.

Even with inexpensive gifts, the wise worker is attuned to the frequency and circumstances of gift giving, and the effects on the helping relationship. If these raise concerns, they may decline even a homemade or token gift. For example, a client whose issues involve overdoing may get caught up in baking for the worker in a way that is countertherapeutic. Or a client who provides vegetables from their garden may need to hear that, while the worker appreciates such thoughtfulness, such gestures aren't necessary remuneration for the worker's service.

And some gifts are never okay. An expensive gift, even if it is given to signify cross-cultural acceptance, raises the potential for problems. Likewise, monetary gifts, heirlooms, and items on which the client's family members might have a claim are also problematic. It is incumbent on the skilled worker to become comfortable at exploring and tactfully declining such offers. The ability to gracefully decline gifts and other overtures is essential because, as we discuss later, ethical practice cannot be separated from good clinical practice (Gottlieb, 1994), and the process by which we enact our ethical decisions is often as important as the decisions themselves.

So, is it ethical to accept a gift from a client? Sometimes it is and sometimes it isn't: addressing the "it depends" will help you understand the conditions under which it and other actions are and aren't okay. The emphasis on context isn't intended to suggest that every ethical dilemma requires an examination of all the factors impinging on the choice. As you develop as a professional, patterns of practice will evolve that suit you, your field, and the populations and issues with which you work. We assume the patterns you develop will be ethical ones. Within those, though, unique variations will emerge from time to time—challenges you hadn't considered, or new client needs that don't fit in your existing model. Having the capacity for ethical decision making will help you not only establish habits for ethical practice but also adapt those habits to novel situations as they arise.

In some ways, it may be helpful to think of ethics as a continuum, where the potential choices and actions are arranged on a spectrum ranging from highly unethical to highly ethical, or from ethically unwise to ethically sound. Where your choice falls on that continuum may depend on the factors surrounding the case, or the context, and may depend on your own level of comfort with your options. As such there may be several right answers, but finding them requires a systematic method for addressing the "it depends," and this is where ethical decision-making models come into play (see Figure 2.1). As Reamer (2018) notes, "Reasonable minds can differ. . . . Clients and other affected parties have a right to expect that social workers involved in the decision will be thorough, thoughtful, sensitive, and fair" (p. 105).

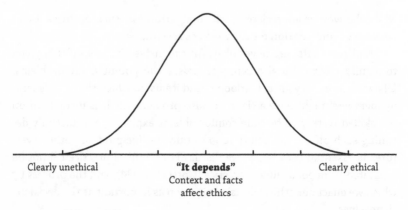

Clearly unethical   **"It depends"**   Clearly ethical
                                      Context and facts
                                      affect ethics

FIGURE 2.1 "It Depends"

Ethical Decision-Making Models

Ethical decision-making models teach us how to carefully weigh the relevant factors in a dilemma and develop an ethically sound course of action. These models come in various forms (D'Aprix, 2005; McAuliffe & Chenoweth, 2007). One type is the decision tree, in which the user is led through different courses of action based on their judgments or answers at various points along the tree (Alagoz et al., 2010; Steinman et al., 1998). Other authors present a list of steps in hierarchical but not contingent order (Dolgoff et al., 2022), and still others offer ordered decision-making processes, some of which include schemata where memory devices are embedded in the steps to assist with recall. For example, Congress's (1999) ETHIC model stands for examine values, think about ethical standards, hypothesize about different courses of action, identify who would be harmed and who would be helped, and consult with a supervisor or colleagues, and in Gallagher and Sykes' (2008) model, ETHICS represents enquire, think through, hear views, identify principles, clarify meaning, and select action.

A challenging aspect of ethical decision-making models is that they are often so cumbersome that people fail to use them or fail to remember what the steps stand for. Another challenge occurs when the user, having proceeded diligently through the steps, still ends up with no clear path to a decision. The key, then, is to adopt a model that helps to reveal the important considerations and yet is simple enough that it can become a ready resource to be used reflexively whenever a dilemma arises.

The Six-Question Model

The model I developed for this book, which I call the six-question or 6Q model, incorporates the steps and features most commonly found in decision-making models for the helping professions (D'Aprix, 2005). It requires you to ask yourself six questions to ensure that you think through the considerations necessary to determine an ethical course of action. These questions are modeled on the imperatives for telling a story or writing a news article—who, what, when, where, why, and how. For the purpose of ethical decision making, the questions in the model are best summarized in Figure 2.2.

Preliminary testing of the model indicates support for its relevance and ease of use. Forty-one master's-level practitioners were trained in the use of the 6Q model; forty-four were trained in another model. When asked to list factors that might affect their future use of a model, the two

Who will be helpful?
- Consultation
  - Supervisor/colleagues
  - Specialists
  - Written and organizational resources
- Generate options, evaluate options, plan process, practice, debrief
- Before or after the decision
- Use discretion

How should I enact my decision?
- Process matters!
- Consider ultimate objectives
- Use social work knowledge and skills
  - Human behavior
  - Strategy
  - Empathy
  - Communication
  - Culture
- Remember to document

What are my choices?
- What additional information is needed?
- Generate alternatives, including non-action
- What will each choice mean for those involved?
- Timing of action? Urgency?

Why am I selecting a particular course of action?
- Examine motives
- Examine rationale
- Self-understanding
- The right thing for the wrong reason?
- Principle of publicity

Where do ethical and clinical guidelines lead me?
- Rule-based/outcome-based philosophy
- Values (professional, cultural)
- Professional standards (NASW, CASW)
- Practice principles
- Ethical principles
- Laws and policies
- Convergence or trade offs?

When have I faced a similar dilemma?
- Examine past dilemmas/experiences/readings
  - Were choices effective?
  - If not why not?
- How is this similar to past choices?
- How is it different?
- Have personal "policies" been developed for this issue?

FIGURE 2.2 The Six-Question Model

most common concerns were "time" and "difficulty remembering steps in the model." Concerns about time generally focused on the timeliness or urgency with which a decision must be made.

At the conclusion of each 6Q training, subjects were randomly selected to participate in the process evaluation of the model (n = 8). For six months, the research participants maintained diaries about their ethical dilemmas and the usefulness of the models in practice. The diaries consisted of sixteen scaled and open-ended questions; participants recorded the dilemmas, the steps used in resolution of the dilemma, the desirability of the decision that resulted, the elements of the model used, and the perceived efficacy and utility of the given element. The questions were drawn from the literature on decision making and the barriers to using decision-making models.

Average ratings were relatively high for each step in the 6Q model across each of eight criteria. The criteria were whether each of the six steps is easy to recall, necessary, intuitive, relevant, clear, comfortable, reasonable, and consistent with values. The 6Q model steps can be ranked in order from highest to lowest in overall utility (as measured by an overall average rating across all criteria) as follows: what, why, where/how (tied), who, when.

Although users found the model effective and helpful, diary keepers provided narrative descriptions of factors that dissuaded or prevented them from fully implementing the model in daily practice. Examples of personal or internal factors included discomfort with confrontation or sensitive topics; fear of judgment, retribution, or overstepping authority; lack of previous experience on which to base the decisions; and a desire to avoid legal involvement. External influences included lack of support from colleagues or supervisors, limited access to consultation, limited time (e.g., the time required to research laws/policies, immediacy of the decision deadline, caseload), and institutional policies.

Some Provisions for Using the Model

You should be aware of four features before embarking on the 6Q model:

- The model is not linear.
- It requires reflection and self-awareness.
- Some steps are implicit and are not specified in the model (addressing unknowns, documenting).
- The value of the model is in the process, not simply the outcome.

Nonlinear. The six questions are not ranked in an order of priority, or in an order for action. While who, what, when where, why and how may be easy to remember, the 6Q model is not a linear process. Each element may support the others. For example, consultation (who?) can help identify options (what?), weigh options (where?), prepare for difficult conversations or strategy selection (how?), and evaluate the process when it is over (what?). You should consider all elements, but different circumstances will dictate that you address them at different times in the decision-making process, and that you give different weight to the various options. In some cases you will be examining a decision retrospectively that you had to make in the moment it arose (such as if you arrived for a home visit with a pregnant teen and found that several members of the extended family were gathered in the kitchen and living room, anticipating inclusion in the meeting). In a case such as that, the worker does the best they can to balance competing goods (confidentiality, cultural humility, and self-determination) based on existing knowledge and ethical wisdom, and then returns to the office to reflect on the incident, using the six questions, in supervision and staffing.

Self-awareness. Another premise is that 6Q users possess self-awareness and capacity to identify and act on ethical dilemmas. These are elements of professionalism and qualities of virtue. They are the focus of socialization as individuals learn about and join a profession. Sensitivity to the presence of dilemmas and understanding of our own capacities and blind spots will help flag issues when they arise. We can then subject the issues to the model for assistance in decision making. For example, a worker on a home visit must realize that the presence of extended family members has ethical and clinical implications. The worker should also be aware of their own positionality, strengths, and weaknesses, particularly in terms of raising this issue with the client and working through to a sound solution. With those fundamentals in place, the 6Q model can assist in examining the pros and cons of various possible responses.

Implicit steps. Social workers often have imperfect information when addressing ethical dilemmas. We may wish we knew more about the client's background and experiences, the other people involved, the agencies or resources we might refer to, and so on. Sometimes we need to proceed without all of the information we desire. Waiting for certainty leads to analysis paralysis. However, it is important to identify the unknowns and the information we most need in case it is crucial for ruling an option in or out. Throughout the applications of the model later in this book, you will see questions raised that identify relevant information to pursue. These can affect any of the steps in the process, so researching information is not aligned to a particular stage.

Similarly, documentation is part of sound practice and may take place at each step of the process, depending on the information the worker receives and considers, and the resources she consults. It may involve notes in clients' records about conversations with the client, entries in private psychotherapy notes on consults received in the case, and personal notations and insights recorded in a journal identifying why a particular option was selected (Zuckerman & Keeley, 2017). Rather than prompt you to document at each step, you are encouraged to build it into your practice as a matter of habit.

Process. While the ideal of any decision-making model is to lead to a decision, the 6Q model, like others, is most effective as a guide to evaluating choices. It is intended to uncover the various dimensions of the "it depends" and in doing so help you weigh the various options, and perhaps rule some out. At the conclusion of the steps, you should know what the relative benefits and risks are for your choices and make a decision in which the reasoning is sound and the outcome thoughtfully derived.

Let's now examine what the elements of the model mean and then put them into practice with an example.

Who Will Be Helpful?

Even the experienced practitioner should not make ethical decisions in a vacuum. Discussing the issue with appropriate individuals or entities (sometimes called the dialogic process) may bring forth information, obligations, or alternatives we haven't previously considered. By discussing the dilemma with others, we are able to unravel the knot of issues that may be tied up in the case. We get assistance in examining the case from various perspectives. We open the door to the generation of more creative solutions, and we have the opportunity to anticipate and rehearse how we will carry out our decision. Dialogue can also help us evaluate a decision after the fact, consider the outcomes, and, if they were unfavorable, strategize any possible ways to make things right. This reflection helps increase our capacity for addressing future dilemmas as we sort out how we'd want to handle things the next time around (see Figure 2.3).

Who will be helpful?
- Consultation
  - Supervisor/colleagues
  - Specialists
  - Written and organizational resources
- Generate options, evaluate options, plan process, practice, debrief
- Before or after the decision
- Use discretion

FIGURE 2.3 Who Will Be Helpful?

Who is an appropriate person or entity for consultation? The answer clearly is, "Not just anyone." You should consult only those people who are well versed in ethical and clinical practice in the setting where you practice. Hopefully, you have an ongoing collegial or supervisory relationship with them, so that the dialogue takes place in an atmosphere of professionalism, familiarity, and trust. That person should be clear on the responsibility to maintain confidentiality on the issue you are sharing, but it is still wise for you to reveal only the information necessary to effectively examine the case. You should avoid mentioning names and other specifics.

It may be tempting to speak to your partner, spouse, or best friend when such dilemmas are on your mind. It is human nature in times of trouble to turn to those we know best. You may reason that you value their advice or that they have a lot of common sense and creative ideas and thus can help you think clearly about your situation. All those things may be true, but unless they are in the same field as you are, the questions they ask and the advice they give are not going to be grounded in the principles of your profession. Even if they are in the same field, that may not translate into having expertise in ethics. And, their allegiance to you may color their ability to provide an objective sounding board. Beyond this, you are breaching your client's privacy by revealing personal information, even if you believe you've obscured identifying information. Think about it another way: Would you want your physician to decide how to manage your care by talking it over with their hair stylist? Would it bolster your confidence in the doctor's professionalism or the quality of her care?

Many agencies today are overworked, and in many cases the quality of supervision has been scaled back to the basics of administrative or dashboard data reviews. Sometimes supervisors do not share the same professional background as their supervisees or are otherwise ill suited for relevant, competent consultation. Or the people whose primary roles are supervision or administration may have no direct supervision themselves. If any of these scenarios is the case at your workplace, you need to make alternative arrangements to develop a skilled, trustworthy, and consistent resource for consultation. One model may involve purchasing supervision. Another option for seasoned practitioners is peer consultation, one on one or in a group format. In developing either of these arrangements, it is wise to create a contract so there is a common understanding of expectations, including those for maintaining confidentiality (Reamer, 2021b). Some even suggest going a step farther and routinely notifying clients about the arrangement and the qualifications of those who serve as supervisors or consultants (NASW National Council on the Practice of Clinical Social Work, 1994).

Sometimes the difficulty arises not from a lack of good resources on which we can call but from having the courage to use those resources. Whether it is because of professional ego, personal hubris, or the fear that we have erred, it can be difficult to say, "I'm confused" or "Something happened in my session yesterday and I'm not sure I handled it the right way." Yet unless professionals are willing to confront the issues, there is no way to begin the **dialogic process**. Without that initiative, all involved are deprived of an opportunity to do better—to flex their thinking and generate ideas and alternatives on vexing issues. This goes back to the concepts of virtue ethics and moral courage raised in Chapter 1. Being an ethical practitioner means constantly opening yourself to learning and input from others.

Supervisors and colleagues aren't the only resources for consultation. Other individuals involved in the dilemma, whether a client or colleague, have a stake in the decision and should be consulted when feasible. The concepts of equity, respect, and reciprocity support such conversations (Grossmanss, 2010). A familiar saying in the disability rights community is "[Say or do] nothing about me without me." Ethical dilemmas, where the outcomes will impinge on others' rights and well-being, are ripe for shared problem solving. These conversations may be uncomfortable and the other person's wishes may be distorted by the power dynamics with the social worker, but those are always hazards in consultation and decision making and should not constitute an automatic reason to rule out discussion, however difficult or uncomfortable the conversation may be. Consider a new employee who is partnered with a veteran practitioner to learn how to deliver a manualized training, but who notices troubling signs of forgetfulness and repetitiveness by the co-trainer. A consultative conversation, in the right time and place, might start with, "Elaine, I have a dilemma, and I wonder if I could talk with you about it?" "I've had some observations over our last few sessions. I'm not sure what to do and I would value your help." The worker could then describe the observations and share the challenge—for example, "I respect you and your reputation as a trainer, but I am also concerned about the needs of the trainees and the quality of our program." In an example involving a client and the prospect of a dual relationship, the invitation might go as follows: "Jerome, I learned yesterday that my husband hired you to do our mowing and plowing this year. He does not know I'm your social worker, and I am always careful not to talk about my work at home, but there can be complications in mixing business relationships. I wanted to discuss any concerns you might have and get your thoughts about continuing your work with me or the work at the house." To be clear, the social worker should use the other decision-making steps and resources to consider whether this dual relationship is problematic or what boundaries should be put into place to protect the integrity of the helping relationship. Jerome may want to continue being a client and working at the home, but if the worker ultimately decides that is untenable, they should revisit the issue and one of the dual relationships might be ended.

In answering the "who" question, you may also consult entities designed to assist in ethical dilemmas. These may include formal ethics committees, such as those that are often found at hospitals and other large organizations. Licensure boards, professional organizations, and attorneys who specialize in professional conduct are also resources for consultation. Be aware, though, of two things. First, you need to take extra care to protect patient identities and avoid revealing excessively personal case information. Second, bear in mind that these entities may have their own agendas or priorities that may influence the nature of the advice they provide. For example, an organization's ethics committee may be more of a risk management device than an opportunity to open up a dilemma for examination. If that's so, the nature of their advice will be oriented toward protecting the organization's interests and liability, not necessarily honoring patient wishes or upholding the highest professional standards. This doesn't mean that you shouldn't consult them, only that you may want to evaluate their advice in light of their stake in the decision.

Other resources for consultation include professional networks developed among former classmates or faculty, with other practitioners in the community, or via associations such as NASW or CASW. By reaching out to colleagues with expertise in particular issues or interventions, or experience in specific settings, social workers facing ethical dilemmas can get consultation specific a particular dilemma. For example, consider the case of a sixteen-year-old client who divulged having been raped by her brother's teen friend but refused to say more and said that she would deny it if her parents or other authorities were informed. In addition to talking to the supervisor about parental rights, informed consent, and confidentiality issues, the social worker also consulted colleagues in trauma-informed care, child protection, law enforcement, and rape crisis services for their advice. The worker revealed minimal information (only the background described above) and asked how their respective services would respond to such a case and to reports made against the client's wishes. The information the worker received indicated futility in reporting without the client's consent and possible re-traumatization in taking the reporting decision out of the client's hands.

A variation on using these formal personal networks for advice involves posting queries to closed or open online forums. As with relying on known professional networks, it is incumbent on the social worker to do the following:

1. Do their own homework to be educated about the issues and common practices in the domain they are asking about.

2. Assiduously guard identifying information in making the query (even saying "I saw someone today who . . ." is too much information).
3. Be attentive to the qualifications of the people giving advice. "Qualifications" go beyond professional credentials: they may be lived experience from consumers of social services, or their family members, or groups that represent their interests. But, especially online, the intentions and wisdom of respondents can be indeterminate or deceptive, and thus must be adopted with care.
4. Document the contact and content in the case record if appropriate, or in a journal or files as one would for the minutes of committee meetings. Documentation should cover the ethical issue and how it arose, the steps taken to assess the situation, the options considered and the mitigating factors for each, and the ultimate action taken and the results (Barsky, 2019; Reamer, 2018).

Seeking consultation is not a substitute for being knowledgeable and developing sound skills for identifying and evaluating dilemmas. It is one part of the ethical decision-making process, not necessarily the first step nor the last, but one which you should approach well-prepared to consider the advice you are given. And, consultation is not just a one-way street. Reciprocal relationships with colleagues will give you the opportunity to think though issues they may bring to you and advise them, and through this dialogue your capacity will also increase.

What Are My Options?

To effectively examine your options for solving an ethical dilemma, and the wisdom of each choice, you need to get the options on the table (see Figure 2.4). Consulting with others is one way of doing so. Consulting books, articles, or other written resources may also help generate ideas. Brainstorming means generating options without regard to feasibility, probability, or cost. Consider also the option of nonaction. The important part at this stage is to think creatively about an array of possibilities.

Once you have generated the options, you should examine the pros and cons of each. What could the options possibly mean for those involved? The case of an accidental dual relationship in Box 2.1 helps illustrate the process of generating and weighing options.

One option in this situation is to do nothing. Another is to terminate the client relationship and keep the client as a personal employee. Another

What are my choices?
- What additional information is needed?
- Generate alternatives, including non-action
- What will each choice mean for those involved?
- Timing of action? Urgency?

FIGURE 2.4 What Are My Choices?

BOX 2.1

An Accidental Dual Relationship

Let's say you've just found out that your spouse or partner hired one of your clients to do yard work at your home. You doubt your client realized it was your home they'd be working at. Still, it presents a dual relationship, and one that is potentially complicated by the fact that the landscaper is a current, not former, client. Similarly, the fact that you didn't initially know about or create the dual relationship doesn't change the fact that the two relationships exist.

is to tell your spouse and ask them to rescind the agreement. Another is to speak with your client and explain the complications, hoping they will cancel the agreement with your spouse. If the client refuses to withdraw from the landscaping agreement, you might ask your spouse to find a new landscaper, without explaining why. Another option is to discuss the issue with the client, allowing them to make the decision to maintain both relationships. Each of these options presents various merits and difficulties for the people involved:

- Doing nothing might preserve the client's confidentiality in that you need not say anything to your spouse. Perhaps the client needs the work and will never find out it's your house. Besides, it's your spouse who made the arrangement, not you. You may prefer not to have to deal with this. Still, your client could feel deceived and exploited if they do find out it's your house and you knew they were hired. This could lead to a loss of trust. Also the knowledge that they are an employee could affect your ability to treat them fairly in the helping relationship or to take action if there are problems with their performance as a landscaper.

- Assuming the client is not ready for termination, ending your relationship to facilitate the role as landscaper could be considered abandonment. Even if they are ready to terminate, the dual relationship concern remains, as dual relationships can occur subsequent to the helping relationship as well as concurrently with it.

- Telling your spouse and asking them to un-hire the landscaper keeps you out of it, but at the expense of the client's confidentiality. And the client/landscaper may want to know why they are being let go. If your spouse tells them, the client knows you breached privacy. If your spouse lies, you both would be treating the landscaper dishonestly.

- Sharing the dilemma with your client is empowering. Explaining the reasoning against dual relationships demonstrates your integrity and your dedication to putting their needs as a service recipient above your need for a landscaper. A discussion about what to do helps to model effective problem solving. Hopefully, your client will volunteer or agree to withdraw from the landscaping job. In doing so, they need not reveal the reason to your spouse, thus preserving confidentiality. If they do tell your spouse, that would be their choice, not yours.

- If your client is not willing to withdraw from the agreement, you should discuss the problems a dual relationship would pose for your work together and consider terminating one or both of the relationships. This is a variation on informed consent, wherein the client knows the actions you will take if they continue to work at your home (for example, you might ask your spouse to cancel the agreement without revealing their status as a client). At that point your client will understand the importance of these boundaries and the implications of the choice not to resign from the landscaping job.

- Consulting with the client about the dilemma and allowing the client to decide if a dual relationship is acceptable would be forthright and empowering. However, the decision about how to conduct the helping relationship rests on more than the client's self-determination: it also relies on the clinician's understanding of their responsibilities. The CASW Guidelines for Ethical Practice (2005b) states that social workers are required to "evaluate the nature of the various contacts to determine whether the social worker is in a position of power and/or authority that may unduly and/or negatively affect the decisions and actions of their client" (2.4). The NASW Code of Ethics (2021) also makes it clear that it is the professional's responsibility to "set clear, appropriate and culturally sensitive boundaries" (1.06c). You may want, for a variety of reasons, to leave the decision to the client, but you are the one who can best foresee the difficulties that can arise from such arrangements. Furthermore, asking the client to decide means that they are forced to choose between their financial well-being and well-being as a service user. In trying to preserve both (or the relationship with you), the client may not act in their long-term interests.

You may be concerned that giving the client this ultimatum could negatively affect the helping relationship. It may, but if discord occurs as a result of you setting a firm boundary around the dual relationship, discord was probably there already. As you are weighing your options, you should certainly anticipate the risk of disruption and consider the ways to manage it if it occurs. It's doubtful, though, that this tension or conflict is a worse price to pay than the greater disruption that might occur if the client ended up employed at your home on a regular basis.

Another issue to consider is how quickly you need to act. Some ethical dilemmas are slow-moving targets. They emerge gradually and require (or allow) a thoughtful, planned response. For example, an agency director might need to decide how to deal with a regulation that challenges ethical practice, or a clinician might anticipate receiving a subpoena with a broad request for client information.

Other dilemmas pop up unexpectedly and require a nimble, immediate response (such as going on a home visit to investigate a child abuse complaint and finding that the father, who answers the door, is in your policy class at school). Still other dilemmas feel urgent but really aren't. A social worker who is instructed to contact other service providers to determine whether clients followed through with referrals, though no client consent was obtained for such calls, might feel obliged to agree or disagree immediately with that direction. However, the worker may have other choices that can be played out by not responding immediately.

You will be best equipped to deal with ethical crises as well as less-pressing dilemmas by having a good command of your options and a cadre of resources (supervisory, consultant, written, and experiential) that you draw on whenever dilemmas arise. As to the last feature, the role of experience in resolving dilemmas, this applies to the next decision-making question.

When Have I Faced a Similar Dilemma?

This question calls for examination of precedents in your own experience and critical thinking about how the current dilemma fits or does not fit with those experiences (see Figure 2.5). Its effectiveness relies on your track record in making ethically sound decisions in the past, and on your ability to identify meaningful differences between the situations. Imagine that you work in a mental health clinic and a client you've seen off and on for a few months invites you to attend her upcoming wedding. This is the first time you've been invited to a client's wedding, though in your previous work with teens you were often invited to graduations and quinceañeras. You usually attended those because they were significant milestones for your clients in which you shared their pride in their achievements. You were careful, though, only to attend the public or ceremonial portion of their event, not the private or more personal, portions, such as gatherings at their families' homes or at local restaurants. You usually gave them a card with a note of congratulation and a bookmark with a symbolic message (rather than a gift of financial value) for the occasion.

In deciding on this course of action, you were mindful of confidentiality, which was easier to maintain by avoiding the family gatherings. You avoided the potential for confusing the client or muddying the therapeutic boundaries by giving a gift of recognition rather than a monetary

When have I faced a similar dilemma?
- Examine past dilemmas/experiences/readings
  - Were choices effective?
  - If not, why not?
- How is this similar to past choices?
- How is it different?
- Have personal "policies" been developed
  for this issue?

FIGURE 2.5 When Have I Faced a Similar Dilemma?

or material gift. Realistically, you also avoided a potentially unmanageable level of expense and the danger of unfair treatment that might arise in buying different gifts for different youths. The decisions to attend the graduations and quinceañeras seem clinically, culturally, and ethically sound, in that they support strengths and developmental milestones, while maintaining boundaries around privacy and conflicts of interest.

How does the wedding invitation fit with these past ethical decisions? It might raise confidentiality complications that could be lessened if you attended the ceremony but not the reception. The complications of gift giving might be resolved in the same fashion as the graduation gifts. The sense of affirmation the clients received by your attending might happen in this case, too.

How is this situation different? The event is not as closely related to the goals of the helping relationship. In fact, you probably don't even know a major player in the wedding—the spouse. The client's purpose in inviting you to the wedding may not be as clear as the youths' intentions in inviting you to their graduations or quinceañeras. Perhaps the client is just being polite but is not especially comfortable at the thought of you accepting the invitation (or has not really considered the implications of your attending). Or perhaps your approval is important to the client, and your presence will add meaning to the event. A further difference between the wedding and other events is the degree to which they involve therapeutic goals. The service objectives might be affected positively or negatively by your decision to attend the wedding. Because the relationship is still in process, there may be time to work those issues out, or the wedding attendance could create a distraction in service or a shift in the helping relationship. These issues need to be sorted out in a different fashion from how you sort out the graduation and quinceañera decisions.

Although the precedent in this example involves accepting invitations to personal events such as graduations and quinceañeras, that is not the only ethically sound option. Another social worker could certainly have a policy of declining such invitations on the bases of firm boundaries, avoiding the risk of compromised privacy, and the sheer unfeasibility of taking time to participate in client activities outside the service environment. The social worker might still acknowledge the life event through a card or other symbolic gift, and can skillfully incorporate the significance of the event and the kindness of the invitation into the clinical work. When face with subsequent invitations, such as to a wedding, this existing stance also forms an ethical and reasonable basis to turn them down.

If you are relatively new to your professional role you may not have a large pool of experiences to draw on for this step of the process. However, class discussions and texts such as this one can provide cases that require you to employ critical thinking and consider your possible actions. These steps help build the foundation of ethical practice for the dilemmas you will face in practice.

Answering the "when" question involves drawing on exemplars, using reflection and critical thinking to see how those inform the current situation. Other considerations require the application of theories, laws, regulations, standards, and principles, as demanded in the next question in the decision-making framework.

Where Do Ethical and Clinical Guidelines Lead Me?

Social workers can draw on an array of resources to provide perspective on ethical dilemmas and to weigh the advisability of different choices (see Figure 2.6). The field of moral philosophy provides historical perspectives

Where do ethical and clinical guidelines lead me?
- Rule-based/outcome-based philosophy
- Values (professional, cultural)
- Professional standards (NASW, CASW)
- Practice principles
- Ethical principles
- Laws and policies
- Convergence or trade offs?

FIGURE 2.6 Where Do Ethical and Clinical Guidelines Lead Me?

through which professionals can determine right actions. Values, standards, and the principles that support them help guide our decision making. Our personal philosophical frameworks are at play here, as well. Laws, regulations, and policies may also shape our choices. The facts of the case, including our knowledge of social work practice and human behavior, help us understand the motivations of people who have a stake in the dilemma, anticipate the effects of our decisions, and craft strategies for effectively carrying out our decision. Let's examine each in turn.

Philosophical approaches. In Chapter 1 we discussed the notion of virtue and the characteristics social workers must develop and sustain to be persons of integrity, and not simply to conform to ethics codes. We also addressed approaches to ethics from perspectives such as justice, care, resistance, rules, and outcomes. While virtue, care, activism, and justice are endemic to social work practice, people commonly rely on rules and consequences to guide their decision making. Those two perspectives often lead to different conclusions and thus they receive the most explicit attention in the model, at least as discussed in this text. In adopting and internalizing the model, users can and should expand their repertoire to include theories that resonate with their practice perspectives and settings.

Values, standards, and principles. Values are our beliefs about what is right and wrong, desirable and undesirable, good and bad. Our values guide our individual choices and behaviors. If I value financial security, my decisions about what jobs I take and what expenditures I make will reflect that value. If I value fairness, I will be attuned to situations where people are being disadvantaged and will take action to right those wrongs. Some values are held more strongly than others. That is, while I may care about both fairness and financial security, I would not choose to treat someone deceptively in order to obtain financial benefits. If I don't embrace the values as equally important, a conflict between them is not likely to result in distress. However, when I hold values with equal strength but then the values clash in some way, ethical dilemmas result. For example, if I value honesty and I value loyalty to my friends, which will take precedence if I find out a friend is having an adulterous affair and is using me as an alibi?

Dilemmas can also arise when the individual's values are in conflict with those of other people (clients, supervisors, colleagues) or with other institutions (regulatory boards, legislative bodies, accrediting organizations). A natural first step in ethical decision making thus involves our self-awareness about the values we hold, the origins and implications of those beliefs, and the ways in which they are congruent with or in conflict with those of others around us (Banks, 2021; Hepworth et al., 2022).

Like individuals, professions also have core values. In social work, these values are service, social justice, dignity and worth of the person, importance of human relationships, integrity, and competence (NASW, 2021). These values define the profession and serve as the basis for the ethical standards embodied in the NASW *Code of Ethics*, which helps workers enact the profession's values in their daily lives. The Canadian Association of Social Work also presents six values within its *Code of Ethics* that govern social work practice: respect for inherent dignity and worth of persons; pursuit of social justice; service to humanity; and integrity, confidentiality, and competence in professional practice (CASW, 2005a).

Codes of professional conduct date back at least to the physician's Hippocratic oath, which emerged around 400 BCE (Sinclair et al., 1996). Codes of ethics can be developed and put forth by professional organizations or associations. These codes generally apply to members of the organization and students who are preparing for professional practice in that field. To the extent that they represent commonly accepted standards for the profession, all members of the profession may subscribe to the code (and may be held accountable to its contents) whether or not they actually belong to the organization that developed the code. For example, social workers are expected to abide by the standards put forward by the Canadian Association of Social Workers (CASW) or the National Association of Social Workers' (NASW) codes of ethics, whether or not they are members of those organizations.

Codes of ethics are also promulgated by licensure or regulatory boards at the state, provincial, or national level. People who are licensed or certified to practice in those jurisdictions are expected to comply with the code for their discipline, and they are accountable to those standards, such that failing to adhere to them may result in a license revocation, suspension, or some other disciplinary action. Because such bodies have the protection of the public as their primary mission, these codes of ethics generally focus on appropriate behaviors in relation to one's clients, rather than on the broader range of responsibilities that concern professions' codes of ethics. The standards referred to in this text are drawn from the NASW and CASW codes of ethics. Because they have a great deal in common with the standards for other helping professions and regulatory boards, knowledge of these codes provides a solid foundation for ethical practice. However, it is important for professionals to be familiar with all the standards that guide their practice. For any given practitioner, this may include adhering to several codes, as when one is functioning as a licensed professional or within a specialty certification (such as marriage and family therapy or school social work). In Canada, regulation is divided between federal and provincial authorities. Each province has enacted unique legislation and has put in place regulatory bodies. Social workers must register as members of the governing body in their individual province.

The CASW *Code of Ethics* (2005a) organizes its standards under the key social work values. Each value also includes a list of principles that social workers must uphold as a part of that value. CASW expands on the implications of these values and principles in the *Guidelines for Ethical Practice* (2005b), which serves as a companion document to the *Code of Ethics* (2005a). These guidelines are not ranked in order of importance but are organized categorically as they relate to the specific value being addressed, and include standards that are both **prescriptive** (tenets that tell you what to do) and **proscriptive** (tenets that caution you *not* to do something).

NASW's *Code of Ethics* contains 174 standards. These standards concern (1) social workers' ethical responsibilities to clients, (2) . . . to colleagues, (3) . . . in practice settings, (4) . . . as professionals, (5) . . . to the social work profession, and (6) . . . to the broader society (2021). Thus, when it discusses a concept such as conflict of interest, NASW covers that concept under each of those sections as it applies to the particular role or responsibility rather than ranking its standards in order of any kind of priority. The code contains standards that are prescriptive and proscriptive: for example, "Social workers should obtain client consent before conducting an electronic search on the client. Exceptions may arise when the search is for purposes of protecting the client or other people from serious, foreseeable, and imminent harm, or for other compelling professional reasons" (NASW, 2021, 1.03i) is a prescription, and "Social workers should not disclose confidential information to third-party payers unless clients have authorized such disclosure" (NASW, 2021, 1.07h) is a proscription. To effectively uphold the standards, professionals must be aware of errors of both omission and commission. The latter term refers to mistakes that occur when the worker does something that the code says they should not do, such as communicating case information to an insurer without patient permission. Errors of omission occur when we fail to take actions directed in the standards, such as failing to provide all the elements of informed consent.

The standards in the NASW and CASW codes are both aspirational and enforceable. Aspirational standards are those that set forth ideals for the profession; unlike enforceable standards, they are not employed as an accountability mechanism for members. While the NASW code does not differentiate between the two, it states, "The extent to which each standard is enforceable is a matter of professional judgment to be exercised by those responsible for reviewing alleged violations of ethical standards" (NASW, 2021). In general, aspirational standards are the more abstract items, encompassing issues of social justice and general welfare, as opposed to those that set forth specific rules that carry an expectation of compliance (Reamer, 2018).

As you review the standards in professional codes, you will notice the use of qualifiers, terms such as "appropriate," "undue," "unwarranted," "reasonable steps," and "professional judgment." Here's an example: "Social workers should inform clients, to the extent possible, about the disclosure of confidential information and the potential consequences, when feasible before the disclosure is made" (NASW, 2021, 1.07d). A second example, this one from the CASW *Code of Ethics*, states, "Social workers contribute to the ongoing development of the profession and its ability to serve humanity, where possible, by participating in the development of current and future social workers and the development of new professional knowledge" (2005a, p. 8). The complexity in interpreting professional standards comes, in part, from the fact that qualifying terms can be fairly elastic, and their meaning is open to interpretation. What exactly does "to the extent possible" mean? In what situations would informing the client be appropriately deemed impossible? What if your notion of possible differs from your colleagues' notion? Does it vary by social work setting or the population seeking services? Where is the benchmark in comparing your interpretation of such terms with the interpretations of fellow professionals? Your use of critical thinking, past experience, consultation, and written resources is vital in effectively interpreting these qualifiers for any given case.

Moral principles transcend the helping and health professions, providing overarching guidance for our ethical choices. You can see these virtues reflected in professional values and ethical standards. They can also be used independently to guide our decision making as we weigh our options (E. Cohen & Cohen, 1999; Kenyon, 1999; Reamer, 2018). Five principles are particularly noteworthy (Beauchamp & Childress, 2012).

- **Autonomy** refers to the helper's responsibility to maximize an individual's right to make his own decisions. In examining a choice according to the principle of autonomy, the worker might ask, "Is it client centered? Does it foster the other person's freedom to make decisions about their life?"
- **Fidelity** is the duty to keep one's promise or word, or to uphold a trust. In upholding fidelity, the worker should weigh choices by asking, "Is it honest? Am I behaving in a trustworthy manner?"
- **Beneficence** is the duty to promote the good or enhance another's wellbeing. It is contrasted with **nonmaleficence**, or the responsibility to prevent or reduce harm. The test for these principles is reflected in questions such as, "Is it helpful?" or, "Is it in the client's best interest?"
- **Justice** refers to fairness, or the duty to treat all equitably, distributing risks and benefits equally (Forester-Miller & Davis, 1996). Simply put, this amounts to asking, "Is it fair? If I do this for this client or employee, would I do it for another in the same circumstance?"

Laws, regulations, and policies. Beyond viewing our dilemmas and options through the lens of moral philosophy, values, professional standards, and principles, we must consider the laws, regulations, and policies that may come to bear on the situation. Laws or statutes are developed at the federal, state, provincial, and local levels. Case law is shaped by court decisions, not the actions of a legislative body. Regulations and administrative codes are typically issued by agencies with financial or other rule-making authority over an area and are intended to interpret, specify, or codify legislation. For example, according to Canadian Criminal Law, an alleged perpetrator cannot be convicted of murder if they were unconscious of the act at the time of the crime. As evidence grew for psychiatric conditions which impacted consciousness, the defense of **automatism** increased, and individual courts were obliged to interpret the law in the context of each case (Cosh, 2020).

While laws, statutes, and regulations cover geographic jurisdictions, policies are typically formulated at the organizational level. Policies create institutionalized answers to common questions: they are developed in the context of a program's unique mission, philosophy, funding, and regulatory environment, and therefore usually only influence the practices in that specific organization. The example of sexual assault reports in colleges and universities receiving HHS (U.S. Department of Health and Human Services) funding illustrates the link between laws, policies, and practice.

Title IX of the Education Amendments of 1972 and the related administrative rules regulate a wide array of educational processes in which gender-based discrimination might occur, including recruitment, admissions, financial aid, athletic programs, and research, academic, or employment opportunities (Education Amendments Act of 1972, 2018). Specific to sex-based harassment, federal courts and agencies have determined that Title IX prohibits sexual harassment such as unwelcome and inappropriate sexual comments, advances and/or name calling on the basis of sex, and sexual violence such as rape, sexual abuse and sexual coercion, and gender-based harassment such as slurs, taunts and name-calling or gender-motivated physical threats (Office for Civil Rights, 2021). As you can probably tell, many university policies and procedures are developed in response to Title IX: the implications (and consequences for non-compliance) are substantial and apply not only to campus counselors and administrators but also to other students, faculty, staff, and health-care personnel (Weiss & Lasky, 2017).

The Office for Civil Rights within HHS has jurisdiction to address claims of discrimination or harassment made under Title IX. A 2011 document sometimes referred to as the "Dear Colleague Letter" underscored the OCR's commitment to addressing sexual harassment under Title IX and stipulated steps universities must take to effectively respond to sexual assault (Ali, 2011). A subsequent document in 2014 clarified that certain designated "Responsible Employees" who learned of a sexual assault were obligated to report to a university official "not only relevant facts but also identifying information- including the names of the victim, alleged perpetrator (if known), and any witnesses" (Holland et al., 2018, p. 258). The list of positions that are designated Responsible Employees varies by institution: some schools designate all employees, while others limit it to people with administrative, advising, supervisory, and residential life roles (Holland et al., 2018). The broad mandate for compelled disclosures gave rise to many varied concerns, including creation of a large body of inept and unprepared mandated reporters; disempowerment and paternalism toward adult-age assault survivors; the lack of informed consent and resulting unintentional disclosures by survivors; and the escalation of vague or second-hand reports never intended to be formal complaints (Weiss & Lasky, 2017). On top of all of this, many "Dear Colleague" regulations were rescinded by the Department of Education in August, 2020 under the Trump administration (Code of Federal Regulations, 2022) creating significant confusion. With a new federal administration taking office, further changes are expected, including reversion to the earlier "Dear Colleague" provisions.

Beyond the dilemmas and demands created by shifting, byzantine laws and directives, the sexual assault stipulations of Title IX demonstrate why it is important for social workers to be informed about the laws that affect practice. Mandatory reporting is a frequent cause of ethical dilemmas as social workers balance the importance of protecting vulnerable youth or elders from abuse against the client's autonomy and privacy. While acknowledging the legal mandate to report suspected abuse, social workers may fear that the report will be ineffectual in protecting clients from further harm and may indeed exacerbate risk. Under Title IX, the compelled disclosure policies raise even more questions, in that college students who may have experienced sexual assault do not have the same level of vulnerability as children or frail elders, the policies can actually *discourage* help-seeking following an assault, and the policies may require staff to betray student trust, dignity, and privacy in the interest of protecting the university's good standing with the Department of Education.

Effective, professional decision making demands that we become conversant with the laws and policies that commonly affect our practice settings or the populations we serve. These include provisions on confidentiality, mandatory reporting, the duty to warn, record keeping, licensure and certification, and parental rights (Corey et al., 2019). When faced with novel dilemmas, helping professionals must be able to identify the array of laws and policies that impinge on the decision. Primary sources offer the most reliable information about relevant laws and regulations. These may be through "legal information gateways for particular areas of law ... (e.g., for child welfare laws, see https://www.childwelfare.gov/topics/systemwide/ laws-policies/state/)", legal search engines, or through consultation with librarians familiar with legal research (Barsky, 2019, p. 10). The U.S. Library of Congress operates a site to facilitate access to U.S. and international laws (Library of Congress, n.d.). Canadian resources include an online database of Canadian laws and regulations offered through the Justice Laws Website (http://laws-lois.justice.gc.ca/eng/), and the Canadian Legal Information Institute, a nonprofit organization that makes Canadian law accessible for free online.

It is important to understand the laws and regulations governing your field of practice, but as described in Chapter 1, the resolution of ethical dilemmas is far more complex than simply finding and following the law. For one thing, the law may be part of the problem. If the law forbids placement of foster children with same-sex couples, and you believe this is unethical, discriminatory, and deprives children of viable, loving homes, an ethical dilemma exists in the tension between law and the ethical standards of nondiscrimination and action in the best interests of the clients. Another problem with using the law as a tool for ethical practice is that many acts are unethical or improper but not illegal. Asking a client to provide testimonials to your excellence as a counselor would be one example. Failing to report negative research findings would be another. Inviting a client to your fundraising event is another. The fact that there's no law against these actions doesn't mean they are correct.

Even if the issue in question is covered by a law or policy that is helpful to your decision, it still provides no guidance in carrying it out. For example, you may be compelled to report the suspicion of elder abuse to an adult protection agency, but the way in which you handle this with the family and the way in which you make your report require particular skill and clinical acumen. The understanding of laws and regulations is a necessary but insufficient element of ethical action.

Practice principles. In answering the "where" question in this section, we have focused so far on the theories, standards, and principles that constitute ethical guidelines for decision making. Beyond these, professional knowledge must also be brought to bear in weighing choices. Our fundamental understanding of human nature, of culture and gender, of the effects of trauma and discrimination, of the nature of various social and interpersonal difficulties, and of the goals and strategies for social work practice will help evaluate the efficacy of various choices. Beyond these elements, the facts of the particular case and the wishes and intentions of the client or others involved must be taken into account. Clinical acumen comes into play when we generate options and weigh the likely consequences of a case and develop strategies for enacting the resulting decision. Consider the example in Box 2.2, which is designed to demonstrate the proper use of the "where" question.

Outcome-based ethics. The utilitarian position would lead Kenneth to look at the consequences of his choices. Alerting Sergio to the deficiencies in his application might give him an opportunity to revise the materials and present a more competitive portfolio to the committee. It would be a gesture of loyalty between friends. The good that would come of this includes improving Sergio's chances of obtaining the job and perhaps increasing the likelihood that Kenneth's favored candidate would ultimately get the position. Tipping off Sergio might have the effect of making him more attentive to the requirements of job applications, which would benefit him whether or not he gets this position. On the other hand, it might also lead him to believe that the rules set for others don't apply to him, which could cause problems if he were hired for the position. Should Kenneth's actions be discovered, his reputation and trustworthiness may be damaged, in ways that go well beyond his role on the committee.

The consequences of telling Sergio go beyond Kenneth and Sergio themselves. Giving Sergio a chance to revise his materials disadvantages the other candidates, who were not given the opportunity to do so. It

BOX 2.2

Applying "Where": The Case of the Suspicious Search

Let's examine the factors covered in this section by applying them to a case drawn from administrative practice. Kenneth is the director of a program in a large agency and a member of a five-person team seeking to fill a leadership position that will ultimately report to him. His good friend Sergio has applied for the position, and Kenneth very much wants to hire him. Ken thinks he'll do a fine job and that working with someone with whom he communicates well and has a trusting relationship will make his job easier.

When the résumés come in for review by the search committee, Kenneth notices that Sergio's looks sparse compared to those of the other applicants. Maybe he was careless, or maybe he just underestimated the level of detail required, but Sergio has failed to provide specifics about his relevant past work. Also, his cover letter and résumé have typographical errors and don't list references, which applicants were instructed to do.

At the outset of the search, Kenneth vowed to himself that he would be objective in the process and would not give Sergio unfair advantage—for example, by informing him in advance about interview questions. Kenneth assumed that his friend would succeed on his own merits, but now he believes Sergio may not even make it past the first round of review. What is right for him to do as Sergio's friend, and as the person who must select and supervise the person who gets this position? Can Kenneth ethically return the résumé to Sergio and tell him to revise and resubmit it? Could he encourage the search committee to overlook the problems with the resume and allow Sergio to proceed to the next phase of the process?

violates the standards of fairness on which employment searches rely, and it probably violates implicit or explicit norms within the search committee about confidentiality and the integrity of the process.

On the other hand, if the focus of utilitarianism is on the greatest amount of good for the most people, and Sergio's capabilities and character indicate he would still be a strong candidate for this position compared to the other applicants, one might argue for telling him. In other words, the good that could come from his appointment to the position may far outweigh the significance of any typos in the cover letter. The question is whether it warrants subverting the established hiring process. Perhaps Kenneth's desire for Sergio's well-being clouds his ability to choose the greatest good, in which case he should recuse himself from the search process.

Failing to tell Sergio might damage the friendship, especially if Kenneth had led Sergio to believe he would be a shoo-in for the position. If Kenneth decides not to alert him to the shortcomings in his application, the committee might reject Sergio's application, and another, less-compatible candidate may get the job. Other consequences of this action are that the fairness of the process is preserved, as are Kenneth's reputation and neutrality, and the integrity of the committee's work. Of the two choices, to tell or not to tell, which choice leads to the greater good? Utilitarianism would appear to support not telling.

Rule-based ethics. What about the deontological perspective? What should be the categorical imperative in this case? Would we want all committee members to feel free to tell their favored candidates about the inner workings of the search process and how their candidacy measures up against the others? Would we want all committee members to agree on a process and then follow that process, ensuring that all applicants are treated equitably? Put this way, the rule-based perspective would support not alerting Sergio.

Values. Clearly the social work value of integrity would prevent Kenneth from talking with Sergio about the application. Upholding the dignity and worth of others means treating them in a respectful manner. Telling Sergio is respectful of him, but not of the other candidates or the other search committee members, who must rely on Kenneth's trustworthiness. Nor is it just. Similarly, though social workers value human relationships, this does not mean that Ken can ignore his relationship with his colleagues or the other applicants in favor of his bond with Sergio.

Professional standards. The NASW *Code of Ethics* (2021) has some standards that might apply to this case:

- "Social workers should not participate in, condone, or be associated with dishonesty, fraud, or deception." (4.04)
- Social workers will not "practice, condone, facilitate, or collaborate with any form of discrimination." (4.02)
- Social workers will "act to prevent and eliminate discrimination in the employing organization's . . . employment policies and practices." (3.09e)

Similarly, the CASW *Code of Ethics* (2005a) expects that social workers will

- "Place the needs of others above self-interest." (p. 6)
- "Promote the qualities of honesty, reliability, impartiality and diligence." (p. 7)
- "Value openness and transparency . . . and avoid relationships where their integrity or impartiality may be compromised, ensuring that should a conflict of interest be unavoidable, the nature of the conflict is fully disclosed." (p. 7)
- "Consider carefully the potential for professional conflicts of interest where close personal relationships exist or where social, business or sexual relationships with colleagues are contemplated or exist." (CASW, 2005b, 2.3.3)

The relevance of some of these passages hinges on the determination of whether the advantage given to Sergio is discriminatory in some fashion toward the other candidates. The sections of the codes that address confidentiality with colleagues might apply if Kenneth's discussion with Sergio is seen as a breach of the committee's deliberations. Certainly the concept of conflict of interest applies in Kenneth's case, in that his friendship with and loyalty to Sergio are in conflict with his duties as a supervisor and committee member.

Ethical principles. The moral principles of autonomy, fidelity, beneficence, nonmaleficence, and justice would also seem to weigh against Kenneth's desire to talk with Sergio about his application. While such a conversation might enhance Sergio's autonomy, it would do so at the expense of the other applicants: while it would be beneficial for Sergio, it would be to the others' detriment. If the decision to allow revised applications is just, the option should be provided to all the candidates, and not only to the one who is friends with the boss. Kenneth's desire to talk with Sergio does not uphold the principle of fidelity, while his refusal to do so would demonstrate his trustworthiness as a member of the search committee.

Laws and policies. Kenneth should examine the relevant laws and regulations regarding personnel matters, including nondiscrimination statutes and affirmative action policies. He may find nothing relevant to support him in his desire to give Sergio extra assistance, though that assistance to Sergio may be discriminatory to others, thereby violating agency policy, the law, or both. Were they to find out, the other applicants could pursue redress through a grievance within the organization or an entity such as the Equal Employment Opportunity Commission or the Canadian Human Rights Commission (Strom, 2021). The information might prove damaging to the organization's reputation (and to Kenneth's), even if no one files a formal grievance. The agency's personnel policies and procedures should also have a bearing on Kenneth's actions, to the extent that they specify the decisions and communications necessary to ensure a fair search process.

Practice principles. Kenneth's decision may be based on other information beyond his understanding of ethics. One example of the ways clinical knowledge might be used is if Kenneth looks into why Sergio turned in a shoddy application. Perhaps Sergio doesn't know how to do a proper résumé and cover letter. Perhaps he managed his time poorly and put it together in a rush. Perhaps he assumed the job was designated for him, and thus the application itself didn't matter. The particular rationale Kenneth selects to explain Sergio's behavior may affect his decision about what to do as a result.

If Kenneth believes the errors were made due to ignorance, he might educate Sergio about effective applications, either after the search is concluded or while the deliberations are taking place. Note that deciding to reach out to his friend in this way does *not* obligate Kenneth to let Sergio submit a new résumé. If he believes Sergio did the application in a rush, he may infer that his friend has poor time management skills, which could be a detriment should he be hired. Or he might infer that the rushed application was an anomaly and not an indicator of future performance. What if Kenneth's knowledge of human behavior (and of his friend in particular) leads him to conclude that Sergio turned in this slipshod application due to certainty that he would get the job regardless of the material submitted? This realization and his experience as a manager and supervisor should serve as a red flag regarding Sergio's suitability for the job and the risk Kenneth is taking in hiring him.

The search committee itself is another area where Kenneth should apply his practice knowledge and case information in making his decision. For example, his knowledge of his colleagues may help him anticipate their reactions if they find out he is biased in favor of Sergio and is providing him feedback about the process. Any specific agreements the committee has had about confidentiality and handling internal candidates or candidates with whom committee members are acquainted, should also inform his decision.

Answering the "where" question is a multifaceted task that draws from a variety of ethical, legal, and clinical resources that can help evaluate the options for solving an ethical dilemma. The many possibilities discussed above regarding a relatively straightforward dilemma involving favoritism in a hiring decision can certainly seem overwhelming. You may feel tempted to just use gut instinct rather than attempting to balance laws, standards, values, principles, theories, and the like. Don't despair! As in any complex task, it takes a period of practice before this step in the decision-making process becomes second nature. As you develop your skills, your gut instinct will incorporate these important considerations as you weigh the options you have generated and address the "it depends." Do the best you can as you gradually incorporate all the elements, and try not to get frustrated if you encounter complexities or contradictions at this stage.

As noted earlier, most ethical dilemmas involve weighing competing goods, not just choosing to do the right thing instead of the wrong thing. Defensible practice involves awareness of conflicting imperatives and the ability to articulate why one was chosen over the other. For example, when the law and ethical standards conflict and both choices are defensible, what considerations influenced the social worker's decision to choose one over the other? As you develop your skills in answering the "where" question, the resources listed throughout the text will be useful in doing legal research, in finding out more about philosophical traditions in ethics, and in properly incorporating clinical case dimensions.

After considering a dilemma by asking who might provide useful consultation, what the options are, when you have had to make similar decisions, and where ethical and clinical guidelines lead, you may have narrowed down your options or settled on a particular course of action. The next question—"Why?"—asks you to engage in critical self-reflection, looking inside to make sure that the basis for your decision is sound.

Why Am I Selecting a Particular Course of Action?

This question is a check on our motivations and asks that we honestly examine our preferences for a particular course of action (see Figure 2.7).

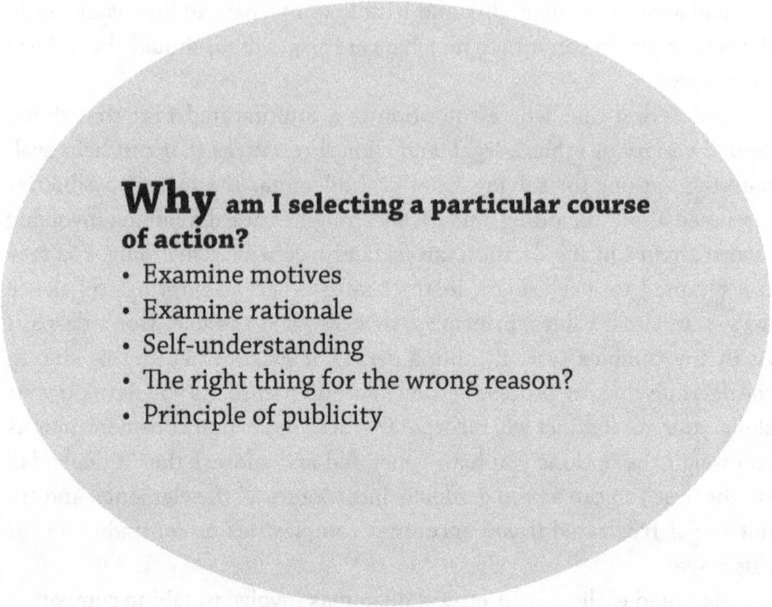

Why am I selecting a particular course of action?
- Examine motives
- Examine rationale
- Self-understanding
- The right thing for the wrong reason?
- Principle of publicity

FIGURE 2.7 Why Am I Selecting a Particular Course of Action?

Sometimes personal beliefs, biases, and preferences can cloud ethical judgment. At other times, errors in critical thinking can lead us to the wrong conclusion or diminish our ability to properly consider all the factors in a case. Table 2.1 offers examples of errors from both categories.

As you can probably tell from these examples, several problems arise when we fail to adequately examine our motivations. Sometimes these biases and distortions will cause us to overlook valid options. They can also lead us to choose actions that are detrimental to certain clients or to make choices that unfairly benefit certain persons over others. Over time, bad decisions and uncritical decision-making processes may become habit, creating unfortunate precedents for future decisions. Conversely, understanding the subtle and overt structural and personal factors that foster inequality leads to critical consciousness (Cook, 2019). "Critical reflection involves learning from and making deeper meaning of experience through a process of unsettling and examining deeply hidden assumptions in order to create better guidelines for action and so improve professional practice and develop a more ethical and compassionate stance" (Beres & Fook, 2020, p. 3).

TABLE 2.1 Errors in Critical Thinking

Error	Thought
Am I acting in self-interest? Is what I'm about to decide or do more *about me and less about my client(s)*?	If a client tells me anything upsetting, I *have* to notify the authorities. I won't have any troubling information on *my* conscience.
Am I putting my personal beliefs ahead of the client's needs or the profession's values?	I have to be true to myself. People shouldn't have more kids than they can afford, so if they need food stamps, that's their problem.
Do I have an ethical blind spot?	I would never misappropriate agency funds, but having my assistant work on my daughter's research paper makes up for all the extra hours I put into this place.
Am I using all-or-nothing reasoning?	Selena is working really hard. If I report her for neglecting her kids, they will be taken away, she'll lose hope, and all that effort will go down the drain.
Am I misapplying otherwise valid concepts?	In my client's culture, physical punishment is a way of expressing love, so it would be culturally insensitive to report them, even if the discipline is leaving welts on the child.
Is my attraction (or aversion) to this person biasing my judgment?	Kitty is such a sweet and friendly young woman. Maybe I can find her a summer job with one of my friends, even if I'm not doing that for the other teens on my caseload.
Am I playing the odds that a wrong won't be discovered?	My former client may find out that I showed a tape of their session in my class on interviewing.
Am I following the crowd?	Everyone on my unit discusses cases in the lunchroom. It's where we get to let off steam.
Am I caught up in relativism?	There are no clear answers about accepting gifts from clients, so why shouldn't I accept these World Series tickets? After all, it means a lot to my client to give them to me!

Let me use an example from my own practice experience. I have especially strong feelings about fairness and a predisposition to support the underdog, whether it is a sports team with a losing record, the duds on a reality TV show, or the client who has not had a fair deal in life. This part of my character is congruent with many principles in social work, but over-reliance on it can distort my decision making. In my BSW field placement, my internship supervisor helped me see this when I was going overboard to providing assistance to a teen from a very impoverished background in a way that was infantilizing and paternalistic to him and unjust to the other teens who needed my help. All these decades later I still need to be mindful of the dynamic of "defaulting to the underdog" so that my administrative, clinical, and supervisory decisions aren't distorted by personal preconceptions.

Another method for rechecking motivations involves applying decision-making tests (Table 2.2). As you think about an option that appeals to you in solving your ethical dilemma, consider whether it passes the **publicity test**, the **reversibility test**, the **smell test**, and the **mom or mentor test**.

The publicity test asks whether our decision can withstand the light of day. If we were to explain our choice to our colleagues, would they understand our rationale and think we had achieved a reasonable solution even if they might choose another course of action? The publicity test doesn't ask whether we are eager to have our dilemmas or decisions broadcast on the internet; few of us would be. Rather, it asks us to determine whether the decision is justifiable and within the norms of the profession.

The reversibility test presents a version of the Golden Rule: "Do unto others as you would have others do unto you." That is, would your choice

TABLE 2.2 Decision-Making Tests

Test	Question
Publicity Test	Is the decision justifiable? How would it be viewed by other professionals or the public?
Reversibility Test	Would I want this done to me?
Smell Test	Does it seem right? Am I trying to talk myself into doing something that is wrong?
Mom Test	How would someone I respect (like my mom or my mentor) think of me if they knew about my decision or action? How would they solve this dilemma?

be the same if you were in the client's shoes or if your child, friend, or parent were subject to the same decision? In submitting your decision to this test, ask, "Would I want someone to do this (or, would I think this was a good choice) if the roles were reversed?" Related to Rawls' veil of ignorance, this test examines the rightness of a choice regardless of one's position (Kidder, 1995, pp. 158–159). In other words, "What would I want to have happen if I didn't know which role I would have in the case?"

The smell test asks whether the choice we are making lives up to community standards, legal standards, or our own gut instincts about right and wrong (Institute for Global Ethics, 2001). The name comes from the instinctive response when something is rotten: "This smells bad." Sometimes this question is reflected in statements such as "It just didn't feel right" or "All the rationalizations in the world can't make this acceptable."

The mom test or mentor test requires us to consider an individual whose integrity we trust, or someone (like a mother) who holds us in high regard. How might that person solve this dilemma? How might that person view us in light of the course of action we are choosing? Is the decision one that lives up to the highest ideals of those people we admire and to which we ourselves aspire?

Examining our motivations and subjecting decisions to these four tests help identify flawed options or flawed decision-making processes. While ruling out or ranking some of our options, these mechanisms may also help draw attention to better options not previously considered. Or, if our decisions are sound, this process of examination can provide reassurance that is the case and bolster the support for selecting one course of action over another.

It is easy to look at this list of questions and tests and find them to be unreasonably complex or idealistic for daily ethical decision making. As with the other elements of decision making, the initial investment in learning (in this case, about personal biases) creates the opening to work on them and incorporate this self-awareness with other critical-thinking skills. Forthright, reliable, and trustworthy supervision and consultation are key to developing self-understanding and exercising self-regulation.

How Should I Enact My Decision?

The final question in the decision-making framework addresses the process by which you will carry out the decision (see Figure 2.8). The professional knowledge and skill base come into play here because often the

HOW should I enact my decision?
- Process matters!
- Consider ultimate objectives
- Use social work knowledge and skills
  - Human behavior
  - Strategy
  - Empathy
  - Communication
  - Culture
- Remember to document

FIGURE 2.8 How Should I Enact My Decision?

"how" question involves taking into account the unique features of the client, your history with that person or system, the intended goals of treatment, and the setting in which you work. Let's say that you are a faculty member at a university, and on the first day of classes you see that a person who was your client three years ago is a student in one of your courses. You notify your supervisor or director about the possible conflict of interest or roles, without specifying who the student is or what the nature of the services were that they received as a client. Through this consultation and by reviewing professional standards you determine that this is an unavoidable dual relationship, but you also note that it is essential to set clear boundaries to acknowledge the former relationship and distinguish it from the current one. How you decide to set those boundaries is key. Thoughtful, sensitive, and adept handling of the conversation will help to reduce any apprehension the student may have, clarify their options should they be uncomfortable with the dual relationship, and clear the air about the new way that you will relate to each other.

A failure to handle this conversation skillfully could be disruptive for both of you. It could make the student feel confused, singled out, suspicious, or ashamed. Ineffective processes for setting boundaries might include calling them out of class, failing to talk in a private setting, acting as if the issues they had when they sought treatment are still in play today, and assuming that trouble will arise from enrollment in the class—for example, if they earn unsatisfactory grades. An effective process for setting boundaries might include privately asking them to meet with you, acknowledging the former relationship, assuring them that you will keep your teaching and counseling roles separate, and discussing how you will relate to each other in your new roles as student and teacher.

As you will see when we discuss cases in the following chapters, much attention must be paid to options for addressing the "how" question, because a process that is thoughtlessly or clumsily handled can turn a good decision into a poor one. Be generous in your reading of these options as we go through them. It is difficult in a written text to convey vocal tone, facial expressions, body language, and other elements that are essential to sensitively conducting difficult conversations. As you consider the process, envision carrying out an ethical decision with clinical acumen and with the utmost attention to the needs of the client and others involved.

The Decisions That Result

Why use the 6Q (or any) framework? How does it enhance the decision that results? Why not just go with your gut, have your supervisor tell you what to do, or simply follow the rules without looking for exceptions and complexities? As noted above and in Chapter 1, good decisions are supported by sound reasoning (Rachels, 1980). Van Hoose and Paradise (1979) contend that a professional "is probably acting in an ethically responsible way concerning a client if (1) he or she has maintained personal and professional honesty, coupled with (2) the best interests of the client, (3) without malice or personal gain, and (4) can justify his or her actions as the best judgment of what should be done based on the current state of the profession" (p. 58). Knowing and using the process consistently will help you to meet those four criteria.

Putting It All Together

Several years ago, my colleague Katie and I wrote an ethics column in which we took questions over the Internet and used them to formulate our topic for the monthly newsletter. The very first question we received was "Is it ethical to pray with a client?" Of course, the immediate answer was "It depends," but we figured the writer would expect more than that. Let's run the situation through the six questions to see where those answers lead us.

The practitioner faced with this question should consult someone in their setting (Figure 2.9). There are some contexts where prayer may be forbidden, unconventional, or disapproved (such as public schools) and others where it is allowed, encouraged, or so common that it is almost a norm of the setting (i.e., a faith-based setting, a hospital, or a hospice).

A supervisor or colleague can help sort out the clinical dimensions of this question and direct the worker to resources to clarify the question. Is the client's request to pray an attempt to distract from or derail the work at hand? Does it convey important information about the client's culture, beliefs, or social supports? Does it require self-disclosure by the worker? Will it be constructive for the relationship and treatment goals of both client and worker? Will it blur the focus of the helping relationship? What are the implications of either accepting or declining the request to pray?

Who will be helpful?
- Consultation
  - Supervisor/colleagues
  - Specialists
  - Written and organizational resources
- Generate options, evaluate options, plan process, practice, debrief
- Before or after the decision
- Use discretion

FIGURE 2.9 Who Will Be Helpful?

A supervisor or colleague can also help us with our own self-awareness. For example, professional norms tend to be more supportive of the use of prayer if it is requested by the client rather than offered by the social worker. If the professional is the one to suggest prayer, a colleague might act as a sounding board on whether that suggestion is appropriate, coercive, an abuse of power, or more indicative of the worker's needs than the client's. Similarly, if the worker is reluctant to support a client's request to pray, what is the basis for that? Is the worker placing their needs or comfort before that of the client, or is there a legitimate clinical rationale supporting one choice over another?

The supervisor or colleague can also help sort out the balance between being attuned to the role that spirituality might play in the client's life and the actual use of prayer in the provision of social work services. Praying in sessions is not the same as being sensitive to spiritual beliefs. Gaining an understanding of the client's faith tradition, if they have one, is an important element in most social work assessments. It aids the worker in understanding how the client makes meaning of adversity, their sources of strength, the supports and resources that are tied to a particular faith community, and the ways these spiritual beliefs intersect with the problem (Bullis, 1996; Canda & Furman, 1999; Carson & Arnold, 1996). While prayer can be an expression of faith, the act of prayer is not necessary or sufficient to understand the client's spirituality. Consultation can help the worker develop skill and comfort with incorporating spiritual dimensions into assessments, and in distinguishing necessary elements of spiritual exploration from expressions of spirituality through prayer.

To pray or not to pray, that is the question. There are several variations on these options, and the choices may depend on the context in which the request for prayer comes up (Figure 2.10). Table 2.3 shows some examples of variations. In each example, the request for prayer originates with the client.

Some of these requests do not ask for an explicit form of prayer or convey an expectation that the helper will take a leading or even an active role in the prayer. The options may be (a) to sit quietly with the clients while they pray, (b) to say, "Yes, I will pray with you or for you," (c) to say something more vague such as "You will be in my thoughts next Thursday morning," (d) to say, "I'm not comfortable with that" or "I'm not able to do that," (e) to say "Let's talk about that further," or (f) to offer a

What are my choices?
- What additional information is needed?
- Generate alternatives, including non-action
- What will each choice mean for those involved?
- Timing of action? Urgency?

FIGURE 2.10 What Are My Choices?

TABLE 2.3 Possible Requests for Prayer

Setting	Request
A mental health setting	"I'm having surgery on Thursday. I hope you'll pray for me."
A community advocacy group	"Can we ask God to be with us in the work we have ahead?"
A home visit	"These Bible passages give me hope that I can become a better parent. Can we call on them when we meet? I need God's help to make me a better person."
An emergency room	"We need to pray that God doesn't take Jeremy from us now."
A group for parents of incarcerated youth	"I'd like to pray that that girl drops the charges she made against my son."
In the car, on the way to a meeting with a medical team where a diagnosis of terminal illness may be discovered	"Will you pray with me on this?"

silent or meditative moment as prayer. Perhaps you have other suggestions as well. It's wise to generate as many options as possible, because
while one might seem inappropriate or callous in a given situation (saying
"I'm not comfortable with that" to a client's plea for the worker's prayers
during surgery), the same option may fit in another case down the road (if
a client's prayer is that harm befall another person).

Your options may also vary by how much time you have to make the
decision. For the worker transporting the client, or the one whose client
is anticipating a court verdict, the response needs to be made in the moment. For the oncology social worker, requests for prayer may be so common that a response becomes part of the worker's repertoire. For requests
that may come as a surprise but have a more lasting impact, the decision
made at that moment may be altered in subsequent sessions. So a worker
who made the decision to go along with a prayer in a community meeting
might reexamine that decision subsequently.

When weighing the options, we're always mindful of what each option
will mean for the client and for the work we're doing together. Refusing a
request for prayer may be devastating to the client or it may be appropriate boundary setting, depending on the contextual factors. This is where
the clinical intersects with the ethical. While it would be unethical to push
our personal religious beliefs on a client, it might also be clinically un-
sound to assume that our response to the request for prayer will have no
impact on the rest of our work with them.

Which of the options is best depends on the worker and the context in
which the request is made. Generally, though, a wise choice involves a response that is focused on the client and that requires a more neutral stance
from the worker. In this case, that may be option a, c, or f as listed above:
to sit quietly as the client prays, to offer a general, supportive phrase such
as "You will be in my thoughts," or to offer a moment of meditative silence
as prayer.

Next the worker should consider if and when they have had similar
experiences and how they responded at the time, as well as the effectiveness of that response (Figure 2.11). The principle of fairness might arise
here: "If I did this for one client, is there a reason I wouldn't do it for another?" The importance of the dialogic process also comes up. Examining
our actions when dilemmas occur helps us evaluate the wisdom of performing the same actions the next time the question arises.

When have I faced a similar dilemma?
- Examine past dilemmas/experiences/readings
  - Were choices effective?
  - If not why not?
- How is this similar to past choices?
- How is it different?
- Have personal "policies" been developed for this issue?

FIGURE 2.11 When Have I Faced a Similar Dilemma?

Once when we were discussing the prayer question in a workshop, a participant gave an example much like the terminal diagnosis case above and said, "I didn't have time to weigh out all these choices. I just did what I believed was best—and in fact, my choices about how to pray were limited, since I was driving the car. I didn't have time for all this, 'it depends . . . on the one hand, on the other hand.'"

Of course she didn't. We are often presented with novel problems that we have to resolve right then. But that doesn't mean that the dialogic process is of no use to her. Good ethical practice means we do the best we can in the moment, document it appropriately, then in our next supervisory or consultation session, say, "You know, something happened when I was driving Mrs. Jones the other day, and I think I handled it okay, but I'd like your help thinking through it for the future." This presents the opportunity to look at the soundness of our choices and to build a repertoire of thoughtful, effective options that we can use even when new situations arise. As noted earlier in this chapter, shame, perfectionism, mistrust, and other reactions can impede workers' willingness to open up those

Where do ethical and clinical
guidelines lead me?
- Rule-based/outcome-based philosophy
- Values (professional, cultural)
- Professional standards (NASW, CASW)
- Practice principles
- Ethical principles
- Laws and policies
- Convergence or trade offs?

FIGURE 2.12 Where Do Ethical and Clinical Guidelines Lead Me?

discussions, yet we must do so if we hope to develop ethical habits to draw
on throughout our careers (Figure 2.12).

Outcome-based ethics. Ends-based moral philosophies would have
us weigh options by the likely consequences. Among other outcomes,
praying with the client may blur worker–client boundaries, obscure the
focus of the relationship and the worker's role, set a precedent for prayer
in future sessions, help the client feel at ease with the worker, demonstrate cultural competence, or center and strengthen the client in facing
the work ahead. Not praying with the client may put up barriers between
the worker and client, create the impression that the worker is insensitive
or culturally inept, or divert the conversation away from the work at hand
and onto the issue of prayer. It may set needed boundaries, provide an
opening to discuss matters of faith, or facilitate referrals to pastoral counselors or assistance in the individual's religious community.

In generating and weighing these possible outcomes, the social worker
must make use of their clinical expertise and knowledge of the particular

case and client. Understanding the basis of the client's request, the importance placed on prayer by the client, and the meaning the client might attach to proceeding (or refusing to proceed) with prayer are all part of weighing consequences and determining which path will carry the greatest benefit.

Rules-based ethics. For a rules-based perspective on the decision, the social worker would look to the existence of policies or guidelines governing such behavior. In the absence of those, the worker might invoke the categorical imperative and consider whether they would want all other social workers to choose the same path.

In sorting out this dilemma, workers must be cognizant of their own values regarding prayer, and sensitive to the importance of prayer to the client. If the worker believes strongly in the power of prayer, it is easy to accommodate the client's request, but perhaps this set of values would lead the worker to introduce or agree to prayer in situations where it is inappropriate. A worker who does not believe in prayer might run the risk of imposing these values on the client and being insensitive to the client's needs while giving precedence to their own.

Values. Three of the social work profession's values have relevance in this case. The commitment to service means that the worker should put the individual's needs or interests before her own, providing services in a client-centered fashion. In upholding the value of competence, the worker should be culturally competent—that is, sensitive to the place that spirituality plays in the life of the client and informed (or willing to learn) about different faith traditions. Competence would also involve having the ability to discern the meaning beneath the client's request and respond to it with skill to preserve and advance the helping relationship. Competence might also mean referring the client elsewhere if their request indicates a desire for faith-based services that the worker cannot provide. Whether or not the worker accedes to the client's request, in valuing the dignity and worth of the person, the social worker will be respectful and attuned to the client's individuality.

Our codes of ethics do not address the issue of prayer, yet they prohibit the use of professional roles for personal gain and recommend that professionals use techniques that are supported by research. Using the helping relationship to advance one's religious agenda might be interpreted as a conflict of interest. Using prayer because it has been demonstrated to be respectful of clients and responsive to their needs would conform with the codes.

Insofar as faith is an aspect of a person's culture, standards on cultural competence would apply. Those standards mandate the following:

- "Social workers recognize and respect the diversity of Canadian society, taking into account the breadth of differences that exist among individuals, families, groups and communities." (CASW, 2005a, p. 4)
- "Social workers shall demonstrate an appreciation of their own cultural identities and those of others. Social workers must also be aware of their own privilege and power and must acknowledge the impact of this privilege and power in their work with and on behalf of clients." (NASW, 2015a, p. 24)

The worker would need to interpret if and how cultural humility and sensitivity impinges on the specific request for prayer.

Laws and policies. There are probably no laws that apply here, but the regulations governing various settings might include rulings on the appropriateness of prayer. What about principles? Which choice would be considered beneficial or harmful to the client? Is your decision fair? Is there a legitimate reason why you would (or would not) agree to pray with this client if you haven't (or have) done so with others in the past? In praying with the client, or in declining to do so, are you appearing to be a trustworthy individual?

Practice principles. Clinical knowledge and case knowledge are central to this dilemma. As noted earlier, our understanding of the case, the setting, and the client will help us to understand the basis for the client's request, the cultural and biopsychosocial elements involved, the practice norms of the setting or geographic region, and the implications of our decisions. Strong communication and assessment skills will help the worker interpret the meaning the request has for the client and, subsequently, the meaning any response will have. The timing of the request and the specific nature of the request all help shape the response.

Depending on the context, one might choose not to pray with a client for a number of legitimate reasons: it is inappropriate for the setting, it could exacerbate problems the client is having (such as with religious ideation associated with psychotic disorders), the use of prayer is obscuring the focus of the helping relationship, the prayer is overtly aligned with a particular religious tradition in such a way that the worker is uncomfortable participating, or the worker's participation or the client's need for prayer is

Why am I selecting a particular cours
of action?
- Examine motives
- Examine rationale
- Self-understanding
- The right thing for the wrong reason?
- Principle of publicity

FIGURE 2.13 Why Am I Selecting a Particular Course of Action?

best addressed by someone from the client's faith community or a pastoral counselor rather than the particular social worker involved (Figure 2.13).

There may also be legitimate reasons for choosing to pray with a client: it is congruent with the goals of work, it brings familiarity and comfort to the client (Great Spirit prayer or "saying grace" before breaking bread), or praying is a norm of the setting (such as the Serenity Prayer in twelve-step meetings). It is important for workers to be able to articulate the reasons that underlie their ethical choices. However, reasons based primarily on the worker's own needs or agenda would not suffice.

In looking at the decision-making tests, you should ask yourself, "If the client tells others about the prayer, will I be comfortable with my decision? If I explain it to my supervisor, will they understand (will it meet the principle of publicity)? Would I be comfortable if others decided to pray with clients in the same circumstances that this client is requesting prayer? Would I want the worker to agree if I were in the client's position? Is this a legitimate and legally sound decision? Is it in the client's interests? Or, does it smell bad and look bad? Would people I respect take a similar action? Would they understand the actions I am taking?"

How should I enact my decision?
- Process matters!
- Consider ultimate objectives
- Use social work knowledge and skills
  - Human behavior
  - Strategy
  - Empathy
  - Communication
  - Culture
- Remember to document

FIGURE 2.14 How Should I Enact My Decision?

How to handle the decision depends on what the decision is (Figure 2.14). Agreeing to pray, making time for meditative or silent prayer, or being with the client in the moment are all relatively straightforward actions. They are low risk in that they accede to the client's request but require limited involvement or exposure by the social worker. The decisions to question the request or decline to pray may be more complicated.

Let's say the client's request to review passages from a holy text and pray to enhance her parenting is not an appropriate activity for your limited time during home visits. You might ask her to talk about what these wishes mean to her in her struggle to become a better parent. If you find her beliefs are sources of strength as she works toward those goals, you might suggest that she review the passages and pray before your visits. You could then begin the session by asking about what she read and how it relates to the issues with which she is struggling. For the client who wants to base sessions on scripture or prayer, the better choice may be to refer them to someone in their faith community who can offer that, while you provide the assistance appropriate to your professional training. If you were the client, what would you want the worker to do?

The effective process for handling the prayer question depends on your respect for the client's wishes (even if you can't accede to them) and your sensitivity in understanding what the request means to this individual in light of the work that you are doing together.

Conclusion

What is best to do when one is presented with an ethical dilemma? It depends. What it depends on and how you generate and weigh options is the crux of thoughtful ethical practice. In this chapter we examined the various considerations for processing ethical dilemmas, and introduced you to the six-question model that will be used in this book. The first key is to apply that model so that it becomes a natural extension of your decision making. Remember, the correct choices (and there may be several) depend on contextual factors, which you must uncover and weigh. The remainder of the book is dedicated to the goal of finding and assessing.

Each of the chapters in Part II introduces a core ethical concept, standards from the code of ethics that relate to the concept, and examples of cases where the standard is upheld and where it is violated. Building on these cases, each chapter presents a dilemma involving the particular standard and examines it using the "who, what, when, where, why, and how" decision-making model. The goal is to dissect the "it depends" for the case, building your comfort with ethical decision making and your confidence for taking on dilemmas of your own.

For Continuing Conversation

1. Who is helpful to you when you face ethical dilemmas in your personal life? Who is or could be helpful with professional dilemmas? What qualities are you looking for in a consultant or supervisor?

2. What laws or policies have you encountered that get in the way of meeting the best interests of clients?

3. The staff at your agency discuss clients in the break room. Is this ethical? How would you decide? If it is not, how would you address it?

4. You have an old laptop you are not using. Is it ethical to give it to your client?

5. Ethics and practice standards advise social workers to engage in self-care. What dilemmas might arise if this imperative conflicts with client needs and the value of service?

Key Concepts

Automatism. The theory that actions are performed automatically.

Autonomy. Freedom from undue influence from the state or others (Barsky, 2019, p. 37).

Beneficence. Working for the good of others.

Boundary. A guideline, rule, or limit that identifies reasonable, safe, and permissible ways for people to behave around each other.

Conflict of interest. A situation in which an individual or organization is involved in multiple interests, one of which could corrupt the motivation for an act in another.

Dialogic process. Ethics that are grounded in communications and understanding between people, rather than in a philosophical tradition.

Fidelity. Faithfulness to a person, cause, or belief, demonstrated by continuing loyalty and support.

Justice. Behavior or treatment that is morally right and fair and the laws and policies that maintain this.

Mom test. A conceptual strategy for ethical decision making that involves asking oneself "What would my mom (or any moral exemplar) do in this situation?" Also called the *mentor test*.

Nonmaleficence. An ethical precept that suggests, given an existing problem, it may be better not to do something, or to do nothing, than to risk causing more harm than good. It serves to remind helping professionals to consider the possible harm any intervention might do.

Prescriptive standards. Tenets that impose or enforce correct behavior or actions.

Proscriptive standards. Tenets that forbid or caution against particular actions or behaviors.

Publicity test. A conceptual strategy for ethical decision making that involves asking oneself if a decision is justifiable, and how other professionals would view it.

Reversibility test. A conceptual strategy for ethical decision making that involves the decision maker asking if they would want a particular action done toward them if the roles were reversed.

Smell test. A conceptual strategy for ethical decision making that involves asking whether the choice one is making in line with community standards, legal standards, or our own gut instincts about right and wrong.

PART II

Applying Standards for Ethical Practice

CHAPTER 3

Self-Determination

Introduction

The principle of **autonomy** reflects individuals' fundamental rights to have control over the decisions that govern their lives. Autonomy is linked to the United States' constitutional principles of liberty and privacy, and to similar principles of liberty and freedom of thought included in the Canadian Charter of Rights and Freedoms (1982). Only in exceptional circumstances should professionals, as agents of society, act paternalistically to restrict the individual's freedom or **self-determination**. Usually, individual autonomy is limited only when the person presents a compelling danger to themself or to others in society. When a client is actively threatening suicide or murder, the choice to overrule autonomy is clear. When a person chooses to live in dangerous conditions or refuses to take medication because of personal desires or religious beliefs, self-determination usually wins out, even if it may cause the helper great discomfort and a sense of foreboding for the future.

Elements of self-determination are as follows:

- Respecting clients' autonomy: the fundamental right to control the decisions that govern their lives
- Assisting clients to identify their goals and make informed decisions
- Overruling clients' self-determination only when the risk of self-harm or harm toward a third party is clear, serious, and imminent

The essential standards relating to patient autonomy encourage professionals to

- "Promote the self-determination and autonomy of clients, actively encouraging them to make informed decisions on their own behalf." (CASW, 2005b, 1.3.1)

- "...[R]espect and promote the right of clients to self-determination and assist clients in their efforts to identify and clarify their goals." (NASW, 2021, 1.02)

These codes also articulate the limits of self-determination:

- "Social workers who have reason to believe that a client intends to harm him/herself are expected to exercise professional judgment regarding their need to take action consistent with their provincial/territorial legislation, standards of practice and workplace policies." (CASW, 2005b, 1.6.3)
- "... when ... clients' actions or potential actions pose a serious, foreseeable, and imminent risk to themselves or others." (NASW, 2021, 1.02)

The ideal of self-determination is constrained by societal and individual factors. Laws and cultural norms balance the individual's desires with the safety and well-being of others. Personal options and choices are restricted by resources and capacities, such that a person's career, health care, or residential preferences are limited by their abilities, opportunities, and socioeconomic status. An individual's autonomy may be further restricted when they lack the capacity to make safe decisions. Whether or not a person is competent to exercise autonomous decision making rests on many factors: the nature of the decision being made (inconsequential or reversible versus life or death), age and maturity (young children are typically not viewed as capable of making health-care decisions), the person's capacity to appreciate the consequences of various choices (to ask "What will this mean for me?"), and other factors (Kuther, 2003; Konrad, 2020; Manning & Gaul, 1997; Reamer, 2018).

The determination of a client's **decisional capacity** is an individualized process specific to a particular decision and moment in time, and specific to the individual involved. That is, a person may not be competent to manage their money but could still be ruled competent to make healthcare decisions. When a person is deemed incompetent, other individuals act as proxies to carry out that person's wishes. For example, parents make decisions on behalf of their children, spouses are designated to speak for each other when one is incapacitated, or adult children may be assigned to speak on behalf of elderly parents.

Individuals can prepare for the possibility of incapacitation by creating living wills and making provisions for an enduring power of attorney, also called durable power of attorney. These processes specify the person's wishes in health care, finances, and life-extending treatments. In a variation of these processes, psychiatric advanced directives are employed by persons with severe and persistent mental illnesses to specify the steps they wish to have taken in the event that they are unable to make those choices (Swanson et al., 2006). For example, a psychiatric advanced directive would alert emergency room personnel that the patient desires a particular form of treatment or prefers a particular type of medication, in line with current medical practices.

Self-determination is a complex philosophical, ethical, legal, and practical issue, with relevance for all domains of service delivery. Helping professionals must be vigilant in protecting the client's wishes against the intrusion of others' beliefs and preferences, expediency, and organizational interests. They must also hold individual will in balance by intervening paternalistically when self-determination puts the client or others in harm's way. The case of Mrs. Mayberry in Box 3.1 illustrates how to uphold the standards surrounding self-determination.

BOX 3.1

Upholding the Standard

Mrs. Mayberry is an eighty-eight-year-old Black Canadian woman who dislocated her shoulder and broke her elbow after slipping on the ice while walking out to her mailbox. Her hospital discharge plan includes a brief stay at a rehabilitation (rehab) center to make sure that her shoulder heals properly and that she does not reinjure it. When she met with Cal, a young, white social worker assigned to make arrangements for the referral, Mrs. Mayberry flatly refused to agree to placement at the rehab center. Cal did not know Mrs. Mayberry well but wondered if their differences in age, gender, and race might be contributing to her distrust of him and this plan. He also wondered if she was resisting because of concerns about her home; sometimes people are reluctant to leave their houses because they are worried about pets, break-ins, or other factors. He explored these questions with Mrs. Mayberry.

She replied, "It's nothing like that. My mama died in one of those rehab places and if I'm going to die, it'll be at home, not with a bunch of strangers at a place like that." Cal tried to clarify that her condition was not that severe, and that her stay would probably last less than two weeks. He shared his concern that if her shoulder failed to heal properly she might ultimately need to be hospitalized or admitted to an assisted living facility anyway. He said that the re-mote location of her home, and the fact that she lived alone, led the hospital staff, including her doctor, to fear that she would overwork the injured arm and cause more damage.

Mrs. Mayberry replied, "Well, I thank you very much for your con-cern and for all these folks have done for me here, but I'll be fine on my own."

Cal acknowledged Mrs. Mayberry's decision then asked if they might come up with a compromise. Could a physical therapist visit her home to work on her recovery and check on her progress? Mrs. May-berry agreed to this option, and Cal began to make the arrangements. He also shared Mrs. Mayberry's decision with the treatment team and his supervisor and documented their conversation in her record.

Tensions in self-determination often arise when helping profession-als believe the client is not acting in their own best interest. Cal's concern for Mrs. Mayberry's well-being is understandable. While he and the other members of her treatment team understand the desire for independence and her apprehensions about the rehabilitation center, they also believe that her condition will improve best if she is placed there before returning home. While they view it as a brief stay, Mrs. Mayberry's fear that it will be a life sentence fuels her rejection of the placement.

Cal is wise to wonder if their differences and the absence of a trusting relationship with Mrs. Mayberry might contribute to her reluctance to take his advice. In such circumstances, Indigenous leaders from the person's cul-tural community; other professionals; or the client's family, friends, or spir-itual leaders might become involved, with the client's permission, to help facilitate communication and negotiate a mutually agreeable outcome. The nature of Mrs. Mayberry's concerns and the vehemence of her response seem to indicate that lack of trust and understanding is not the problem.

Professionals can intervene paternalistically if they believe a client is incompetent to make a health-care decision. Cal was wise not to pursue this course of action. His preliminary interactions with Mrs. Mayberry indicate that she understands her condition and is aware of the risks inherent in her choice to return home. Pursuing further assessments of **competence** would have been fruitless and would have further alienated the client from the health-care team. Cal or another worker with an ongoing relationship with Mrs. Mayberry might want to have a conversation with her about the point at which she would seek further professional assistance or placement. The treatment team may also discuss the point at which they would deem Mrs. Mayberry's decisions to be so flawed that they warrant intervention to assess her decisional capacity.

While the offer of in-home services is, to Cal, a less desirable option, it is in keeping with Mrs. Mayberry's wishes. If she is happy and comfortable at home, it ultimately may be a more effective option for healing than a setting she finds foreign and frightening. And Cal has demonstrated respect in honoring her wishes. He has also adhered to informed consent processes in explaining the client's options and documenting her decision. The following case (Box 3.2) demonstrates actions that violate standards associated with self-disclosure.

BOX 3.2

Violating the Standard

Tonya and Randy are both twenty-eight years old. They work part time at a returnable-bottle sorting center in a small town. They both were born with Down syndrome. They are in love, have been married for several years, and are eager to start a family. They are aware of their conditions but are confident in their ability, as a team, to successfully raise children. Vanessa is their caseworker from the developmental disabilities council. During a recent meeting, Tonya confided in Vanessa that they are concerned about their inability to conceive and asked for help in accessing resources to pursue fertility treatments.

Privately, Vanessa cringed. She had been hoping that this notion of parenting would go away over time. While she respected Tonya and Randy's abilities and dedication to each other, her previous work in child protection had left her very discouraged about the capacity of most people, much less those with the conditions Randy and Tonya have, to parent effectively. Her past conversations with them about her concerns have failed to change their plans, and she secretly longed for the days when sterilization was routine for certain populations. In responding to Tonya's request for assistance, Vanessa decides to contact a physician who shares her views and who will not actively assist the couple with their quest to have children. She is reluctant to deceive her clients but believes she is acting in their long-term best interest.

Cal's dilemma with Mrs. Mayberry arose from their differing beliefs of what is best for the client. Vanessa's dilemma, while veiled as protecting the clients' interests, stems from the clash of her values with her clients' decision to have children. It is not uncommon for social workers and other professionals to struggle with the choices that their clients are making and to have strong feelings about those choices. Vanessa's error is not in her intense reaction to the case but rather in her failure to address their requests for help and in her surreptitious actions to undermine her clients' rights.

Vanessa's values have been shaped by many experiences, including her upbringing, her education, and her work—for example, in CPS. It is unclear what preparation she has received for working with people with Down syndrome, her sensitivity to the biases of ableism, and the degree to which she understands the history of oppression and discrimination this group has experienced, particularly around reproductive rights (Buchanan et al., 2000; Caplan, 2000). It is also not clear how well she understands the capacities of parents with Down syndrome, and the abilities of this couple, in particular (Preston, 2013). Is she underestimating their abilities and the supports they will draw on in raising a family? Is she placing her judgments ahead of their needs and desires? Supportive and probing supervision is essential in helping workers like Vanessa address value conflicts and reconcile their beliefs with their professional responsibilities. Vanessa could have benefited from such conversations before the situation reached a point where she believed her only choice was to stonewall or deceive her clients.

Even with ample reflection, knowledge, and understanding, Vanessa may still believe that her clients are making a poor choice and that they are unworthy of services that will help them conceive children. If, ultimately, she is unable to assist her clients in exercising their right to services, she must transfer the case to someone who can help them. It is not her role to determine their capacity to pursue fertility treatments and ultimately parent and deceiving them by colluding with another professional against their wishes is a violation of her fiduciary responsibilities.

There are situations in which the client's judgment is sufficiently impaired to warrant intervention against the individual's wishes. In cases of reproductive rights, "any restriction or denial of decision-making authority to a disabled woman should be the consequence of an objective procedure, containing proper legal safeguards against every form of abuse. This procedure must be based on an evaluation of the capability of the mentally disabled person by qualified experts, subject to periodic review and to appeal" (Center for Reproductive Rights, 2002, p. 2). These due process protections are intended to ensure that individual rights are not usurped by family members or representatives of social agencies purporting to know the best interests of others. Vanessa can be assured that Tonya and Randy's capacity will be evaluated, as necessary, in a transparent and empirically supported manner as they progress through the various processes necessary to pursue their goal of parenthood. Sometimes, decisions about self-determination are not clear-cut. The case "Hostile in Hospice" (Box 3.3) illustrates such a dilemma.

BOX 3.3

Resolving Dilemmas in Self-Determination: Hostile in Hospice

Mr. Lee is a fifty-six-year-old man in the last stages of lung cancer. His physician has made a referral for hospice services to supplement the care that his ex-wife and adult children are providing. When Joan, the hospice social worker, arrives for a first visit, she notes a Confederate flag from the American South waving from Mr. Lee's front porch. She finds Mr. Lee in a hospital bed in the living room. His daughter is sitting nearby, and the two are watching the news. Both are smoking cigarettes. In the brief time before the interview starts, Mr. Lee reacts negatively to news stories on immigration and same-sex marriage, using slurs to refer to the people involved and saying loudly to his daughter, "Now that's just plain wrong."

Joan is taken aback by the dense smoke, by Mr. Lee's language, and by his unabashed bigotry. During her one-on-one time with the daughter, she observes, "Your father sure has some strong opinions." The daughter shrugs and says, "Always has. We'll know his days are numbered when he doesn't give a rip anymore." When Joan voices her concern about the smoking, the daughter replies, "Yeah, some others don't like it, either, but if it makes him happy, why not? It's not going to kill him. And if he's going to smoke, why can't I? Don't worry about us blowing the place up, though. We turn off the oxygen when we light up."

In her interview with Mr. Lee, Joan mentions her earlier observation. "Those news reports seemed pretty upsetting to you. What other programs do you like to watch?" In response, Mr. Lee springs into an obscenity-laced diatribe about people who are ruining America. Joan is a member of two of the groups he names, lesbians, and Indigenous people. Her negative reaction to Mr. Lee is so strong that she can't muster a response. Instead, she concludes the interview early and spends the whole ride back to her office thinking of what she wishes she'd said.

Does respect for client self-determination require Joan to endure comments she finds offensive? Does it mean that the workers should accept risky behavior, such as smoking in the vicinity of an oxygen tank? Can professionals carry out their responsibilities in an atmosphere where they are uncomfortable and defensive? In sharing their discomfort with clients, are workers misusing power, placing their needs and rights above those they are intended to serve or are they guarding their own well-being through self-care? Conversely, in withholding their candid reactions, are professionals acting dishonestly, doing a disservice to their own humanity, and harming the relationship anyway?

Joan is understandably upset and unnerved by her client's attitudes and his vehemence in expressing them. She is also concerned about his smoking and home environment, in light of his condition. Her responsibility is to help Mr. Lee and his family as they prepare for his impending death, not help him become a more tolerant and open-minded citizen. Nevertheless, how can she overcome her reactions to him and create an environment in which she and others can effectively deliver services? Is she being dishonest in allowing him to condemn groups of which she is a part without alerting him to that fact? Or would such a conversation be in service of her needs instead of her client's?

Applying the Six-Question Model

Who Can Help Joan with Her Decision?

Joan's supervisor should help process her experience at the intake interview. She should empathize with Joan about the feelings it engendered and help her depersonalize Mr. Lee's statements or put them in other contexts. The supervisor must also determine if resources exist to transfer the case, should that become necessary.

Joan's colleagues will be an important resource in sorting through her reactions to Mr. Lee and determining if she can effectively serve him. They may offer perspectives on his actions and needs in light of his culture and his terminal condition. They can help her weigh her options and appropriately balance her needs with his. Other service providers who are working with the family may be able to assist her in responding to him and will benefit by being prepared in advance for his invectives. Colleagues who have known Joan for a long time or who know her well will be especially helpful in assessing her reaction and providing her with frank feedback. Is this a new issue for Joan, or has she often struggled with strong reactions to clients or the inclination to self-disclose to them?

Joan may find that written resources help broaden her understanding of Mr. Lee; she might consider and apply concepts such as honesty, authenticity, and confrontation (Farber, 2006). Resources in palliative or end-of-life care provide insight into the issues that arise in this area of specialization (Sendor & O'Connor, 1997). Ethics operationalize the principle of client autonomy and the limits on that when others' rights are being abridged. Social work values speak to individual dignity and worth, the importance of human relationships, and the imperative of social justice.

A review of the professional standards and competencies will present Joan with a mixed picture of her obligations. Social workers are expected to demonstrate cultural competence and humility, be self-aware about the dynamics of power and privilege (CASW, 2005b; NASW, 2015a), and adapt their techniques for clients from "different age groups, . . . socioeconomic and educational backgrounds, lifestyles and differing states of mental health and disability" (NASW, 2004, p. 20). They should not impose personal values in practice (NASW 2015a). Conversely, "Social workers oppose prejudice and discrimination against any person or group of persons, on any grounds, and specifically challenge views and actions that stereotype particular persons or groups" (CASW, 2005b, p.5) and "promote sensitivity and knowledge about oppression and cultural and ethnic diversity" (NASW 2021, p. 5). First-person accounts and blog posts may prove useful to Joan in choosing among the competing imperatives present in her dilemma. As Janssen so thoughtfully elaborates, being true to oneself and to the needs and vulnerabilities of the client can feel like walking a rope bridge in high winds (Janssen, 2021).

What Are Joan's Options?

Joan essentially has four options.

1. She can continue to serve Mr. Lee without addressing his inflammatory comments. The rationale for this choice is that addressing his comments would divert the focus from the intended purpose of her visits and might alienate Mr. Lee or violate standards of respect.

2. As a second option, Joan can continue to work with him and ask him not to use racial or other kinds of slurs in her presence. This option sets ground rules for their work together and may facilitate Joan's ability to be of help to Mr. Lee.

3. A third option is to return to his home for the next session and notify him that she is a member of two of the groups he scorns. Doing so treats Mr. Lee with honesty without expecting a change in his behavior, but it is a self-disclosure on her part that she may not wish to reveal and which may be irrelevant to the working relationship.

4. The final option is for Joan to seek a transfer of the case. Given the breadth of Mr. Lee's contempt, it is unlikely that any worker will be immune from his harsh words, but some might be better equipped to deal with them than Joan.

When Has Joan Made a Similar Decision?

Joan has no doubt experienced prejudice against her race and condemnation of her sexual orientation in the past. As a result, she has probably developed strategies for responding to such statements and for inuring herself to their impact. These strategies may include confronting the perpetrator or venting to her social network, colleagues, or others who share her background. The extent to which those strategies are relevant to this situation depends on how well Joan is able to separate her personal reactions from her professional responsibilities. Is complaining to friends about a bigoted comment by a client the same as complaining about the same comment from a store clerk? Whether she is typically forthright or passive when confronted with prejudicial comments, her responses to Mr. Lee will represent not only her personal position, but also that of her agency and profession. While she may feel victimized by Mr. Lee, she has particular power in this situation in that he and his family need the services she is equipped to deliver. Any comments that she makes or declines to make will carry the weight of her role.

An additional dimension differentiating her past personal responses from her reaction to Mr. Lee is that some past slurs may have occurred outside the context of an ongoing relationship. In those cases, Joan's intent may have been to remedy the immediate situation by removing herself or rebuffing the offending person. Different strategies are needed when the intent is to preserve a relationship—in this case, one involving professional services. As such, Joan must take a longer-term view, recognizing that her in-the-moment responses will have long-term consequences.

Joan's experiences with adversity may also play a role in this decision. While she may wish to resign from Mr. Lee's case, will that put her anger at Mr. Lee to rest? Will it perpetuate a pattern where Joan seeks the path of least resistance rather than struggling with and potentially growing from a dilemma? On the other hand, it may not be wise to try to work through Mr. Lee's anger if Joan's pattern is to stay in a toxic situation at the expense of her own health and well-being. Her knowledge of herself and her supervisor's knowledge of the areas on which she needs to work are therefore relevant to the current decision.

In addition to having experienced personal insults, Joan has probably also experienced patients who fail to follow the instructions of their medical team. She has likely encountered clients, like Mr. Lee, who continue the very behaviors that contributed to their current conditions. In a classic struggle with client self-determination, Joan must reconcile her client's insistence on smoking with the other needs he presents. Making too big an issue of his behavior, particularly in light of his terminal status, will probably be fruitless and may alienate him and his family at the very time they should be engaging with the helping network.

Joan's personal and professional experiences shaped her response to Mr. Lee's diatribe, and they can also be marshaled to move purposefully and effectively beyond the difficulties of the first session. Joan should reflect on them in weighing her options, and she should include those insights in her consultations with others about the case.

Where Do Ethical, Clinical, and Legal Standards Lead Joan?

Rule-based ethics. Deontology suggests that right courses of action should hold under all circumstances (Dolgoff et al., 2022). What rules might be formulated from Joan's four options? We will examine each in turn.

The rule embedded in the decision to stay with the case and ignore Mr. Lee's invective might be phrased as "Professionals must rise above their personal distaste for clients' opinions." It would mean putting clients' needs ahead of workers', thus ensuring that people whose habits, appearance, and attitudes are undesirable are not precluded from care. Those are good rules and, in fact, accepted aspects of service delivery. However, there are also legitimate reasons that they are not universal law.

The first involves the fair distribution of scarce resources. People cannot be forced to comply with treatment; however, such patients may removed from care so that providers can reallocate services to others who can make better use of them. Another exception to the rule occurs in instances where the client's intentions place the worker's physical and emotional safety at risk. Generally, clients should come first, but there are situations in which the worker's interests and society's should not be subjugated to the client's. Clinical and ethical examination will help tell us if Mr. Lee is one of those cases.

Joan's second option, wherein she would address Mr. Lee's slurs and ask for a moratorium on them during their sessions, might be translated to a rule stating, "Social workers have a right to work in an environment free of harassment and offensive speech." Again, this is a reasonable rule and one that in the United States and Canada is codified into prohibitions against racial and sexual harassment. The twist in universalizing the rule is that there are some conditions where workers may withstand personal affronts in the course of doing their jobs. Clients may become angry at a worker's actions, or their own conditions or pain may cause them to lash out at others. Because helping and health professions exist in service to others, there may be times when the worker cannot or should not exercise control over the client's speech and actions.

For Joan's third option, alerting Mr. Lee to her background, the rule might be construed as "Social workers should be truthful with their clients" or "A social worker's background should not be objectionable to the client." It is essential that the social worker utilize the principles of honesty and genuineness to convey their desire to help to their clients. Yet like many concepts, there are circumstances where these tools lose their utility. For honesty, those circumstances might include situations that demand excessive self-disclosure by the worker or instances that divert attention from the client to the worker. While candor is good, it is not always good. As such, a conversation about backgrounds may perpetuate prejudice and stereotypes, undermine the worker's credibility, divert attention from the problem for work, and suggest client choice where none exists.

The hypothetical rule embedded in Joan's fourth option, to transfer the case, might be stated as "Social workers can terminate a client whose thoughts, statements, and behaviors are objectionable." A more positive wording might be "Social workers are not required to continue working with clients whose thoughts, statements, and behaviors are objectionable." As in the first option, the extension of these rules to universal law might mean that clients must conform to workers' expectations in order to receive care, which is a violation of the service ethic of the profession. Furthermore, it might jeopardize care entirely for clients who are in some way called undesirable.

Outcome-based ethics. An examination of Joan's options from the deontological perspective helps to highlight the hazards associated with each of them. What consequences are implied by each of the alternatives? If Joan stays with the case but is mute about Mr. Lee's derogatory comments, she may suffer from the abuse, and she may be tempted to shortchange his care because time with him is so repugnant to her. There may also be adverse consequences for the helping relationship if Mr. Lee eventually learns of Joan's background and feels deceived by her silence about it while he went on with his slurs. A positive consequence might occur if Joan learns to handle challenging clients, redirect and to effectively manage her own strongly negative emotional reactions.

What might be the consequences if Joan raises her concerns with Mr. Lee and asks him to restrain his comments during their visits? He might comply, appreciate her candor, apologize, or explain, thereby facilitating a more positive relationship without requiring Joan to reveal her background. Or he might ridicule her request, question it, and refuse, driving a further wedge between the two. If improperly handled, the request may seem petty, self-centered, or patronizing, and an abridgement of free speech rights. The conversation may detract from the original purpose of the visit, meaning Mr. Lee and his family are deprived of needed assistance due to the worker's agenda.

In disclosing her background to Mr. Lee, Joan faces some of the same risks and benefits as she does in asking him to cease the comments during her visits. Additional consequences arise from her personalizing the concern by revealing her own background. Mr. Lee might realize that his slurs refer not to faceless groups but to real people, and that those people are hurt by them. At its most ideal, this could be a transformative moment for him. On the other hand, Joan's self-disclosure may mean that he turns his derision on her and refuses to work with someone of her race or sexual orientation. The resulting rift would clarify the future of their relationship but perhaps result in professional damage to Joan.

Transferring the case before the next session would free Joan from having to face Mr. Lee's wrath and would spare him a worker from groups he scorns. The next worker would be better prepared to help him, despite his prejudices, and so service delivery may be more effective. However, transferring the case may set an untenable precedent for the hospice agency, and it would extinguish the opportunity for Joan to overcome challenges with clients such as Mr. Lee. While the greatest potential good appears to come from scenarios where Joan shares her concerns in some way with Mr. Lee, they also appear to be the scenarios that are the most risky for the relationship and for Joan personally.

Values. What does an examination of values say? Joan's values regarding racial and other minority groups are at odds with those of her client. As she strives to reconcile those differences, several social work values are relevant to the case. The value of service is enacted through the principles that state in part, "Social workers elevate service to others above self-interest" (NASW, 2021, p. 5) and "Social workers maintain the best interests of clients as a priority" (CASW, 2005b, p. 3). Valuing the client's inherent dignity and worth means treating "each person in a caring and respectful fashion, mindful of individual differences and cultural and ethnic diversity" (NASW, 2021, p. 5), or striving for "a working knowledge and understanding of clients' racial and cultural affiliations, identities, values, beliefs and customs" (CASW, 2005b, p. 4). The value that emphasizes the importance of human relationships adds yet another dimension to the case, identifying relationships between people as the vehicle for change and encouraging the engagement of clients as partners in the helping process. This value would appear to encourage Joan to form an alliance with Mr. Lee to overcome their differences in service of his needs. Alternatively, it may be interpreted as encouraging her to transfer the case to a worker who can better forge a constructive bond with the client. Adherence to these values would favor options that keep the focus on Mr. Lee and his needs.

Professional standards. In addition to the ethical standard on self-determination noted at the outset of the chapter, three other standards might apply to Joan's dilemma:

1. When to transfer or terminate:

   - "Social workers renegotiate or terminate professional services when these services are no longer required or no longer meet the needs of clients." (CASW, 2005b, 1.8.1)
   - "Social workers should refer clients to other professionals when the other professionals' specialized knowledge or expertise is needed to serve clients fully or when social workers believe that they are not being effective or making reasonable progress with clients and that other services are required." (NASW, 2021, 1.1.6b)

2. How to terminate:

   - "Social workers should take reasonable steps to avoid abandoning clients who are still in need of services. Social workers should withdraw services precipitously only under unusual circumstances, giving careful consideration to all factors in the situation and taking care to minimize possible adverse effects. Social workers should assist in making appropriate arrangements for continuation of services when necessary." (NASW, 2021, 1.1.6b)
   - "Whether the decision to renegotiate or terminate is that of the client or the social worker, social workers (where appropriate) initiate a discussion with the client to appreciate, and if possible, address any difficulties or misunderstandings that may

have occurred. If the client desires other professional services, the social worker may assist in referral." (CASW, 2005b, 1.8.3)

3. How to avoid discrimination:

- "Social workers do not discriminate against any person on the basis of age, abilities, ethnic background, gender, language, marital status, national ancestry, political affiliation, race, religion, sexual orientation or socio-economic status." (CASW, 2005b, 1.1.2)
- "Social workers should not practice, condone, facilitate, or collaborate with any form of discrimination on the basis of race, ethnicity, national origin, color, sex, sexual orientation, gender orientation or expression, age, marital status, political belief, religion, immigration status, or mental or physical disability." (NASW, 2021, 4.02)

Practice principles. Guidelines for effective practice might oblige Joan to narrowly focus her time with Mr. Lee on his needs rather than her personal discomfort. An alternative approach would contend that discussion of these value differences is in fact part of the work (Doherty, 1995; Koenig & Spano, 2003). The point of such moral dialogue is not to convert Mr. Lee to her point of view, but rather to foster a discussion of their perspectives in service of the work that they are going to be doing together. "Social workers are not obligated to endorse clients' views blindly, particularly if social workers do not agree with them. Social workers should have confidence in their clients' ability to accept or reject social workers' views. Clients also have the right to know about practitioners' biases that may influence their work in any given case" (Reamer, 2018, p. 134–135).

Ethical principles. In applying ethical principles to Joan's options, we note that the preservation of autonomy is the core issue in the dilemma. While autonomy of beliefs or speech may be less compelling as an ethical issue than autonomy over life-and-death decisions, it is still a bedrock concept associated with "Western values of individualism, independence [and] interdependence" (Corey et al., 2014, p. 17). As Mr. Lee exercises his autonomy through his vitriol, the effects on others are not significant enough to warrant limiting his autonomy. But do any of Joan's options do that? Even in the options where she might speak with him about her concerns, her intent is to provide for her own self-care and humanity, not to abridge his rights. Transferring the case (assuming there is a capable worker to receive it) or remaining silent upholds Mr. Lee's autonomy.

None of Joan's options is overtly deceptive or in violation of the principle of fidelity, but those where she voices her concerns are the most forthright in honestly and respectfully reacting to Mr. Lee's actions. Those options also appear to best promote positive outcomes in the case and prevent the harm that Mr. Lee's invectives will cause or that Joan will provide substandard services in light of them.

The principle of justice calls for Joan to engage in reflection about the nature of her reaction to Mr. Lee. Is she acting out of her own form of prejudice or personal hurt? Or, in contrast, does her reaction occur in defense of a larger principle? Why is Mr. Lee's behavior a particular point of contention compared to that of the myriad other clients she has served? In other words, is her choice to transfer the case or to object to his attitudes just? Would she do the same with other clients, or is she unfairly singling him out for his disagreeable comments?

Laws and policies. Several laws and regulations stand out in this case. As is true for other citizens, Mr. Lee has a constitutional guarantee of free speech. This does not mean that Joan can't exercise her right in expressing her position, but if she is representing a government agency, she cannot abridge his rights to services on the basis of his offensive language. The sources that are funding Mr. Lee's care may also have regulations about the provision of services and about the degree to which a provider can decide who to serve and who not to. Joan's agency likely has policies establishing the basis on which cases can be transferred or terminated. They may also have policies for service delivery when clients fail to follow health and safety standards, such as smoking in the presence of an oxygen tank. These policies will provide Joan with guidance and support in her decision making.

Synthesis: Ethical, clinical, and legal implications. Of Joan's four options, the one to transfer the case appears to have the least support in an ethical analysis. Even if it were feasible, it does nothing to remedy the core conflict except move it on to someone else. To continue the case and remain silent also has less merit in that it also fails to address the conflict and runs the risk of taking a toll on Joan and on her care of Mr. Lee. Both options that involve Joan voicing her concerns have multiple benefits. They can be combined if needed, they offer the possibility of reconciliation and understanding, and they do not preclude the option of transferring the case if an impasse is reached.

Why Is Joan Selecting a Particular Course of Action?

Because the conflict arises out of value differences between Joan and her client, she must carefully evaluate her preferred actions in terms of her client's interests. What are her motivations in preferring one option over another? Whether she is disclosing her reactions to Mr. Lee or her personal background, it must be in service of facilitating their working relationship, her own emotional catharsis, or a replacement of her needs over his. Choosing to stay silent or to leave the case demonstrates all-or-nothing reasoning: that she must either capitulate to Mr. Lee's behaviors or retreat.

The principle of reversibility seems to favor Joan's choice to speak up. If she were to put herself in her client's shoes and imagine how she would want to be treated, it is likely that she would prefer to be dealt with forthrightly and respectfully. The first and fourth options (ignoring the comments or transferring the case) give Mr. Lee no capacity to defend his views, explain them, apologize, or rectify them. Those favoring the principle of publicity and mom/mentors would likely suggest that these options are less desirable, at least as a first course of action, for the same reasons.

How Should Joan Carry Out Her Decision?

Attention to process will be essential for the success of this decision. Joan is balancing concerns that are very personal (the slurs about race and sexual orientation) with concerns that are grounded in health and safety (the smoking). Joan must prepare for a conversation about which she has strong emotions and consider whether she has the emotional regulation to broach it neutrally. She must manage the risks that Mr. Lee will feel attacked or judged by the conversation. She must be clear about the objective of the conversation and keep that goal in mind, whatever path the actual discussion takes. Joan should prepare carefully for the interaction by considering all the directions the discussion may take and her responses to Mr. Lee's possible reactions. If her intention is simply for the troubling comments to cease during her visits, she can probably achieve this without revealing anything about her own background. However, she will need to decide if and when she would disclose that information, prepare for Mr. Lee's reactions, and determine in advance the point at which she will limit further self-disclosure.

It is possible that Mr. Lee will say, "Oh sure, I can stop. I didn't mean anything by it" or "I didn't mean I wouldn't like you, just those other gays and Indians." Joan should consider whether this is sufficient to achieve her goals and, if it is, thank him for hearing her out and move on to the purpose of her visit.

If, however, Mr. Lee becomes enraged or disgusted by the conversation, Joan must have a simple response and follow-up plan prepared. For example, she might thank him for his honesty and ask whether it is feasible for them to continue working together. If they conclude that it isn't, she should explain the next steps, and the timeline for facilitating them. (This is expedited by Joan having sought out the options in advance.)

It may be tempting for Joan to lash out at Mr. Lee if her concerns are rebuffed, and anger would certainly be an authentic response in that circumstance. However, in being mindful of her client's vulnerability, her ethical responsibilities as a social worker, and her role representing the agency, she would need to maintain a calm and focused tone and use other venues to appropriately address her hurt or fury.

Box 3.4 provides readers with an opportunity to work through a case involving dilemmas in self-determination.

This case is complex because of the age of the client and the potential health and criminal issues involved. As you work through the steps of the ethical decision-making process, consider the following additional points:

- Would consultation with child welfare, police, and rape crisis personnel be beneficial? How can the worker do so without jeopardizing Selma's privacy?

BOX 3.4

A Dilemma for You: The Reluctant Reporter

Selma is sixteen. She was referred to a counselor at the neighborhood family service agency by her family and her parish priest because of her slipping grades and listlessness. In the third session, Selma disclosed to her worker that she had been raped three months earlier by a friend of her brother's, whom she declined to name. She states that she has not told anyone about the assault because "It was my fault anyway for getting wasted and coming on to him." She reports that she is not pregnant and is at no further risk from him, stating, "I'll make sure it never happens again." When the worker suggests that her parents or the police should be told, Selma looks horrified and says, "No way. I'll deny everything."

- What else might the worker need to know about the situation to help with the decision making?
- Does Selma have the legal and developmental capacity to determine who should be told about her attack?
- Is it urgent that the worker make a decision in this situation?

Conclusion

Self-determination is a reflection of the fundamental right of autonomy. It ensures that individuals are able to make decisions about how they conduct their lives free from the interference of others. The bar for intervening paternalistically is high: when an individual's personal agency seriously impinges on their own life and health or that of others. Professionals who are concerned that their clients are making poor and potentially irreversible decisions must utilize available processes to objectively assess the client's capacity for the decision at hand. When the individual involved is judged to be incompetent, professionals can initiate civil commitment or guardianship procedures, intervene to place the person in a secure setting to prevent suicide, or provide life-saving medical treatments. Each of these is considered to ultimately serve the best interests of the client. If the client is judged to be competent, the professional must accept their right to make choices, even those that trouble or offend the helper.

Exercising **paternalism** through deception is inappropriate in that it presumes the worker knows what is best for the client, though the worker will never live with the consequences in the same way the client must. And, in addition to being fundamentally dishonest, deception also destroys the trust that is essential in a professional relationship. Social workers and other professionals can, however, be forthright in expressing their concerns to their clients. They can use informed consent procedures to ensure that the client understands his options and their likely risks, benefits, and consequences.

For Continuing Conversation

1. Describe the situations in which you feel you might have to overrule a client's right to self-determination. How would you do so while minimizing the risks to their privacy, trust, and individual rights?

2. In Box 3.3, "Hostile in Hospice," how could Joan respectfully ask Mr. Lee to refrain from using racial slurs in her presence?
3. Most of Box 3.3 focuses on the client's prejudicial comments. There is also the matter of the client's smoking while on oxygen. Should Joan address Mr. Lee's smoking? If so, how?
4. Having worked through the case in Box 3.4, involving Selma's reported rape, are you confident and comfortable in the decision you reached?

Key Concepts

Autonomy. Freedom from external control or influence; independence.

Competence. The ability to do something successfully or efficiently.

Decisional capacity. An individual or client's competency to make decisions affecting themselves, based on age and maturity, mental ability, or ability to understand the consequences of various choices. Decisional capacity is to be evaluated specific to the circumstances in a particular moment; when that capacity is not present, other individuals act as proxies for decision making.

Paternalism. Behavior, by a person, organization, or state that limits a person or group's liberty or autonomy, ostensibly for their own good

Self-determination. The process by which a person controls their own life.

CHAPTER 4

Informed Consent

Introduction

The doctrine of **informed consent** requires that professionals discuss with clients the nature of procedures to be performed and the attendant risks, benefits, and alternatives to the procedures. Informed consent also addresses the limits of confidentiality; researchers use the procedure with study subjects to ensure that they understand the expectations and consequences of the study, should they elect to participate. Informed consent is linked to self-determination, confidentiality, competence, and other standards in that it forms a common basis of understanding from which the worker and client proceed (see Box 4.1). Equipped with an understanding of their options and the parameters of service, people then have the right to **consent** to or refuse treatment (or research participation). The right to informed consent is also embedded in the nature of **fiduciary relationships** wherein one party has differential power, and thus that party has the inherent responsibility to share necessary information with the other (Barsky, 2019; Kutchins, 1991). Informed consent "is intended to assure the client's freedom, privacy and safety" (Houston-Vega et al., 1997, p. 52).

Effective informed consent is not simply a matter of handing someone a form and asking them to sign it. Rather, it requires that the person:

- possesses adequate information,
- has the ability to understand relevant information,
- is able to appreciate the situation and its consequences,
- has the ability to reason, and
- gives consent without coercion or deception.

BOX 4.1

Elements of Informed Consent

- Ensure that clients have clear and adequate information regarding the risks, benefits, expectations, and alternatives to clinical treatment or research participation.
- Be attentive to the ways that a person's mental/emotional state, culture, language, and past experiences may influence their willingness or ability to give consent.

Informed consent is an ongoing process, as different steps in the helping process require separate discussions, consent, and documentation of that consent. How much information is enough? The basic standard of informed consent is "what a rational client would reasonably want to know to make an informed decision" (E. Cohen & Cohen, 1999, p. 78). Disclosure includes "a description of the proposed procedures, any possible alternatives, risks and benefits of both, the probability of success, and the implications of no treatment" (Manning & Gaul, 1997, p. 106). Resources are available enhance the accessibility of informed consent: text for prospective research participants can range in readability from the fourth-grade level to college level (Government of Canada, 2022a; Paasche-Orlow, Taylor, & Brancati, 2003):

- "Taking part in this study is your choice. If you decide not to take part, this will not harm your relations with your doctors or with the university."
- "We will tell you about new information that may affect your health, welfare, or willingness to stay in this study."
- "There is no benefit to you from being in the study. Your taking part may help patients in the future." (Saint Luke's Health System, 2013, p. 2)

Psychologist Kenneth Pope also offers an online resource for viewing and comparing various consent forms and disclosures used by American, Canadian, and other international organizations, which can be accessed online (Pope, n.d.).

Even under the best of circumstances, obtaining informed consent can be an intricate process due in part to variations in patients' capacity for understanding and the complexities of the choices they are facing (Palmer & Harmell, 2016).

- People in crisis or experiencing other trauma may have difficulty synthesizing and evaluating complex information.
- The person's illness, culture, primary language, and experiences with the health or social service system may affect their willingness or ability to provide consent.
- Legal considerations may result in documents that are so dense and lengthy that clients or research subjects simply sign them without appreciating the issues they address.
- Inconsistent patient–provider bonds and pressures for efficient use of treatment time may erode attention to information sharing and diminish the patient's comfort in providing consent.
- Scarce resources often render the true degree of client choice moot.

Clinicians and researchers may be tempted to shortchange informed consent processes. Perhaps they fear that in describing risks or exceptions to confidentiality, they will frighten the client or subject, bias the results, or lead the individual to drop out of the study or service. Some professionals take the attitude that they know what is best for the other person, and thus the individual's permission is an inconvenient formality. In still other cases, the professionals may reason that the long-term benefits of the study or service provided outweigh the short-term misgivings or discomfort of the participants. Why give them the right to decline if you intend to pursue the project anyway? Unfortunately, such attitudes can lead to grave violations of human rights. A well-known example is the Tuskegee syphilis study. From 1932 to 1972 researchers subjected 399 Black sharecroppers with syphilis to painful and risky medical procedures while allowing their disease and associated conditions to advance unabated. Researchers and health-care providers failed to inform the study participants of the nature of their disease or the true purpose of the research, and did not provide them with potentially effective treatments once cures for syphilis were discovered (National Center for HIV, STD, and TB Prevention, 2005; Newkirk, 2016). The **institutional review boards** and **human subject** protections we have today are due in part to reactions against the exploitation and deception evident in this study.

Under the Canadian Sexual Sterilization Act of 1928, physicians conducted surgical sterilization procedures on individuals with mental or physical disabilities who were considered unfit to parent. These procedures, which were performed primarily in the province of Alberta, continued until the legislation was repealed in 1972 (Tymchuk & Faulds, 2004).

From 1883 to 1997, more than 150,000 children from Indigenous families in the U.S. and Canada were removed from their communities (forcibly and under false pretenses) and placed in residential homes where they were commonly subjected to exploitation, abuse, disease, and for many, death (Mosby & Millions, 2021). Instead of addressing appalling hunger and food services, the head of the Canadian federal nutrition service used the poor health of the children as an opportunity to experiment with untested, dangerous nutrition schemes (Mosby & Millions, 2021). As you might imagine, in a system of cultural assimilation that amounted to cultural genocide, informed consent and other rights were not afforded to Indigenous parents or the children themselves (TRT World, 2021).

More recently, the cultivation and commercialization of an African American woman's cells without her knowledge or that of her family raised significant concerns about exploitation by powerful interests as well as the capacity to patent raw materials in addition to the technologies that succeed making them consequential and salable (Truog et al., 2012). Informed consent procedures are now structured to protect vulnerable, desperate, and poorly educated individuals from abuses of power and position in the name of science, but the procedures offer scant protection when the people who must abide by them are uninformed, unethical, or inhumane.

Professional codes of ethics address various dimensions of informed consent for research participants and social service recipients, as illustrated in the following excerpts:

- "Social workers, at the earliest opportunity, discuss with clients their rights and responsibilities and provide them with honest and accurate information regarding the following:

  - the purpose, nature, extent and known implications of the options open to them;

- the potential risks and benefits of proposed social work interventions; ...
- the client's right to view professional records and to seek avenues of complaint." (CASW, 2005b , 1.3.4)

- "Social workers should use clear and understandable language to inform clients of the purpose of the services, risks related to the services, limits to services because of the requirements of a third-party payer, relevant costs, reasonable alternatives, clients' right to refuse or withdraw consent, and the time frame covered by the consent ... [and] ... provide clients with an opportunity to ask questions." (NASW, 2021, 1.03a)
- "Social workers who have children as clients determine the child's capacity to consent and explain to the child (where appropriate), and to the child's parents/guardians (where appropriate) the nature of the social worker's relationship to the child and others involved in the child's care." (CASW, 2005b, 1.3.3)
- "Social workers engaged in evaluation or research should obtain voluntary and written informed consent from participants, when appropriate, without any implied or actual deprivation or penalty for refusal to participate; without undue inducement to participate; and with due regard for participants' well-being, privacy, and dignity." (NASW, 2021, 5.02e)

The codes also affirm the rights of involuntary clients, the need to obtain consent prior to audio- or videotaping or allowing observation by outsiders, and provisions about electronic service delivery, communications, and data storage. The case in Box 4.2 demonstrates actions that uphold standards related to informed consent.

Establishing the risks and benefits of a particular course of treatment is more familiar, and perhaps easier, in medicine than it is in social and behavioral health services. Physicians can say with some certainty what side effects, risks, and benefits a particular medication or procedure will cause. These predictions are less precise in other helping professions, where the dangers and benefits of interventions are less well established and are more contingent on the individual client and the skill of the worker employing them than on the treatments themselves. Nevertheless, while social workers strive to establish the evidence base to support or rule out

BOX 4.2

Upholding the Standard

Amelia is a child protective worker. Mrs. Lopez had been assigned to her caseload following an investigation that indicated Mrs. Lopez was using forms of punishment that were harmful to her children. Referral to parenting classes is a common element of the case plan for parents in this situation. Involuntary clients such as Mrs. Lopez have no choice about complying with the service plan if they wish to retain custody of their children.

When Amelia met with Mrs. Lopez to review the treatment plan, she was cognizant of her client's involuntary status, and the need for informed consent. She was also mindful of the possibility of language differences and cultural practices that might impinge on Mrs. Lopez' parenting methods and her relationship with Amelia as a helping professional. In both Spanish and English, Amelia described several elements of the case plan then said, "The parenting group we are requiring is an important part of your plan because it will equip you with better alternatives for disciplining your little one. The group I am sending you to is effective for about 50% of the people who attend. What we have found is that the participants' attitude is the big difference between those who benefit from it and those who don't. While attending the group is required for us to be sure your children are safe, you do have a choice about when to start the group and how you will participate. Some of the groups are bilingual and they may have Latina facilitators."

certain interventions, they must likewise work to employ that information in informed consent procedures. To the extent that information on risks and benefits is available, clients have a right to know.

Involuntary clients and others who are mandated to receive services may have limited latitude in accepting or rejecting the interventions proposed by the social worker. However, like other people, they are entitled to information about the risks and benefits of the proposed treatment, and the consequences they will face for not participating. In this case, the worker is forthright in describing what she knows about the efficacy of the parenting classes and the conditions that are related to success (Rooney, 2009).

Some workers might be reluctant to share information about a service with 50% effectiveness, and fear that the rate of failure could become a negative self-fulfilling prophecy for those compelled to attend. Nevertheless, people have a right to know what is known about the treatment, particularly if they are required to participate in order to retain custody of their children. Workers who are reluctant to divulge data for poorly performing interventions might want to consider the rationale for requiring the intervention, given its low success rate. The case in Box 4.3 demonstrates other violations of informed consent standards.

BOX 4.3

Violating the Standard

Lars is a counselor in a program for homeless youth. Because his clients are frequently reluctant to seek services and often distrust professionals, he prefers to work outside the box, relating to them more casually and skipping some of the formalities of counseling sessions. As such, he usually doesn't discuss confidentiality (and the limits of it) at the outset of service, even though such discussions are considered important so that clients know how the social worker may use information, and can judge accordingly what they want to share.

Lars recently began working with Jameis, encouraging Jameis to find stable housing, address his use of alcohol and other substances, and stop his cutting and suicide threats. One day, Jameis told Lars that he is HIV positive and feels his life is, for all intents and purposes, over. Even though he says he loves his girlfriend, Kat, he refuses to tell her of his status, fearing that, as he put it, he will "scare away the only good thing in my life right now." In the region where Lars practices, professionals are required to report situations such as Jameis's to the city health office so that public health workers can notify the partner at risk. However, Lars' failure to inform Jameis of this reporting requirement means that Jameis shared the information with Lars without understanding the potential consequences. How can Lars uphold his legal responsibility so that Jameis does not feel betrayed (or worse)?

The ambiguous nature of the helping relationship and Lars' failure to engage Jameis in a conversation leading to his informed consent for services may now put the helping relationship in peril. A common and important element at the outset of services is a discussion of the worker's intention to protect the client's privacy and the situations in which the worker is allowed or compelled to divulge confidential information. Typical situations addressed in this conversation are the worker's obligation to report suspicions of child abuse, instances where a client is a threat to himself or another, supervisory sessions, parents' rights to information about the services minors are receiving, and statutory obligations, such as the public health disclosure described in Lars' case.

The discussion of these conditions for services can feel awkward and legalistic in a setting such as Lars' or in any first session, where the focus should be on the client's presenting problems and relevant history. Nevertheless, the conversation is important because it allows people to exercise autonomy in determining if they wish to continue services under the conditions set forth by the worker. It also helps alert the client, in advance, to the consequences of certain disclosures, so that the worker's actions, in response to a suicide threat, for example, are an expected response rather than a surprise or a betrayal of trust.

Social workers may intentionally avoid or minimize the discussions around informed consent when they have the impression that such warnings will make the client less forthcoming and less comfortable seeking services. While the discussion might indeed inhibit the client's participation, the principle of autonomy grants people the right to refuse to participate. Because people cannot exercise autonomy without full and clear information about their options, it is unfair for persons in power to withhold or distort the information needed for others to make such a decision.

Lars' approach to informed consent is complicated by his setting and the transient minors he serves. While shelters and other outreach services operate alongside child welfare, public safety, juvenile justice, and traditional social service settings, their responsibility in serving minors is less clear (Staller & Kirk, 1997). Transient and independent clients and an "anti-parent and anti-establishment" organizational culture (Staller &

Kirk, 1997, p. 230) may lead workers to use informal practices around informed consent.

The law in this particular jurisdiction requires that Lars notify public health authorities about Jameis and Kat. Lars may also feel an ethical obligation to protect Kat from harm. At the same time, he has led Jameis to believe their conversations were confidential. In breaking this implied promise, he puts Jameis at risk. The helping relationship is already tenuous, and Jameis's health and emotional well-being may also be compromised by his living conditions and illnesses.

How will Jameis react when Lars tells him of his obligation to file a public health report? While the best scenario would be for Jameis to be relieved to stop living with his secret, and to be given the opportunity to address Kat forthrightly himself, without the intercession of the authorities, this outcome seems unlikely. More troubling potential outcomes are that he will drop out of service and escalate his self-injurious behaviors, or attempt suicide. Even if he makes it through this episode, will his capacity to trust professionals in the future be damaged by this experience? Would he be able to file a grievance against Lars for obtaining his health information under false pretenses? Could he alert other shelter youths that the staff is untrustworthy, moving this group of young adults even farther into the margins of the service delivery system? Lars' failure to obtain Jameis' informed consent clearly has serious and reverberating consequences.

Lars and his colleagues must deal honestly and sensitively with the disclosure of Jameis' status while trying to help him with his preexisting problems. They must also examine their institutional and individual approaches to informed consent and develop protocols so that clients of the shelter understand the constraints on service and on confidentiality whenever they share information.

While informed consent is vital in research and in health and social services, the processes and limits of consent can be less straightforward. The case of "Advertising for Adoptions" (Box 4.4) demonstrates those complexities.

Kathy's complaints may be grounded in a number of ethical issues: concerns about the dignity and worth of vulnerable clients, exploitation of marginalized populations, questions of conflict of interest in the agency's goals for placements and the best interests of the clients involved,

BOX 4.4

Resolving Dilemmas in Informed Consent:
Advertising for Adoptions

New Beginnings is a private child welfare agency that contracts with a state department of social services to facilitate adoptions for hard-to-place youths. Kathy, a new worker at the agency, has raised questions about the strategies New Beginnings uses to reach out to potential adoptive families. In particular, she is troubled by **photolisting**: open online sites providing pictures of the youths, their first names, ages, and profiles including their interests and special needs.

She has also raised concerns about open houses or fairs at which interested adults are introduced to and mingle with children who have been placed for adoption. After attending her first open house, Kathy voiced her objections at a staff meeting, equating the experience to a "meat market where vulnerable children were being given a high-stakes once-over in hopes of adoption." The staff assured Kathy that New Beginnings was not unique in using these strategies, and that they were ultimately in the best interest of the children. She replied, "They may be common, but does that make them ethical?"

and matters of confidentiality and the amount of information the public should have about vulnerable youth. For the purposes of this chapter, we will examine her case through the lens of informed consent. That is, what rights should minor clients have about their involvement in these strategies on their behalf? Do the older children in the hard-to-place group have different rights from those of the younger hard-to-place children served by the same agency? If Kathy's colleagues are correct that theirs are standard practices, what are her chances, as a new worker, of overturning a widespread practice, regardless of how troubling she and others find it? Since the government is both the guardian of the children and a funder of Kathy's agency, does this conflict of interest complicate her approach to the case?

Applying the Six-Question Model

Who Can Be a Resource to Kathy?

Kathy's search for consultation might begin with her supervisor and agency colleagues; she should make an earnest and open-minded effort to learn the history of the fairs and photolisted profiles, the criteria by which the agency selects children for the programs, and the information the clients receive about the process.

- Are all children required to participate if their case worker or guardians approve it? How are the children prepared for the listings and fairs?
- Is it possible the practices damage emotionally fragile children or discriminate against some groups such as children of color?
- What other efforts to enhance placements has the agency tried?
- How effective are these advertising and open house strategies?
- Why are the online listings available to the general public, rather than to only to prescreened potential adopters?
- Does the funding system in any way encourage New Beginnings to shortchange the children's rights to privacy in order to secure placements and advance the agency's well-being?

It would be helpful to know what the youths themselves think.

- Has there been research on advertising for adoptions?
- Have first-person accounts been published about the experience?
- Does Kathy have access to individuals who have participated in the recruitment process (such as adoptive parents, caseworkers, or adoptees) who can provide their perspectives on the practice?

Kathy should be mindful of her professional role and responsibilities in engaging current clients at New Beginnings in such conversations. That is, her research and advocacy on the fairs and postings should not be allowed to interfere with her attention to her clients at New Beginnings and their needs. She should not triangulate the youths against the agency or the advertising practices in her zeal for change. However, her agency might support focus groups on the topic, and she may personally know individuals who can provide feedback from their own experiences.

Kathy might go on to compare New Beginnings' practices with those of other adoption organizations.

- Are the agencies' practices consistent?
- Are there state or provincial regulations or national standards that support this practice?
- Are there recommendations for enhancing the youths' rights while using innovative methods to secure placements?
- And what does the research show? Is there any indication that youths are harmed by the advertising and fairs? Is there a meaningful distinction between the fairs and the ads—that is, is one recruitment strategy more problematic or more successful than the other?
- Have others raised concerns similar to Kathy's? If not, why is it troubling to her, but not to her colleagues or employer? Are people working on this issue on a large scale?

Each of these questions may indeed lead to more questions, but they are all a requisite part of the information that Kathy should gather to clarify her concerns and understand the efforts that New Beginnings staff might have already made to address them.

What Are Kathy's Options?

Through the ethical decision-making process, Kathy must determine what rights, if any, children have in deciding to participate in adoption advertisements or fairs. If she determines they have a right that is now being abridged, she must decide what procedural changes are called for. These choices may include ceasing the practices that concern her or building in acceptable measures of consent and competence for the children involved. Regardless of the change to be pursued, Kathy will need to decide if she is equipped to alter the practice and what strategies she might employ to create change.

When Has Kathy Made Similar Decisions?

What experiences and lessons can Kathy draw on in considering her current dilemma? Perhaps she has personal experience or professional expertise about adoptions or children's services that can help her understand the limits of informed consent for minors, particularly those in state or provincial territorial custody. Maybe she has had experience in advocacy for vulnerable groups against the status quo. Has she been able to effectively communicate her concerns and seek alternative, more ethical, ways of proceeding? Does she have a passion for social justice that allows her to take unpopular stances and adopt strategies for long-term change? Is she able to forge strategic alliances with people who share her concerns about issues such as this? Even if Kathy has been unsuccessful in past change efforts, she may draw lessons from those experiences that she can apply to this case.

Where Do Ethical and Clinical Guidelines Lead Her?

Kathy's positions can be categorized into three broad areas: (a) advertising children for adoption is unethical and should be halted; (b) adults who are acting in the children's interests have the right to make decisions about their care, and therefore the youths' consent is not required for adoption publicity; (c) minors have an ethical right to informed consent that can be exercised within the practice of adoption publicity efforts.

Rule-based ethics. How would the deontological perspective view each of these positions? Most broadly, should it become law that humans, and particularly children, can be unknowingly (and perhaps knowingly) marketed? This conjures horrific, yet real, images of the public bidding on and selling of slaves, sexual trafficking, and mail order brides. While these practices are all different, each treats humans as products to be marketed. More narrowly, would we want the advertisement of potential adoptees to become a universal law? Aren't there any circumstances (a child's safety, emotional fragility, or potential for humiliation) where even discreet marketing should be deemed inappropriate? Should adults be given the universal right to act on behalf of minors without their consent? Clearly there is some discomfort in rendering this a universal law, in that there are already a variety of exceptions to parental or guardian rights (Pimental, 2016; Polowy & Gorenberg, 2011).

What about a rule that minors have the right to informed consent in adoption advertising? Were that to become a universal law, there might be situations in which the minors' youth or immaturity would lead them to make poor decisions. Similarly, the withholding of consent might prove damaging to the child's prospects for permanency and exacerbate the backlog in the service system if foster homes are filled with youths who are eligible for adoption but invisible.

A rule-based examination of Kathy's options renders all of them wanting in one way or another; however, the process of examination also reveals the risks and challenges in each of the options. This may be helpful to Kathy because some risks may be more desirable than others. The deontological perspective, then, helps her decide what rules she might be willing to live with.

Outcome-based ethics. What are the consequences of each of Kathy's options? The first option, ceasing public listings of children available for adoption would vastly diminish the pool of interested families and thus the number of children who could be placed in permanent homes. It would also close off a popular avenue for informing the public about the crisis of children in need of placement (Freundlich et al., n.d., p. 11; Samuels, 2018). On the other hand, cessation of such practices might result in more-innovative and less-potentially exploitive recruitment procedures. It might also protect some children from harm or humiliation at the hands of classmates or others who do not have the youths' best interests at heart. From a macro perspective, an end to "electronic child shopping" may amplify the rights of children and reverse a culture of commodification and racialization in adoption matching (Milovidov & Treitler, 2014, p.104).

The second option, not allowing the youths themselves to consent to the service, might be construed as further victimizing an already fragile and powerless population. Such disempowerment might result in poor mental health outcomes for these youths and resentment toward the system and workers who have forced the publicity. Proceeding with the photolistings despite the children's reservations might expose them to embarrassment or risk from public exposure of their personal information, including foster care status.

Possible outcomes must also be considered for the third option, allowing youths to consent to publicity. Creating and implementing consent procedures may be cumbersome and time consuming, particularly for an already overburdened child welfare system. Workers might need training to assess the child's developmental capacity for consent. Another likely consequence is that some children may refuse consent. How would this affect the efforts to secure them permanent homes?

Values. Many individual and institutional values are at play in the issue of advertising children for adoption. Foster families, adoptive families, and social workers in the child welfare field value placement in permanent and loving homes (Thomas & Scharp, 2017). Their agencies value efficiency and resourcefulness in successfully matching children with adoptive families. The children themselves likely value placement with a family, but they also value privacy and dignity, particularly following traumatic events and bureaucratic processes that have affected their safety. The practice of photolisting is congruent with the value placed on prompt and effective placements (Adoption.com LLC, 2020). Prohibitions on how much information is shared through those processes help to honor the children's safety and privacy. However, questions remain about the extent to which photolisting promotes the value of client empowerment if youths do not have the right to object to the practice (Samuels, 2018). Especially in the context of transnational adoptions, concerns exist regarding "the (economic, political and racialized) inequalities of power between sending and receiving nations" (Milovidov & Treitler, 2014, p. 84).

Social work values related to the dignity and worth of individuals expect that professionals will

- "Promote clients' socially responsible self-determination ... [and] seek to enhance clients' capacity and opportunity to change and to address their own needs." (NASW, 2021, pp. 5–6)
- "Respect the unique worth and inherent dignity of all people and uphold human rights." (CASW, 2005a, p. 4)

In sustaining the importance of human relationships, social workers

- "Believe in the obligation of people, individually and collectively, to provide resources, services and opportunities for the overall benefit of humanity and to afford them protection from harm." (CASW, 2005a, p. 5)
- "Seek to ... promote, restore, maintain, and enhance the well-being of individuals, families, social groups, organizations, and communities." (NASW, 2021, p. 6)

These values may be construed to support any of Kathy's three choices. Social workers may uphold clients' dignity and worth through the cessation of the adoption advertising or the utilization of informed consent measures. Giving precedence to human relationships might support the use of advertising practices in service of the good of securing an adoptive family.

Professional standards. The ethical standards on informed consent cited at the beginning of this chapter have relevance for this case. Social workers should allow for informed consent. In cases where clients are not legally or clinically competent to render consent, social workers should ensure that their guardians and others are acting in the clients' best interests and include the clients themselves in the process to the extent possible.

Ethical standards on confidentiality also apply to this case since the essence of the adoption advertising controversy involves how much information should be shared without the consent of the youths involved. Key provisions suggest that

- "Social workers should avoid posting any identifying or confidential information about clients on professional websites or other forms of social media." (NASW, 2021, 1.07r)
- "Social workers may disclose confidential information ... with valid consent from a client or a person legally authorized to consent on behalf of a client." (NASW, 2021, 1.07b)
- "Social workers should inform clients, to the extent possible, about the disclosure of confidential information and the potential consequences, when feasible before the disclosure is made." (NASW, 2021, 1.07d)
- "Social workers should discuss with clients and other interested parties the nature of confidentiality and limitations of clients' right to confidentiality." (NASW, 2021, 1.07e)
- "Social workers should be aware that posting personal information on professional websites or other media might cause ... harm to clients." NASW, 2021, 1.06f)
- "Social workers review with clients when disclosure of confidential information may be legally or ethically required." (CASW, 2005b, 1.5.1)
- "When social workers provide services to children, they outline for the child and the child's parents (where appropriate) their practices with respect to confidentiality and children. Social workers may wish to reserve the right to disclose some information provided by a young child to parents when such disclosure is in the best interest of the child." (CASW, 2005b, 1.5.5)

How might these ethical standards influence Kathy's decision? While they make no distinction between adult and child clients, the standards clearly emphasize the need for restraint by social workers and the rights of clients to be informed about their entitlements, options, and the actions being taken on their behalf. In most cases, minors are not considered competent to render consent for medical and social services, and therefore an adult's permission is required for the minor to receive care or participate in research (Barsky, 2019; Strom-Gottfried, 2008). Nevertheless, the execution of the legal right to act on behalf of minors is strengthened when youths are afforded an ethical right to participate in the decision making. The standards would therefore seem to uphold the use of adoption fairs and photos with the consent of the child's guardians, but they would also encourage the youths' involvement to the greatest extent possible.

This involvement might be expressed in one of two ways. **Assent** "recognizes that minors may not, as a function of their developmental level, be capable of giving fully reasoned consent but may still be capable of reaching and expressing a preference" (Koocher & Keith-Spiegel, 1990, p. 10). A second mechanism for involvement would be to provide each youth with the right to decline inclusion in the listing. While only a legal guardian could provide consent for inclusion, allowing the youths to opt out of the service would empower the client and provide maximum protection and respect for the youths' concerns. In addressing minors and health care, the American Academy of Pediatrics (1995) suggests, "A patient's reluctance or refusal to assent should also carry considerable weight when the proposed intervention is not essential to his or her welfare and/or can be deferred without substantial risk" (p. 316).

In Kathy's case, the negative effects of such a provision would be that the child's likelihood of placement would be diminished and the provision of services in an impermanent setting would be prolonged. As in other cases involving competence and informed consent, an assessment would be required to determine whether the child was capable of comprehending the risks and benefits in order to make a reasoned decision (Barsky, 2019; Devettere, 2000; Newfoundland & Labrador Association of Social Workers, 2018b; Richards, 2003). Manning and Gaul (1997) suggest, "The touchstone of assessing competency is to look for a 'thoughtful' decision making process, taking into account reversible versus irreversible conditions, and the level of preparedness for the decision versus impulsiveness that affects the quality of the decision" (p. 109). Assent and dissent effectively broaden Kathy's original three choices by elaborating on the different forms that clients' consent might take.

Ethical principles. The concern for the principle of autonomy is at the core of Kathy's dilemma. On the one hand, individuals should have the maximum degree of choice in the matters that affect them. The third option (allowing consent) would provide the greatest autonomy for the minor clients. However, in both the United States and Canada, minors are accorded limited rights. Furthermore, the child welfare system, having intervened paternalistically to rescue youths from abuse and neglect, is charged with their care and well-being. In Canada, a child living in foster care or a group home is the responsibility of the Ministry of Children and Family Development or a Delegated Aboriginal Agency (Ministry of Children and Family Development, n.d.). As such, the system considers the long-term advantages of permanent homes to outweigh the short-term challenges inherent in finding such homes for individual children.

Assuming that whatever privileges New Beginnings and other agencies afford minor clients, they are forthright about what the specific options and processes will be, all of Kathy's choices are in keeping with the principle of **fidelity**. Kathy's choices are consistent with the principle of justice as well. That is, whichever option she chooses, there is no indication that New Beginnings will implement it unevenly, except as is necessitated by differences in a child's decision-making capacity. However, the element of justice that is concerned with the fair distribution of scarce resources might be detrimentally affected by Kathy's third choice, that of offering the youths' consent, if the refusal to render consent means that a logjam occurs with foster homes occupied by those youths who are ready for more permanent form of placement.

How the options measure up on the basis of beneficence and nonmaleficence will depend on one's evaluations of what is "good" in the case. That is, each option offers some kind of benefit for the clients, the youths in the child welfare system: a stronger possibility of placement in a secure home, the right to exercise self-determination, and improved protection of their privacy and dignity. Each offers potential harms, too: a diminished pool of families interested in adoption, increased difficulty of finding homes for hard-to-place children, vulnerable youths put in positions that might be embarrassing or hurtful, and a paternalistic override of children's wishes about photolisting or fairs. Like the utilitarian analysis, the principles of beneficence and nonmaleficence help us weigh these outcomes.

They may also help Kathy craft a fourth option that preserves the practice of advertising for adoption matches while ensuring that young children have the opportunity for assent, and that older children have the opportunity for consent.

Laws and policies. Adoption-related websites can be divided into several categories based on their function: information and referral, mutual contact between birth parents and potential adoptive parents, brokering, chat rooms, and photolisting (Roby & White, 2010). Photolisting has a fifty-year history, and the practice has evolved as information-sharing technologies have become more sophisticated and the needs of children for placement have continued unabated (Freundlich et al., n.d., pp. 6–8). The practice has been endorsed and financed by child advocacy groups such as the Child Welfare League of America (CWLA), by the Adoption Council of Canada, and by governmental entities such as the federal Children's Bureau (Freundlich et al., n.d., pp. 7–8). The North American Council on Adoptable Children has recommended caution in selecting and preparing children for individualized promotion activities, though it endorses those practices as worthwhile (Schuerger, 2002). While official bodies shape the rules and procedures governing adoptions, Kathy is not alone in the concerns she has about the process (Milovidov & Treitler, 2014; Scarth, 2004).

Federal and state laws on confidentiality regulate the information that can be shared during child-specific recruitment. Such laws prohibit disclosure of information about HIV status, substance abuse treatment, and other conditions until later in the adoption process. The Health Insurance Portability and Accountability Act of 1996 (HIPAA; 1996), regulates the use of health information but has not resulted in uniform state practices with regard to adoption advertising (Freundlich et al., n.d., p. 14). In Canada, information sharing is regulated on the federal level by the Office of the Privacy Commissioner (OPCC), and at the provincial level by Freedom of Information and Protection of Privacy Acts (OPCC, 2013). Despite these attempts at regulation, photolisting and profiling of children still creates ethical concerns regarding misrepresentation, exploitation, and disclosure of sensitive information without the child's consent (Roby & White, 2010).

Each jurisdiction has its own regulations about the use of advertising for adoptions. Some prohibit advertising by those seeking to adopt or by their representatives, such as physicians or attorneys. Others restrict the right to advertise to public agencies or those with licensed or contractual arrangements to provide adoption services in the state (Child Welfare Information Gateway, 2012). Canadian policy requires that visitors wishing to view a child's adoption profile online must first provide personal information and obtain a password, thus reflecting a "higher level of concern regarding information disclosure" (Freundlich et al., 2007, p. 15).

Each of those statutes is intended to protect participants in the adoption triad from unscrupulous practices. It appears that no statute addresses Kathy's concern about the rights of children in custody to consent to advertisements or to participation in recruitment activities.

Common law principles and civil and criminal statutes have been used to prosecute wrongful adoption cases involving the Internet, but difficulties in policing online activity have made it difficult to enforce this type of regulation (Roby & White, 2010). Where government regulation falls short, specific agencies may have policies or procedures that address Kathy's concerns. Kathy would need to investigate those that apply to her region and consult with other jurisdictions to learn about models her region might utilize. While arduous, this process might help her to learn more about the regulatory employees and processes in her state or province. These contacts will enable her to craft a more effective strategy for change, should she decide that informed consent provisions are required in the photolisting system.

Practice principles. In addition to legal and policy considerations, Kathy must also take standards of practice for photolistings into account. For example, social workers must consider the disclosure of personal and potentially harmful information in light of the entire adoption process. Adoption workers should share limited and generally positive information at the recruitment phase, while disclosing more comprehensive information about the child as the process unfolds, based on a family's intent to pursue adoption (Freundlich & Gerstenzang, 2004). Social workers should include the children involved to the extent possible and should give them the opportunity to express concerns and provide input on their postings. Freundlich et al. (n.d.) suggest that adoption staff do the following:

- Discuss the purpose of photolisting with the child and show them examples. This might involve talking about what the child likes and dislikes about different forms of photolistings and what they want to include or exclude in their own description or having them review the photolisting and pick the photo to be used.

- Consider the information to be shared in light of the worker's own family. Workers should ask themselves, "Would I want such information posted about my child?"
- Be prepared to address a child's reluctance. This may include exploring the nature of their apprehensions, answering questions, acknowledging fears, and adjusting the process to address the child's concerns (for example, by using pseudonyms).
- Demonstrate restraint in the portrayal of the child. Even though professionals could share information, sometimes they should not do so. Imagine how the child would react if certain facts or characteristics were available through the Internet, adoptee brochures, or public service programming on TV. Even if children are too young to appreciate the consequences now, how might they feel about such disclosures later in life? (pp. 19–21, 33).

Kathy may find additional practice standards helpful. For example, the *NASW Standards for the Practice of Social Work with Adolescents* addresses confidentiality and client empowerment (NASW, 2003, p. 12, p. 15). Practice standards in individual social service departments may stipulate how children should be selected, screened, and prepared for photolisting or adoption fairs. Canada's Ministry of Children and Family Development and other resources offer guidance for the fair and effective presentation of children for adoption. For example, children chosen for child-specific recruitment should be representative of the larger population of available children and actually be available for adoption (rather than already in line for a **kinship placement**). Social workers must ensure an individual child's safety so that publicity does not put them at risk at the hands of angry relatives. Furthermore, recruitment publicity is premature and possibly damaging if the child's caretaker opposes it or if the child is not ready for placement (Schuerger, 2002).

Why Would Kathy Select a Particular Course of Action?

If Kathy's exploration of the ethical, legal, and clinical advisability of the choices leads her to conclude that youths deserve the right to provide assent or dissent for photolisting and adoption fairs, she must still examine her own motivations in pursuing that path. For example, does her personal history predispose her to advocate inappropriately for the youths involved? In other words, does she care about it more than they do? Is she appropriately applying the concept of informed consent in such a way that youths are protected and empowered, in keeping with their developmental capacities?

Does her plan treat the youths in the way that she would want to be treated? Are the basis of her concerns and the rationale for her plan understandable to others? Is she comfortable asking others to work with her on this issue? Is she behaving in a way that reflects the best standards of the profession? Are her decisions and actions in line with her beliefs and those of people she respects?

How Should She Carry It Out?

As a new employee at the agency, Kathy is probably not strategically poised to bring about the organizational change she desires. As she conducts the research suggested here, she should build social capital in the organization, forge relationships with people who share her concern or have decision-making power, and educate others about the options for reconciling client rights and agency practices.

The change needed will depend on how divergent the agency's current practices are from her ideal. If the agency already screens youths and prepares them for in-person recruitment events, and if the youths are actively involved in the photolisting process, then instituting an assent–dissent provision should be a relatively minor change in both policies and practices. The process of effecting change will take longer and require more steps and strategies if the agency tends to act on behalf of, rather than with, the clients, particularly if it does so with the approval of the state child welfare agency.

The next case (Box 4.5) provides an opportunity for you to practice your decision making skills on a scenario involving informed consent and an older adult at risk.

As you apply the decision-making model to this case, consider the following:

- What does the research say about the risks associated with restraining orders?
- How should the social worker present information from the research to Carolyn and her family?
- What are your thoughts about Carolyn's capacity to make a sound decision about her safety? Is she equipped to render informed consent? How would you determine her capacity to give consent.?

BOX 4.5

A Case for You: "Can a Paper Protect Her?"

Carolyn is a married woman, eighty-six years old, who has been hospitalized following a fall in her home that resulted in a broken collar bone and dislocated shoulder. Initially she reported to medics that she had woken up disoriented at night and fallen down the stairs. Later, based on prompting from her daughter and granddaughter, Carolyn admitted to the social worker that there was a history of abuse by her husband, Nelson, resulting in past fractures. She acknowledged that her current injuries were the result of an assault by him, but she demonstrated reluctance to leave him or file for orders of protection, based on fears that "it will just make him madder," and the belief that "now that people know, he won't do it again." Carolyn's offspring are adamant that she "leave before he kills her" and want the social worker's assistance in convincing her to take action. They maintain that she is "so brainwashed by him she can't make a rational decision." The social worker knows that some women are put at increased risk if they file for orders of protection but does not want to discourage Carolyn from seeking safety.

- What alternatives exist to balance Carolyn's safety with self-determination? Are these different for her, as an older woman, than they would be for younger women in the same circumstance?
- If you find the case compelling and you worry for Carolyn's safety, how might those reactions affect the way you resolve the ethical dilemma?

Conclusion

Informed consent processes are essential for personal autonomy. People cannot exercise self-determination in the absence of honest information about their choices and the related risks and benefits. True informed consent requires that the information be presented to the person in an understandable fashion, that consent be rendered voluntarily and without coercion, and that the individual be competent to provide consent. The assessment of capacity is specialized and individualized to the case in question. It depends on the state of the client (age, cognitive functioning, and ability to weigh alternatives and compare outcomes) and the nature of the decision. Capacity may change (improve or deteriorate) over time.

When clients are not competent to provide consent, other individuals may be legally or ethically empowered to do so on their behalf. Even under these conditions, however, social workers should be mindful of the client's stake in the decisions, ensuring that the third party is acting in the client's interests. In some clinical and research settings, clients have the opportunity to give assent (that is, informed agreement with the consent that a guardian provided for them), or dissent (the right to refuse or withdraw from the service suggested). Many resources are available to help clinicians and researchers institute the proper protocols for protecting clients and human research subjects (Agency for Healthcare Research and Quality, 2018; Anesthesia Key, 2020; Coyne, 2009; Government of Canada, 2022b).

It is essential that social workers obtain informed consent at the outset of service because it provides the ground rules about confidentiality, treatment criteria, and other policies that lay the foundation for the helping relationship. The client and social worker then revisit informed consent throughout the duration of the therapeutic process as changing circumstances require new decisions and as the client's understanding and interests evolve.

For Continuing Conversation

1. How are **evidence-informed practices** related to informed consent?

2. Ethical standards suggest that professionals ensure that third parties who are entitled to give consent do so in keeping with the wishes of the client. How might you determine whether such third parties are or are not entitled to give consent?

3. As you work through the cases in this chapter, practice what you would say when providing information to the client to obtain informed consent. Is your presentation understandable, thorough, and noncoercive, in keeping with the parameters of informed consent?

Key Concepts

Assent. The expression of approval or agreement.

Consent. Permission for something to happen or agreement to do something.

Evidence-informed practice. Using the best available research to guide the selection, planning, and implementation of interventions, while allowing space for innovation and adaptation based on clinical experience as well an individual client's circumstances, culture, or desires.

Fidelity. The degree of accuracy with which something is followed or copied.

Fiduciary relationships. A legal or ethical relationship in which one party places complete trust in the actions or decisions of the other to act on their behalf.

Human subjects. The term used to describe persons who are the subjects of or participants in clinical research.

Informed consent. Permission granted in the knowledge of the possible consequences, typically that which is given by a patient to a doctor for treatment with full knowledge of the possible risks and benefits.

Institutional review board. A committee formally designated to approve, monitor, and review biomedical and behavioral research involving humans. The number one priority of IRBs is to protect human subjects from physical or psychological harm.

Kinship placement. The full-time care and protection of children by adult relatives other than parents by formal arrangement with the child welfare system.

Photolisting. Providing photographs and brief descriptions of the children in the public foster care system who are available for adoption.

CHAPTER 5

Conflicts of Interest

Introduction

Conflicts of interest occur when workers' needs or interests threaten to take precedence over those of their clients or otherwise impede the practitioners' ability to carry out their professional responsibilities. For instance, a worker who is hired to develop housing for people recovering from substance addictions may experience a clash of values and conflict of interest when one of the group homes is targeted for their neighborhood. Conflicts can also occur when the worker's loyalties to clients are split in such a way that upholding the interests of one client would disadvantage another. Difficult situations arise in family therapy when the interests of the children may be at odds with those of the parents, and the worker owes loyalty to the entire family. The overlap between personal and professional relationships and roles is a particular form of conflict of interest which will be addressed in the next chapter.

Conflicts of interest can give rise to a loss of professional objectivity and compromises in professional judgment (Fisher, 2003). As discussed in Chapter 2, accepting a gift from a client may be clinically and ethically sound, depending on contextual factors, or it may create a conflict if the social worker is then reluctant to make appropriate therapeutic demands of the client or reinforce agency rules, because accepting the gift has undermined the worker's ability to carry out their responsibilities. When there are personal or financial stakes for the worker, other conflicts of interest can occur such as when the worker receives commissions from the sale of books or vitamin supplements that are recommended to clients, or when a researcher has a stake in a treatment that is being investigated

BOX 5.1

Conflicts of Interest

- Professional responsibilities to different parties are in tension with each other.
- Professional relationships with clients have the potential to impact the clinician's privacy, relationships, finances, or well-being.
- Personal and professional relationships overlap.
- The worker is unable to effectively fulfill their responsibilities due to biases or irreconcilable differences with the client's intentions, actions, or beliefs
- Employer expectations conflict with the best interests of the client or other professional obligations, creating divided loyalties for the worker.

Avoid conflicts when possible; when conflicts are unavoidable, inform the client and take steps to resolve the issue in accord with the client's best interest. (Banks, 2021; Barsky, 2019; Reamer, 2018)

and skews findings to obscure the treatment's shortcomings. Conflicts can also occur when loyalty to one's employer (and the need for a job) conflicts with the best interests of the client, with one's professional expertise, or with one's ethical obligations. Box 5.1 describes different types of conflict of interest.

Ethical tenets on conflicts of interest stipulate that social workers

- Should "not take unfair advantage of any professional relationship or exploit others to further their personal, religious, political, or business interests." (NASW, 2021, 1.06b)
- "Do not exploit professional relationships for personal benefit, gain or gratification." (CASW, 2005b, 2.2.1)
- "Should be alert to and avoid conflicts of interest that interfere with the exercise of professional discretion and impartial judgment . . . inform clients when a real or potential conflict of interest arises and take reasonable steps to resolve the issue in a manner that makes the clients' interests primary" even if that means terminating the helping relationship. (NASW, 2021, 1.06a)

• "Consider carefully the potential for professional conflicts of interest where close personal relationships exist or where social, business or sexual relationships with colleagues are contemplated or exist." (CASW, 2005b 2.3.3).

Ethics codes clearly describe the variety of ways the worker's interests can intersect with the client's interests and places responsibility on the professional to detect and address potentially compromising situations. Recent political scandals have called attention to the ethical imperative of avoiding conflicts of interest. Even if it is legal for politicians to accept contributions, or vacation junkets from groups they regulate, these are ethically troubling practices. The rejoinder "I would have supported that legislation anyway" doesn't remove the cloud of suspicion that the support was facilitated by the gift. The cumulative result of such practices is an erosion of public trust in the individuals involved and in the profession and institutions they represent. The case described in Box 5.2 illustrates adherence to standards affiliated with conflicts of interest.

BOX 5.2
Upholding the Standard

Mountain Vista Assisted Living is run by a for-profit corporation that is intent on generating goodwill and referrals for its programs. Iris works on the renal dialysis unit at the local hospital and thus does extensive business with the area rehab facilities. She is impressed with Mountain Vista's services. Though its fees are much higher than those of other facilities in the region, she suggests it to patients and their families as one of several options to consider.

Last year during the end-of-year holidays, Mountain Vista sent her a large fruit basket with a note thanking her for her referrals. Iris is accustomed to getting office supplies, lunches, and coffee breaks from the various pharmaceutical companies that do business with the hospital, so she thought nothing of accepting the basket and sharing it with the workers on her unit. In December this year, Mountain Vista sent Iris a gift certificate for $100 to the local mall. Iris did not want Mountain Vista, her colleagues, her patients, or staff at other nursing homes to think that she practiced favoritism toward Mountain Vista because of its generous gifts. Nor did she want the gift from them to put her in a bind if for some reason she needed to stop her referrals or confront Mountain Vista in some way in the future. She returned the gift card to Mountain Vista with a note thanking them for their thoughtfulness, and noting that giving clients referrals is part of her job and that it would be improper to take gifts for doing so.

Iris exercised a good deal of self-restraint in returning the facility's gift. It would have been easy to rationalize that her hard work and insufficient salary warrant a little extra recognition now and then. She might be confident in her ability to resist any influence Mountain Vista seeks to exert with its gift and could argue that as long as her practices are unassailable she shouldn't care what others think. Or she may assume that no one will find out about the gift and take it, reasoning that it is easier to ask forgiveness than permission.

However, taking it might not pass the smell and publicity tests with her colleagues and patients. Not being transparent about the gift further raises suspicions that Iris knew that it was wrong to accept it. And perceptions matter. Iris is in a position of authority, and she is a representative of her profession and her organization. The acceptance of a gift from a community agency reflects on those entities as well as on Iris herself.

Some might question drawing the line at the gift certificate. Because she had accepted a fruit basket in the past, perhaps Mountain Vista believed Iris was comfortable with such transactions. Why does a gift certificate create a conflict of interest when a fruit basket doesn't? Depending on the fruit basket, price may be a differentiating factor. However, this incident might cause Iris to rethink her habit of accepting the fruit baskets. Even though she shared it with the unit rather than keeping it for her personal use, Mountain Vista probably does not know that, hence the current gift. It would be wise for her to discuss the various gifts in supervision to determine any explicit policy or guidelines that might help to differentiate among the various gifts that unit personnel receive. Such a discussion (with documentation) also puts on the record the fact that the gift was received and returned.

Iris's attention to process in declining the gift is also noteworthy. In returning the gift, she expressed appreciation for the gesture and avoided condemning Mountain Vista or impugning their motives. However, she set a clear boundary regarding the appropriateness of such gifts in the future. In contrast, the case in Box 5.3 demonstrates the failure to address conflicts of interest.

The premises underlying Andrew's compensation system are not unusual or inherently unethical. Performance-based compensation is a common feature of many workplaces. Bonuses, commissions, and profit- or

BOX 5.3

Violating the Standard

Andrew is the administrator at a pioneering multiservice center that receives state funds to provide a continuum of services to children with emotional and behavioral problems. Because of the funding structure, any resources Andrew saves by moving a child to a less-intensive, less-expensive service create additional funds for services for those who need them (and for the agency's reserves). Having done a good deal of research in personnel management and staff retention, Andrew has come to believe that innovative compensation systems lead to better employee morale and greater efficiency and productivity. Therefore he has instituted a compensation system whereby any staff member who places a child in a less-restrictive setting in three days or fewer receives a $200 gift certificate to the local mall or the restaurant of their choice. Some high performers under this system receive such a bonus for almost all of their cases.

Andrew's fellow agency directors question this system. They are concerned that it provides an incentive for premature discharges and shoddy placements. They suspect that some workers encourage hospitalizations on the front end so they can get credit for more discharges, and that others avoid high-need clients because their conditions preclude successful attainment of the bonus. Andrew notes that the gift certificates cost a fraction of the money saved by reduced hospitalizations and that less-restrictive settings are healthier for the clients themselves.

gain-sharing arrangements base varying proportions of workers' pay on efficiency or productivity targets. Managed care systems are predicated on rewarding providers and users of care for the judicious use of services. Cost reductions resulting from the elimination of unnecessary service usage can conserve scarce resources for other uses. Such incentive systems can help encourage productivity and reward excellence in meeting organization expectations.

The danger, as Andrew's critics note, is in the behaviors that are rewarded. The incentive system must be aligned with the agency's mission and goals so that it reinforces the proper activities. If the agency's goal is to provide the best possible care for children, then such care should be the standard by which workers are rewarded. To distribute rewards based on expediency, or to give expediency improper weight, is to depart from the primary mission of caring for children. That the rewards are individual and case-based instead of for aggregate team performance increases the likelihood of conflicts of interest.

Improper specification of expectations can lead workers to cut corners in order to meet performance targets to qualify for financial rewards. Sometimes these systems can lead to fraudulent practices, as one retailer learned when it rewarded its auto mechanics for their automotive parts sales. The unintended consequence was that thousands of customers were encouraged to purchase parts they did not need (Halverson, 1992). In Andrew's case, the consequences of a poorly conceived reward structure will be played out in the lives of vulnerable children. While Andrew may believe he can rely on the integrity of his workforce, money, even in the form of gift certificates, can motivate inappropriate as well as desired behavior.

It does not appear that Andrew has built into his system the necessary checks and balances to ensure that it is free of financial conflicts of interest. **Utilization reviews** would help identify troubling patterns of admissions and discharges. **Quality assurance** reviews could examine randomly selected cases to ensure that their discharges were appropriate and made to suitable settings. A system of penalties could be instituted for adverse findings. Additional rewards could be employed for work on complex cases or hard-to-place clients, so that the level of difficulty is factored into the compensation schema.

If the revamped compensation system seems difficult or costly to administer, that is because it is. A simple single-outcome system cannot take into account the complex tasks of social work in the same way it might effectively reward car sales. A more sophisticated system is fairer for employees and safer for clients. Perhaps simply having it in place will deter workers who are inclined to put their well-being ahead of their clients'.

Ethical dilemmas arise when no clear strategies exist for social workers to avoid or address conflicts of interest. "The Case of the Angry Parent" (Box 5.4) illustrates decision making in conflict of interest dilemmas.

BOX 5.4

Resolving Dilemmas in Conflicts of Interest: The Case of the Angry Parent

Gia and Alex Rawlings sought counseling from Jeffrey Williams for two years as they tried to work on their marital discord and disagreements about how best to discipline their two sons. During treatment, Jeffrey perceived that Alex's parenting style was unnecessarily harsh, especially when contrasted with Gia's nurturing, supportive style. Despite their best efforts, the couple decided to divorce and ceased sessions with Jeffrey, refusing to attend a termination session. Today Jeffrey received a subpoena from Gia's attorney requesting his records and testimony for the child custody proceedings, particularly those concerning Gia's suitability over Alex as the custodial parent.

As noted earlier in the chapter, some ethical dilemmas arise when the interests of clients are at odds with those of the worker. In other cases, dilemmas pit the interests of clients against each other. Such is the case with the Rawlings, who both began service as Jeffrey's clients. Now Gia's request puts Jeffrey in the position of acting in favor of one client at the expense of the other. Without a waiver of confidentiality from Alex, Jeffrey would be violating his privacy, ostensibly for Gia's benefit. A complicating factor is Jeffrey's opinion that Gia's case has merit. If he declines to take a partisan role in their dispute, it will mean remaining silent about his substantive concerns in the case.

Applying the Six-Question Model

Who Can Be a Resource to Jeffrey?

Triangulation of the therapist between parties in custody disputes represents a growing area of malpractice risk for psychologists and social workers (Gould & Martindale, 2013). Therefore one of Jeffrey's first calls should be to his attorney for advice about how to proceed. This consultation should not only help him weigh his options but also offer procedural guidance so that whatever course he chooses is done in the proper manner. For example, should he communicate with Gia or her attorney about the subpoena, explaining the problem it presents and his corresponding responsibilities to Alex as his client? What notification, if any, should Jeffrey provide to Alex?

With or without legal counsel, there are several other steps Jeffrey should take. He should consult the privilege statutes in his state or province, which may expressly prohibit disclosure of confidential material in divorces and related actions unless a judge compels him to do so. Jeffrey could cite the statute in refusing to comply with the subpoena.

As in other cases in this book, Jeffrey will find consultation with colleagues and ethical and practice standards helpful in sorting out his options and generating alternatives (Reamer, 2021b; Smith, 2003). He should also review the informed consent procedures and documents he used at the outset of the Rawlings' treatment. What was their understanding about confidentiality and the stance he would take in any actions they might take against each other? A clearly specified policy will provide Jeffrey guidance in responding to the demand for information from Gia's attorney. For example, some clinicians state at the outset of conjoint work that the focus of service is on the relationship and on the couple, not the pair as two individuals. The clinician then clarifies his intent as bipartisan, in that he will address the issues observed rather than taking sides in the couple's disputes. Some practitioners may go farther and specify that they will not serve in an adversarial capacity for or against either partner.

Informed consent procedures also address information sharing, for example, stating that the clinician will not keep secrets from one party on behalf of the other. Thus, individual communications with the therapist would routinely be shared with the other member of the client system. If Jeffrey had a well-founded informed consent procedure and if he followed it in his treatment of the Rawlings, he could reference it and provide documentation about it in his communications with Gia and her attorney.

What Are Jeffrey's Options?

Jeffrey essentially has two options: he can comply with the subpoena, or he can refuse to comply. Within these two contrasting alternatives there are several variations in substance and process. For example, if he decides to comply, he must decide whether he will seek to limit the disclosure required (only supplying records rather than verbal testimony, for example). He must also decide what he will tell Alex about his decision and what his stance will be if Alex's legal team subpoenas him for their cause.

If Jeffrey decides not to comply, will he urge Gia and her attorney to rescind the subpoena, or will he take other steps to resist it? What basis will he use for declining? Will he simply refuse to participate, citing the treatment contract, legal, ethical, or informed consent provisions, or will he try to broker a middle ground, for example encouraging the court to assign a custody evaluation to an impartial clinician hired for that specific task?

When Has Jeffrey Faced Similar Dilemmas?

Two issues are central to this dilemma. One involves neutrality in serving multiperson systems such as groups, couples, and families. The second involves containment when the clinician possesses troubling or unsettling information. Even if Jeffrey has never before been subpoenaed in a client dispute, he has likely faced the underlying issues in the case, and his position on those issues will shape his response this time. Let's examine each issue in turn.

A crucial element of professional development involves addressing the reality of the worker's partiality for some clients over others. While affinity for some clients may create difficulties in a caseload, it leads to unique tension when differential connections exist within a client system such as a family. Partiality can come from a variety of sources. **Countertransference** can lead the clinician to identify with some individuals more strongly than others, or to have negative reactions to particular clients (Bruscia, 2018). The research on clinician attraction to clients indicates an array of sources, including the client's physical attractiveness, intellectual stimulation, similarity in life experiences and interests, and motivation for treatment (Fisher, 2004; Ladany et al., 1997; Nickell et al., 1995). One's affinity for particular clients may be linked to positive therapeutic attributes such as enthusiasm, warmth, and increased empathy. The clinician may be more invested, caring, and attentive to such a client, and more willing to go the extra mile for the client's success. On the other hand, such partiality may blind the worker to the client's needs and difficulties and may hinder the worker from carrying out her professional responsibilities (Hepworth et al., 2022). Taken to the extreme, affinity may lead to boundary transgressions, including harmful dual relationships and sexual impropriety. Within client systems, partiality may lead to feelings of rejection, anger, and confusion on the part of the nonfavored client(s). It may exacerbate existing fissures within families and couples, and it may irreparably undermine the clinician's effectiveness in the treatment process.

Jeffrey should reflect on his work with the Rawlings and on his conclusion that Gia is the more suitable parent of the two. On what does he base that conclusion? Is Alex an unsafe or harmful parent, or simply one whose style is different from the type Jeffrey favors? In taking stock of his treatment of them, Jeffrey should consider whether his partiality may have played a role in their decision to discontinue treatment and in Gia's belief that Jeffrey will support her bid for custody. This reflection will require Jeffrey to examine his assumptions about their suitability as parents and his responsibility for testifying about the custody matter. The reflections will also help Jeffrey to refine his practices in the future, should he find that partiality played a negative role in their care.

Beyond reexamining the Rawlings' case, Jeffrey should consider other cases where he has felt an affinity for one member of a client system over others. How has he managed the helping relationship in light of that connection? Has it led him to make decisions that favor the client he preferred, or conversely, to rule in favor of the less favored client in an attempt to compensate for the slight? This reflection will increase Jeffrey's understanding of his inclinations in the current dilemma.

The second issue in this dilemma involves his sense that Alex is the less desirable parent. Jeffrey is being asked to share his assessment of Alex's suitability as a parent when that was not the focus of treatment. Is it fair or appropriate for Jeffrey to testify as to his impressions of Alex's parenting when he has received that information secondarily in the context of his work with the couple on their relationship? Has he seen Gia and Alex in interactions with their children? When parenting issues were discussed in therapy, were the clients aware that Jeffrey might ultimately be passing judgment on their respective fitness as parents? These questions are intended to assess the soundness of Jeffrey's assessment that Gia's parenting is preferable to Alex's.

In addition to examining the rationale for this conclusion, Jeffrey must also look at situations in the past where he has had to contain information or opinions that he is not at liberty to share. This is a common phenomenon in clinical practice. Clients may, for example, disclose troubling fantasies; reveal past crimes or describe disturbing behaviors, such as driving while intoxicated; or report taking jobs or positions for which the clinician feels they are patently ill-suited. In these and similar scenarios, social workers may wish that they could speak up and tell someone, when practicalities, ethics, and roles require that the worker share the concerns only with the client or in the confidence of supervision or consultation, and not with an outside party. Jeffrey's temptation to comply with the subpoena stems in part from his sense that Gia's claim has merit. However, as in other situations requiring containment, that apprehension is not an adequate justification for breaking Alex's confidentiality. Jeffrey may find, in reflecting on other disquieting experiences, that the tools he used to manage those dilemmas are appropriate for this case as well.

Where Do Ethical and Clinical Guidelines Fit with Jeffrey's Decision Making?

Rule-based ethics. At least two rules are embedded in the option to comply with the subpoena to testify for Gia in the custody dispute: that professionals are obligated to render assessments in cases affecting their clients, even if those opinions are based on confidential information and may be detrimental to the client, and that social workers should comply with subpoenas. Two rules are also reflected in the option to resist the subpoena: that professionals should always maintain the privacy of material received in confidence, and that professionals should not violate the trust of their clients.

In a deontological framework, what would be the implication of transforming these rules into universal laws? Clearly, social workers should behave lawfully and comply with subpoenas, maintain privacy, and be trustworthy, though in ethical practice, professionals may find exceptions to these rules in upholding other goods, such as public safety or client well-being. We might be comfortable with these rules as guiding principles, but not without exceptions.

In contrast, the rule permitting social workers to speak up, even against the client's interests, is problematic as a universal principle, though there may be times when the social worker might rightfully do so. To create a universal law that would allow professionals to freely share their impressions without the affected client's permission would undermine the basis on which the helping relationship is grounded. For that reason, professional ethics permit such disclosures only when required in extreme circumstances to avoid greater harms, such as injury or death. If Jeffrey believed Alex to be a harmful parent, he should have used mechanisms such as a child welfare report and/or referral for services to address the problem. If he is not harmful, but is merely less appealing to Jeffrey as a parent than Gia, Jeffrey has little basis on which to enter into the custody dispute.

Outcome-based ethics. Using a utilitarian position, we might envision numerous consequences of Jeffrey's two choices. If he complies with the subpoena, he might influence the custody process in favor of Gia, which might ultimately be a favorable outcome for the children if the assessment is well founded. If he is wrong in his impressions of Gia's and Alex's relative abilities as parents, his involvement might result in poor outcomes for the children and the parents. His testimony would probably distress Alex, and we can envision numerous deleterious consequences from that, including distrust in the therapeutic process, a sense of betrayal, and perhaps even a lawsuit or licensure action for breach of privacy. Another result of Jeffrey taking a partisan role in the custody case is that his participation adds to the fissures in the family rather than helping to create a constructive outcome for all concerned.

If Jeffrey fails to respond to the subpoena, he could be held in contempt of court. If he responds but refuses to testify, the result may be that his clinical observations are kept out of the custody decision-making process when they might have had bearing on the case. His refusal to participate might anger Gia, resulting in attempts to compel his testimony or retaliation in the form of negative comments or a complaint to Jeffrey's regulatory board. If Jeffrey argues for an independent clinician to do a custody evaluation and that process is in some way flawed, the children may be harmed by a poor placement or parenting arrangement.

Of these outcomes, which is the most troubling? While either party in conjoint treatment or a custody matter may lash out against the professional, Jeffrey is on safer ethical ground protecting his clients' confidentiality than breaching it. This is not to say that a complaint may not be filed, only that Jeffrey's actions in maintaining Alex's privacy are in keeping with the standards of the profession, and abridging it is not. Jeffrey's apprehensions about Alex as a parent must take a backseat to his fiduciary responsibility to him and other clients who must trust his discretion. Likewise, Jeffrey must trust that an impartial evaluation focused specifically on the question of custody may yield a more thorough and accurate appraisal of both parents than any impressions gleaned secondarily from the couple's treatment.

Values. Both personal and professional values are at play in this case. The social work value of integrity speaks to Jeffrey's responsibility to treat both members of this client system in an honest, fair, and trustworthy manner. In practice, that would mean adhering to commitments he made about confidentiality, impartiality, and his intentions in the treatment process. The value would also seem to require him to be forthright about his intentions, and to inform Gia and Alex about his response to the subpoena.

Jeffrey's personal values and life experiences no doubt play a role in the case. Those values and experiences may lead him to favor a warmer, more maternal style of parenting over a more aloof, directive style. They may bias him in favor of granting custody to mothers. His values may also make him responsive to authority in such a way that he'd be unlikely to question the validity of the subpoena. Hopefully, supervision and self-awareness have sensitized Jeffrey to these preferences and qualities, and as a result he has developed strategies to manage their impact on his work. While these values may have a useful place in some activities, such as follow-through and client advocacy, in this case they may lead him to reach poorly founded conclusions in the custody matter, and the biases may disadvantage his client Alex.

Professional standards. Ethical standards provide guidance on avoiding conflicts of interest throughout the helping process. The NASW code requires social workers to clarify which individuals are considered clients and "the nature of social workers' professional obligations to the various individuals who are receiving services" (2021, 1.06d). It explicitly directs workers who anticipate "having to perform in potentially conflicting roles (for example, when a social worker is asked to testify in a child custody dispute or divorce proceedings involving clients)" to clarify the roles with the parties and minimize the conflict of interest (NASW, 2021, 1.06d).

Provisions about confidentiality are also relevant to the Rawlings' case. "Social workers should protect the confidentiality of clients during legal proceedings to the extent permitted by law. When a court of law or other legally authorized body orders social workers to disclose confidential or privileged information without a client's consent and such disclosure could cause harm to the client, social workers should request that the court withdraw the order or limit the order as narrowly as possible . . ." (NASW, 2021, 1.07j). "Social workers protect clients' identity and only disclose confidential information to other parties (including family members) with the informed consent of clients or the clients' legally authorized representatives, or when required by law or court order. . . . In all instances, social workers disclose the least amount of confidential information necessary to achieve the desired purpose" (CASW, 2005b, 1.5).

In light of the codes' provisions, Jeffrey should have explicitly addressed issues of confidentiality and loyalty at the outset of treatment. For example, he may have stated that he viewed information shared as open for disclosure within the entire client system. Similarly, it would have been ethically wise to clarify his intention to avoid triangulation between the clients in disputes in sessions or following treatment. Professional standards would suggest that Jeffrey seek to have the subpoena withdrawn or require a court order for his testimony, in that complying with the subpoena without Alex's permission is a violation of his privacy.

Ethical principles. How do ethical principles align with Jeffrey's choices? Three have particular relevance for his decisions in this matter. The principle of fidelity, and the related concepts of honesty and trustworthiness, would encourage him to act in congruence with the understandings set forth at the outset of his service in the case. That is, which decision regarding the subpoena is consistent with the informed consent agreements he made with the Rawlings? If the informed consent promised privacy and neutrality, it would be proper to resist the subpoena and keep the promises made to his clients.

Which choice leads to the well-being of the parties or avoids harm to them? The principles of beneficence and nonmalfeasance appear to support not testifying. While Gia (and potentially the children) are helped by Jeffrey's testimony, Alex is harmed by it. If Jeffrey fails to testify, he is neither harming nor helping Alex: his case and Gia's will be judged on their merits. Failing to testify would not necessarily harm Gia and the children, unless Jeffrey has a powerful perspective on the case that no other testimony would equal.

Justice, the duty to treat all equally, would also align with a decision not to testify for Gia. Theoretically, justice might be served if Jeffrey shared his impressions of both Gia's and Alex's parenting. However, being even-handed is not the only principle at stake in this case. It would still be inappropriate for Jeffrey to testify if his assessment of the parenting was not central to his work with the couple. Furthermore, testifying about the strengths and weaknesses of both parents doesn't negate the fact that one parent has not permitted such disclosure. Put another way, it is not fair to work with the couple on one issue then testify about other observations learned in the course of that treatment, nor is it fair to breach a client's privacy without compelling professional reasons to do so.

Laws and policies. Laws and regulations are also germane to this case. The Health Insurance Portability and Accountability Act of 1996 (HIPAA) established federal standards in the United States to protect personal health information in all forms, including paper records, electronic data and communications, and verbal communications (HIPAA Medical Privacy Rule, 2003; HITECH Act, 2009; U.S. Department of Health and Human Services, 2003b). Information sharing is similarly regulated in Canada, at the federal level by the Office of the Privacy Commissioner of Canada (OPCC) and at the provincial level by Freedom of Information and Protection of Privacy Acts (OPCC, 2013). These provisions would appear to restrict Jeffrey's ability to share information in the custody suit without both clients' permission. As noted earlier, State or provincial laws may specifically address disclosures in divorce and custody matters. Even if they do not, state confidentiality provisions, if more stringent than HIPAA, would apply to Jeffrey's dilemma. There are no apparent statutes that would support Jeffrey in choosing to testify for Gia and against Alex in this dispute.

Practice principles. Like legal standards, there is also a robust body of clinical wisdom about managing confidentiality and conflicts of interest in conjoint and family therapies. Many point to the initial sessions and informed consent processes as the foundation for clear expectations about the clinician's loyalties and responsibilities. Whether the clinician treats each member of the system as individual clients or sees them only as a system, focusing on the interactions and relationship, the chosen perspective should be explicit from the outset and revisited throughout treatment as possible conflicts of interest emerge (Gottleib, 1996).

Why Is Jeffrey Selecting a Particular Course of Action?

The temptation to abridge a client's privacy often arises from a sense of duty, notions of the greater good, or the clinician's belief that they are averting harm. While there is nothing inherently bad in any of these motivations, the intentions are often misguided. Too often, the urge to break confidentiality reflects distortions in a professional's sense of self-importance ("Only I can stop this disaster from happening") or in the risk involved ("What if there's *any* chance of harm coming from my silence about what I know?"). Social workers and other helping professionals are privileged by society and the clients they serve to enter people's lives, learn their deepest secrets, and address their most profound concerns. Because of this power, ethical and legal protections are in place to ensure that these intimacies are not violated. This is not simply to preserve the client's privacy but to reinforce the sanctity of the work with which the profession is entrusted. Therefore, the contracts such as those established through informed consent notify the client about the nature of the work, the ways that the worker will use information, and the worker's intent to protect information (Smith, 2003). Occasionally, professionals may need to break that agreement to avert an imminent, serious, and immediate threat to the life of another or a credible suicide threat, but by and large they must exercise fidelity to the agreement and refrain from sharing information (Edwards, 2012; Klinka, 2009). If this threshold for breaking confidentiality seems high, that is because it is!

In the Rawlings' case, Jeffrey may well believe that Gia is the preferable parent, and he may feel torn about withholding information that would help Gia obtain sole custody. However, his professional responsibilities are greater than his desires in the case. He must ask himself if he is in a position to objectively and competently assess appropriate parenting, what specific harms he wishes to avert by testifying, and whether that disclosure is worth betraying Alex and the legal and ethical repercussions of a breach of privacy. Is Alex's parenting detrimental, or simply not Jeffrey's preferred style? If it is detrimental, are there other mechanisms for introducing those findings into court? Could a custody evaluation by a neutral party better address those than Jeffrey could, given the nature of her contact with the parents and the therapeutic privilege barriers to testimony?

Would Jeffrey be comfortable subjecting his choices to review by his colleagues via the principle of publicity? In fact, seeking consultation on the case would help him measure this, and it is likely that most would support him in not testifying, thereby upholding the ethical and legal standards in the case. Otherwise, he would have to convince them that the information he has to share is so compelling that it justifies breaking the law and his promise to his client.

In contrast, the principle of reversibility may be of little help in resolving this dilemma, in that Jeffrey's sympathies may shift depending on whose perspective he takes in the case. That is, if Jeffrey puts himself in Gia's shoes, he might want to testify, but if Jeffrey looks at the situation from Alex's point of view, he would refrain from testifying.

How Should Jeffrey Carry Out His Decision?

If Jeffrey decides that his testimony would undermine the interests of one of his clients, he must contest the subpoena. A first step would involve contacting both clients to notify them of the request for information in this case. Gia, of course, may have already approved of the release in writing. Theoretically, Alex could also permit Jeffrey to share the information in compliance with the subpoena, but it is more likely that he will refuse to waive his privilege of confidentiality. If that is the case, Jeffrey could, with his clients' permission, contact the attorney who issued the subpoena and describe the privacy concerns and the inappropriateness of testifying about custody given the nature of his services. If Jeffrey's knowledge is deemed to be irrelevant for the custody proceedings, the attorney could withdraw the subpoena.

Failing that, Jeffrey or his legal representative should contact the court in writing, specifying the legal and ethical grounds for his refusal to appear. This communication should be made in writing and copied to the attorneys in the case (Zur, 2013). Alternatively, Jeffrey's attorney could file a motion to quash the subpoena, voiding the order to appear. In this, the judge may determine that the goals of Jeffrey's testimony can be met by other means (evaluations or testimony by others without **privilege** exceptions). If the judge affirms the subpoena and determines Jeffrey's testimony or records would be relevant, legal representation would help him in depositions, court testimony, and other matters. If Jeffrey is compelled to testify, representation will ensure that his responses are legally sound and that any refusals to answer are made on solid legal grounds.

Now that you have had the opportunity to review decision making on a dilemma involving conflicts of interest, Box 5.5 provides a practice case involving similar standards.

As you process Evelyn's dilemma, consider cases that cause you discomfort. Is anybody truly objective and free of prejudicial reactions? When is it in a client's interest to refer the case to another professional? When is it appropriate for the professional to address their own conflicting reactions and proceed with a case?

BOX 5.5

A Case for You

A horrific crime fills the local news. The battered body of a missing five-year-old child is found in the woods. Surveillance footage from a local hotel shows a young man carrying her into an elevator. It is the last time she is seen alive. Police allege that her mother gave the child to the man in payment for a drug debt. Both adults are in jail pending murder charges.

Evelyn is a forensic evaluator assigned to the prison for pretrial evaluations. Like the rest of the community, she is distressed by the case and the haunting video images. Though she often deals with disturbing criminal allegations, this case is especially troubling to her because her own daughter bears a striking similarity to the deceased youngster. She is uncomfortable with the prospect of being assigned this case, yet believes it will be difficult to recuse herself. She practices in a remote region and bringing in another evaluator will be expensive and unpopular with the attorneys. She wonders if she is being narrow-minded about the case. Surely professionals can't reject every case that makes them uncomfortable. Perhaps she can manage her aversion to this one, but how?

Conclusion

Many situations can give rise to conflicts of interest, including tensions between the client's needs and the worker's financial or personal interests, and cases where the worker experiences divided loyalties within a client system. Conflicts of interest are often linked to other ethical issues. Professionals are expected to address potential conflicts of interest as part of informed consent procedures. Dual or sexual relationships or other therapeutic boundary crossings inherently create conflicts of interest as the worker strives to reconcile the social, business, or other sorts of ties to the client with her professional responsibilities. In an effort to manage conflicting roles and responsibilities, workers may breach other ethical standards such as those on confidentiality, competence, or professionalism.

Helping professionals are expected to be alert to conflicts of interest and take steps to avoid or mitigate their effects. Sometimes conflicts are apparent because of roles or relationships. An employee declines to serve as a supervisor for his son, who works in the same setting. Or a worker, in reading a referral, recognizes the client as her son's school bus driver. She declines to take the case based on the possibility that the work may reveal information that is difficult for her to contain or keep separate from her interests as a mother. In both of these cases, the worker can divert the conflict by declining a role that creates conflict.

In other cases, conflicts are internal and less easily managed. A worker with a history of sexual abuse berates a client whom they believe to be sexual offender. The hallmark of the conflict is in the worker's own emotional reactions and difficulties in achieving objectivity. Pandemic-related public health measures routinely subjected workers to complex decisions balancing the health and needs of their families with those of their clients (Banks et al., 2020). These implicit dilemmas may reveal themselves in supervisory or consultative conversations, but if they do not, it is the worker who must be aware of the conflict and take steps to ensure that the client's interests are given priority.

Beyond self-awareness and supervision, legal, ethical, and collegial resources are beneficial in identifying and managing conflicts of interest. Solving dilemmas of this type does not require that social workers ignore or negate their own interests, only that they ensure that the interests of clients are protected and preserved.

For Continuing Conversation

1. What is your organization's policy about the receipt of gifts from clients? Is it ethically sound in helping staff avoid conflicts of interest? Is it clinically prudent and culturally responsive?
2. What strategies should workers use when they experience strong reaction (positive or negative) toward clients?
3. Some clinicians refuse to take cases such as couples work or custody evaluations because they carry elevated risk of grievance when one of the parents believes their interests were not valued. Other workers may avoid certain clientele, such as people with anorexia, because of the life-threatening nature of the disorder. What are the ethics of declining cases on these bases?

Key Concepts

Countertransference. A therapist's conscious or unconscious emotional reaction to a client based on the therapist's own life history or developmental conflicts, resulting in the therapist projecting their feelings toward a client.

Quality assurance. The maintenance of a desired level of quality in a service or product especially by means of attention to every stage of the process of delivery or production.

Triangulation. Situations in which one person serves (overtly or unintentionally) as a messenger between others who are in conflict or experiencing other tensions.

Utilization review. The process of evaluating the appropriateness, medical need, and efficiency of health-care services or procedure that have been provided, according to an applicable set of guidelines or established criteria.

CHAPTER 6

Professional Boundaries

Introduction

A particular type of conflict of interest occurs when social workers engage in **dual relationships** with their clients. Dual or multiple relationships occur any time a helping professional has an attachment or affiliation with the client beyond the therapeutic or helping relationship. The other relationship may be social, financial, sexual, or professional in nature. The other relationship may occur at the same time as the helping process or before or after the client–worker relationship. As such, dual relationships may involve a wide array of possibilities. Some examples include accepting a former supervisor as a client, being "friends" with a student intern on social media, hiring a client to do bookkeeping for one's practice, accepting a student as a therapy client, going out to lunch with a client after referring them to another agency, inviting a client to join a church group, inviting a former client to join the worker's cosmetics sales team, having sexual relations with a former client, or accepting an invitation for your family to join your client at a hockey game. The steps in creating firm therapeutic boundaries are listed in Box 6.1.

As you can probably see from this list, some overlapping relationships are more troubling than others. **Boundary crossings** are often distinguished from **boundary violations** in that they have a differential potential to diminish one's professional objectivity and to lead to client confusion and exploitation. As Reamer (2019a) notes, "A boundary violation occurs when a social worker engages in a dual relationship with a client or colleague that is exploitative, manipulative, deceptive, or coercive," whereas "Boundary crossings are not inherently unethical"

BOX 6.1

Strong Boundaries

- Avoid inappropriate dual relationships, such as any attachment or affiliation with the client beyond the helping relationship.
- If unavoidable, does the dual relationship create a real or perceived conflict of interest?
- Make referrals to other service providers when necessary if there is a preexisting relationship with a potential client.
- When dual relationships could occur, discuss concerns proactively with your client, seek input of a supervisor, and set clear parameters for self-conduct and self-disclosure.

(pp. 157–158). In fact, in some rural communities, practice settings, and ethnic or cultural groups overlapping relationships may be unavoidable or even desirable (Gripton & Valentich, 2003; Newfoundland & Labrador Association of Social Workers, 2018a; Piché et al., 2015; Pugh, 2007). Situations such as inadvertently running into a client in the community or at a social gathering are boundary crossings, in that they are usually unanticipated and momentary. Boundary crossings may also include more substantive dual relationships, as when people attend the same house of worship, have children at the same school, or are members of the same civic groups. These crossings may sometimes be uncomfortable and require attention to privacy and respect for the working relationship, but they are not characterized by misuses of power in the way that boundary violations are.

The CASW *Guidelines for Ethical Conduct* (2005b) states,

- "Social workers establish appropriate boundaries in relationships with clients and ensure that the relationship serves the needs of clients." (p. 7)
- "Social workers value openness and transparency in professional practice and avoid relationships where their integrity or impartiality may be compromised, ensuring that should a conflict of interest be unavoidable, the nature of the conflict is fully disclosed." (p. 7)

The NASW *Code of Ethics* (2021) similarly stipulates,

- "Social workers should not engage in dual or multiple relationships with clients or former clients in which there is a risk of exploitation or potential harm to the client … when dual or multiple relationships are unavoidable, social workers should take steps to protect clients and are responsible for setting clear, appropriate, and culturally sensitive boundaries." (1.06c)
- "Social workers should avoid communication with clients using technology (such as social networking sites, online chat, email, text messages, telephone, and video) for personal or non-work-related purposes." (1.06e)
- "Social workers should be aware that posting personal information on professional websites or other media might cause boundary confusion, inappropriate dual relationships, or harm to clients." (1.06f)
- "Social workers should be aware that involvement in electronic communication with groups based on race, ethnicity, language, sexual orientation, gender identity or expression, mental or physical ability, religion, immigration status, and other personal affiliations may affect their ability to work effectively with particular clients." (1.06g)

While many forms of dual relationships can complicate the helping process, some are especially harmful to clients. Situations in which clients are exploited emotionally or financially, where the worker's and client's lives become intertwined, or where professionalism is lost often result in added harm to the clients involved. As a result, dual and sexual relationships constitute a significant proportion of the ethics complaints and liability actions against social workers and other professionals (Boland-Prom, 2009; Daley & Doughty 2006; Guthiel & Brodsky, 2011; Strom-Gottfried, 1999).

Clearly, when dual relationships can be avoided, the social worker should do so. This may mean declining to join a team, club, or committee in which a client is a member. It may mean, for example, transferring a client who lives in the worker's neighborhood, belongs to the worker's place of worship, or serves as the worker's accountant/mechanic/hairdresser if these or other associations might unnecessarily complicate the helping relationship or otherwise affect the worker's ability to act in the client's best interests. Sometimes workers recommend such a referral in order to preserve their own privacy or to keep their personal and professional lives separate, though the ultimate responsibility is to protect the client's interests.

Not all dual relationships are avoidable. A client and their therapist may both be elected to the local school board. A student may be assigned to a class taught by their former caseworker. The building inspector assigned to appraise a worker's house may have attended the worker's support group for grieving parents. The parent of a child hospitalized on the social worker's ward may turn out to be the person who, months earlier, sold that parent a used car (complete with unreported engine problems). A social worker's promotion may mean that they are now supervising their friends and former peers on the direct-services staff. If these relationships can't be avoided, they must be managed in such a way that the other relationships don't present conflicts of interest for carrying out the professional relationship. This involves careful evaluation of the options and appropriate boundary setting by the worker.

Even if the working relationship is in the past, the professional must be alert to and address any ways in which the new relationship may detrimentally affect the gains made in the earlier relationship. For example, having a former client as a student in class might raise concerns about the professor/therapist's objectivity in grading or possibly unfair treatment in the class that could undermine successful earlier therapeutic efforts. To meet the ethical standard, the professor might talk privately with the student about the new relationship as distinct from the past one, assure the student of their objectivity and of the confidentiality of their therapeutic relationship, and offer to make alternative arrangements if the two determine that the professor's instruction or grading might be influenced by the prior relationship. As part of boundary setting, the instructor may alert their supervisor to the fact that a former client is enrolled in class, in order to learn about any policies or options that relate to such situations. For example, the school may recommend using unique identifiers rather than names on papers to ensure anonymity in grading. Or the supervisor might offer to be available for consultation should the student or teacher experience difficulties during the class.

Boundaries and Sexual Relationships

Sexual relationships are a particularly damaging form of dual relationship and are never advisable. Because sexual relationships are a common area of difficulty for helping professionals (Boland-Prom, 2009; Psychotherapy Finances, 2003; Strom-Gottfried, 1999) codes of ethics address them with very explicit standards: "Social workers should under no circumstances engage in sexual activities, inappropriate sexual communications through the use of technology or in person, or sexual contact with current clients, whether such contact is consensual or forced" (NASW, 2021, 1.09a) and "Social workers do not engage in romantic relationships, sexual activities or sexual contact with clients, even if such contact is sought by clients" (CASW, 2005b, 2.6.1). The prohibition also includes supervisees, students, trainees, or other colleagues over whom the social worker has authority.

Sexual improprieties are generally believed to be among the final acts in a slippery slope of boundary transgressions that can include excessive self-disclosure by the worker, seeking contact with clients outside of appointments, seeking favors or influence from clients, sexualizing elements of the clinical interaction, and comparing the client favorably to the worker's loved ones (Gabbard, 1996). While sexual misconduct is generally construed as a phenomenon between male workers and female clients, research indicates the emergence of other patterns, particularly female client–female worker transgressions (Gartrell & Sanderson, 1994; Strom-Gottfried, 1999).

Social workers are sometimes perplexed at the prohibition on sexual relationships with former clients, noting that many state regulatory boards and some other helping professions set a clear ban on sexual involvement within two years (American Psychological Association [APA], 2010) or five years (American Counseling Association [ACA], 2005) of termination, or "for that period of time following therapy during which the power relationship reasonably could be expected to influence the client's personal decision making" (Canadian Psychological Association, 2000, p. 18). CASW and NASW provide standards that are more ambiguous:

- "Social workers should not engage in sexual activities or sexual contact with former clients because of the potential for harm to the client. If social workers engage in conduct contrary to this prohibition or claim that an exception to this prohibition is warranted because of extraordinary circumstances, it is social workers—not their clients— who assume the full burden of demonstrating that the former client has not been exploited, coerced, or manipulated, intentionally or unintentionally." (NASW, 2021, 1.09c)

• "Social workers who have provided psychotherapy or in-depth counselling do not engage in romantic relationships, sexual activities or sexual contact with former clients. It is the responsibility of the social worker to evaluate the nature of the professional relationship they had with a client and to determine whether the social worker is in a position of power and/or authority that may unduly and/or negatively affect the decisions and actions of their former client." (CASW, 2005b, 2.6.2)

Upon close examination, NASW's standard does not differ greatly in substance from standards that set specific time limits. All standards discourage sexual involvement with former clients (even after the two-year or five-year moratoriums) and emphasize the worker's responsibility to demonstrate that they did not misuse power in engaging in a relationship with the client. Clearly, the message to workers is "proceed with caution!" Even relationships built on the best of foundations may come to an end. One built on an earlier client–worker relationship places the professional at particular and ongoing jeopardy for ensuring, even retrospectively, that no harm was done to the former client.

Implicit in NASW's lifetime ban on sexual involvement with former clients are the notions that once a person is a client, the worker will always know them in that way, and that workers must treat all clients the same. Therefore, a social worker who facilitates an educational group for heart attack survivors would be held to the same standard vis-à-vis former clients as an outpatient trauma therapist would be held to with theirs. The standards that set specific time limits acknowledge that not all worker–client relationships have the same depth and duration. Helping relationships that are brief or perfunctory might allow for an eventual intimate relationship, well after the helping relationship has ended. Regardless of the circumstances, the professional who engages in a relationship with a former client would have to demonstrate, if questioned, that the context of the relationship (the timing and circumstances under which it evolved) and the nature of the original helping relationship indicate that the sexual relationship is not predatory, harmful, or exploitive. For an example of proper boundary setting, see Box 6.2.

BOX 6.2

Upholding the Standard

Tim is a social worker in private practice. Several weeks ago, the daughter of his friend Sean died in a car accident. Tim and his wife have been spending a great deal of time supporting and comforting Sean's family in the wake of their tragic loss.

Today, Tim got a call from Sean, who asked to come see him on a professional basis. "You've been such a champion for us these last few weeks, but I know I need extra help to deal with this."

Tim sympathized with his situation and commended him for reaching out for help but said, "I'm happy to help you any way I can as your friend, but I think it would be better for you to see someone else to take it farther than that."

Sean: "Don't you do this kind of work in your practice?"

Tim: "Yes, sure, but because I value our friendship, I can't see you in my practice. I may not be objective enough to help you."

Sean: "But that's just it! I don't want to have to dredge all this up with someone new. I want to see you because you already know all about us and what we've been through."

Tim: "Sean, you have to trust me when I say it's not in your best interest to see me professionally. There are a lot of great clinicians out there who work on just the kinds of issues you are struggling with. I'm happy to suggest some and even go with you on a first visit to see someone, but I can't take on the counseling myself. We're just too close."

It may seem paradoxical to refuse to accept a friend as a client, when the two people involved already have a close and trusting relationship and the worker already knows a great deal about the potential client. Some might argue that rather than causing harm, such an arrangement could allow for efficient and effective service. Even professionals who are conversant with the notion of professional boundaries might share the layperson's confusion as to why such an arrangement is unwise.

Tim addresses one core reason for boundaries when he notes that he may not be objective enough to help with Sean's care (Pugh, 2007). He, too, is grieving the young girl's death.

- How can he distinguish his own reactions from the needs of his client?
- Even if he had no prior relationship with Sean's daughter, due to his friendship with Sean he knows a great deal about his life and past. If he changes hats to become his clinician, what is he to do with that information? Can he put it in the proper clinical perspective?
- Similarly, what is he to do, as a friend, with the information he will learn as Sean's counselor? How can he ignore what he learns in the therapeutic relationship when they are interacting as friends? Even if the chances are small that he will learn something troubling about Sean and his family, is that a risk he wants to take in taking on his friend's case?
- And where does the work end? If Sean is a client and calls Tim one weekend when he is lonely, is he calling his friend or his therapist?

Beyond addressing objectivity and how information is received and viewed, boundaries help regulate the roles and rules that are part of the therapeutic interaction (Reamer, 2018).

- Can Tim ask questions, provide guidance, push for self-examination, and utilize confrontation in clinical work with Sean as he would with any other client in the same circumstance, or are his techniques and decisions limited because of his friendship and history with the client?
- Will Sean view Tim with the same authority with which he would view another worker he knows less well?
- After the counseling, how will their relationship be construed? Will they relate to each other in the future as friends or as client and worker? As Sean reveals himself in the safety of therapy, will he be comfortable resuming his friendship with Tim, or will he eventually seek to put distance between them following his self-exposure in therapy?
- Is having Tim as a worker worth the potential price of losing him as a friend and as a supporter through the grief process?

Those advocating for the dual role might suggest that in his grief, Sean has already poured his heart out to his friend. And no doubt Tim's responses to his friend's loss are influenced by his therapeutic training and his professional knowledge base. But giving and receiving that information in the context of a friendship is still not the same as the process of disclosure in therapy. Advocates for taking the case might argue that the risk of harm to Sean is slight, and therefore therapy would not constitute a dual relationship as described in the social work codes. As the social worker, it is up to Tim to assess the risk, considering such factors as the power differential, the length and intensity of the two relationships, the client's strength and clarity, the likelihood of challenges to his own objectivity, and the message the relationship might send to others (Ebert, 1997; Gottlieb, 1994; Kitchener, 1988; Piché et al., 2015). He should also appraise the reasons for taking the case. His assessment that others can better help Sean with his grief is important here: an abundance of competent resources makes it less compelling for Tim himself to take the case. Ultimately, he is making the selfless and safest choice in supporting his friend's pursuit of counseling with someone else while preserving his role as friend and protecting the friendship. Box 6.3 offers a case in which the social worker fails to maintain boundaries and uphold standards around dual relationships.

BOX 6.3

Violating the Standard

Amelia works in a community program designed to help persons with a history of psychiatric hospitalization develop vocational skills, with the ultimate goal that clients will attain full employment. Her client Honey had worked as a seamstress prior to the onset of her illness, and she hoped eventually to return to that field. One day Honey overheard Amelia talking to a colleague about her search for a wedding dress, and Honey mentioned wistfully, "Those were my favorite pieces to do when I was working—so much creativity, and always for a happy occasion."

It occurred to Amelia that she could develop a win-win scenario if she hired Honey to sew her dress. It would help boost Honey's confidence and give her some extra money and a chance to feel useful again. She suggested it to Honey, who eagerly agreed, and the two settled upon on a price; selected a pattern, fabric, and trim; and talked often about their ideas for the gown. Amelia believed that her employer might disapprove of her paying Honey under the table and might question Amelia's objectivity for taking Honey under her wing in such a fashion, so she also suggested that they reserve their activities and discussions of the gown for nonwork time.

Eight weeks before the wedding, however, Honey's attendance at the vocational program began to drop off. When Diane, the program supervisor, called to check on her, Honey screamed, "Just stop pressuring me!" Amelia became increasingly concerned about the status of the dress, and as the date neared, unable to reach Honey by phone, she went to her home. The apartment was in total disarray, the misshapen bodice of a wedding gown was laid across the back of a sofa, and a pile of tattered fabric lay nearby. Upon seeing Amelia, Honey burst into furious sobs. "This is very bad fabric!" she shrieked. "I couldn't get it to come out right, so I had to keep recutting it and starting over. Now there's not enough left to finish the bottom!"

Amelia was dumbfounded. She had expected to find a finished garment, and she, too, was furious. She gathered her composure and said, "It's okay, Honey. Just give me what you have, and I'll pay someone else to do it."

Honey sobbed, "What about my pay? I've put a lot of time into this—much more than I agreed to. Plus, I've had to miss time at my workshop job because of your project!"

When Amelia resisted full payment and tried to explain the additional costs and delays that Honey's errors had caused, Honey concluded the conversation, shouting tearfully, "That's not fair to just use me like that! I'm telling Diane!"

By entering into a business arrangement with Honey, Amelia created a dual relationship that conflicts with her role as the woman's social worker. While she may have originally rationalized the purchase of Honey's services as congruent with her treatment goals of employment, Amelia could have met that goal more appropriately by helping Honey to find a job or start a business rather than becoming her first and only customer. And Amelia's reluctance for other workers to learn about the arrangement is a sign that she knew the agreement with Honey was inappropriate, however she might try to justify it as therapeutic.

As in this case, a common danger of dual relationships is the exploitation of and harm to clients (Reamer, 2018).

- Did Amelia's authority as Honey's worker lead Honey to take on a task she might have otherwise declined?
- Did it lead her to do the task for less money than she might ordinarily charge, and did it constrain her from speaking up when the project did not go as planned?
- Did the pressure of doing the project for her social worker create an additional countertherapeutic strain on Honey?
- Did it create other harm as she withdrew from the treatment center and experienced increased symptoms due to the pressure of the project?

A second effect of dual relationships is erosion in the social worker's capacity to carry out his professional responsibilities because of the conflict created by the other relationship (Pope & Keith-Spiegel, 2008; Simon, 1999). We have no evidence that Amelia's treatment of Honey was different because Honey had control of the wedding dress, but we can imagine Amelia treating Honey favorably or overlooking problems because of their business relationship. Furthermore, because of her responsibilities as Honey's social worker, Amelia is constrained from treating Honey as she would any other seamstress who botched the wedding dress and failed to deliver on time. How can she help Honey develop her vocational skills while expressing anger and disappointment about the dress? Had another seamstress ruined the dress, Amelia might have posted negative reviews on social media or taken the case to small claims court to recoup the costs. Those avenues, which are appropriate in other consumer transactions would be thoroughly inappropriate when directed against a client. The boundaries that protect the client in the helping process also protect the worker who upholds the distinctions between those she serves as a professional and those she befriends or hires.

While errors can occur when professionals violate therapeutic boundaries, many boundary decisions are ambiguous. The case of "The Sleepless Sleepover" in Box 6.4 is one such example.

BOX 6.4

Resolving Dilemmas in Boundary Maintenance: The Sleepless Sleepover

Gary is a clinician at a child guidance clinic who is assigned to provide consultation for a chain of group homes for children and adolescents with severe emotional and behavioral difficulties. Gary returned home from work one night to find that a friend of his eleven-year-old daughter, Sasha, would be sleeping over. When he met Sasha's new friend, Gail, he realized she was a former resident of one of the group homes where he is a consultant.

Is Gary on the verge of a dual relationship with Gail? His role at the group home where she was placed was that of consultant, so it is unclear whether his contact with her there might be construed as a client–worker relationship. Even if that might be considered a professional relationship, does her friendship with his daughter constitute a social relationship with him? If there is a dual relationship, is it potentially harmful to Gail as a former client? While we may question whether this case fits the criteria for a dual relationship, most parents can identify with Gary's unease about the surprise guest and his desire to set proper, professional boundaries. The question here is less about avoiding a dual relationship and more about the nature of Gary's concerns and the boundaries he must set as a result.

What concerns might prompt Gary to set boundaries in this case? Perhaps his knowledge of Gail's history makes him concerned that she is an unsuitable companion for his daughter. Perhaps his knowledge of her history makes it difficult for him to maintain her privacy during her visits or in conversations with his family. Perhaps he is uncomfortable at the thought of a former client, however remote the relationship, having such intimate involvement with his family, and staying at his home. Perhaps he is concerned that others will interpret the situation negatively and see the relationship as inappropriate or exploitive of Gail.

Applying the Six-Question Model

Who Can Help Gary?

What experiences and resources can Gary draw on to respond in the moment to the dilemma that greeted him at home? It may be possible to call a colleague or supervisor for advice. It will be helpful if it is someone who knows his role at the group home and the challenges of parenting in a community where there are likely to be overlapping relationships between the worker's children and those he serves.

Gary may also consider calling Gail's parents or guardians. They may not know that the sleepover is with the family of someone affiliated with the group home. If they are comfortable with the arrangement, it may alleviate some of Gary's concerns, in that they have consented to the arrangement. If they are uncomfortable with it (or are sympathetic to Gary's discomfort), they may call Gail home from the sleepover or discourage future play dates.

A trickier question is whether Gary should consult his wife, who arranged the sleepover. Saying "Gail used to be at the group home, so it puts me in an awkward spot to have her stay here" alerts his wife to the difficulty and involves her as an ally in problem solving, but it also reveals information about Gail's status as a client that his wife has no right to know, and it may open a deluge of other questions about Gail that he is unprepared and unauthorized to answer.

What Are Gary's Choices?

As noted earlier, Gary's choices vary depending upon the nature of his concerns and the goals he wishes to achieve. If he is concerned about mixing the two roles (counselor and dad), he can withdraw from the role of dad for the night, allowing his wife to supervise the sleepover and deal with the two girls as she would with any other overnight guest. Alternatively, he could speak privately with Gail or her parents and explain that because of their past relationship, having her spend the night in his home would be uncomfortable and ethically questionable. Should he pursue this course of action, he would hope that the child or her parents would end the sleepover and explain to Sasha and her mother their reasons so that he doesn't have to. A third solution would combine these two choices, allowing the sleepover that has already commenced, but ensuring that no overnight visits take place in the future.

Different choices would arise if Gary were concerned that Gail is some-how unstable and a risk to his daughter and his family. First, Gary should be very certain that his concerns are well founded and not a judgmental, knee-jerk reaction based on some distant case history or stereotyped view of clients. He must also consider that in taking steps to insulate his fam-ily from her as an overnight guest, he may be stigmatizing the young girl and providing only limited protection from her in that she and Sasha may continue to be friends and schoolmates with or without his approval. If he determines that she cannot spend the night because of his safety con-cerns, his options are to end the sleepover without explaining why, or to speak with her and her parents about ending it, using the ethics rationale described earlier.

If Gary is simply uncomfortable having a former client in his home, he must weigh the risks and benefits of somehow ending the sleepover for his own well-being with the risks and benefits of allowing it to continue for the well-being of his daughter and her friend. This requires Gary to forth-rightly examine the basis for his apprehensions. Does setting boundaries mean that Gail must be sent home or banished as a friend of his daughter's simply for his convenience or comfort? Can he set boundaries about the ways in which *he* interacts with Gail and demonstrate restraint in what he says about her, in order to let the girls' friendship move forward and run its normal course without his interference?

When Has Gary Faced a Similar Dilemma?

Practice in small communities often requires that professionals develop family **norms** to help maintain boundaries between their work, social lives, and business dealings (Schank & Skovholt, 1997; Strom-Gottfried, 2005). For example, family and friends learn not to ask, "Who was that?" when strangers approach the social worker at the supermarket and say, "I'm doing a lot better now." Partners and spouses ask first, before hiring a babysitter, landscaper, carpenter, and so forth, "Is there any reason I shouldn't get so-and-so to do such-and-such?" This allows the social worker to approve or decline the hire without divulging why such a decision would be unwise. The spouse may assume that an answer in the affirmative is tantamount to identifying the person as a client, but there may be other reasons and relationships that would influence a yes or no answer in this case. This helps families set proper boundaries without requiring them to inappropriately seek or divulge information. In trying to understand the nature of their parent's work, children may also ask about clients and thus learn the norms of confidentiality and boundary setting. As a result of these conversations, children may develop enhanced compassion and understanding about human troubles (Boisen & Bosch, 2005; Brownlee et al., 2012; Burkemper, 2005; Gumpert & Black, 2005; Halverson & Brownlee, 2010; Manning & Van Pelt, 2005; Pugh, 2007; Strom-Gottfried, 2005).

Against this backdrop, we might wonder what the understandings are in Gary's family. Might the family have avoided the awkwardness of the sleepover with better communication? How have similar incidents been handled in this family or in this professional community? Is Sasha's friendship with Gail an artifact of her sensitivity and concern for others? Would she interpret boundary setting as a message not to be kind, not to reach out to others? The precedents in the family for managing overlapping relationships and for the way that the members of the family relate to each other would help shed light on effective strategies for the sleepover.

Other factors that may help the decision-making process include Gary's past experiences with setting limits. Has he had other interactions with youths from the group home, in the community, as classmates of his children, or as direct clients? Have he and his wife regulated Sasha's friends and houseguests before? If there are other friends whom they perceive as a poor influence or an unwelcome guest, how have they handled those situations? Is Sasha mature enough to set limits or communicate with her parents if any friend demonstrates disturbing behavior or proposes inappropriate activities? How might Gary draw on those experiences in this situation?

Where Do Ethical and Clinical Guidelines Lead Him?

We start our examination of Gary's choices with two traditions of moral philosophy.

Rule-based ethics. Looking at Gary's case through a deontological lens, we can ask, "What rules are embedded in Gary's choices, and what choice would he want to adopt as a universal rule?" This case helps demonstrate the complexities of applying theory to practice, in that we could reasonably derive several conflicting principles for any one of Gary's choices. Deciding to tell Gail she can't sleep over might embody rules ranging from "No one I knew as a client can be friends with my daughter" to "No one I knew as a client can spend the night at my house" to "No one who troubles me can stay overnight." Which principle is at stake here?

Deciding to let the sleepover go on may reflect various principles from "My daughter has to be the judge of her own friends. I can't regulate that for her" to "I could never say anything that might hurt Gail's feelings." Both are valid principles, but neither would likely be favored as a universal rule. The advantage of the deontological perspective for Gary is that it requires him to define the basis on which he is making any given choice. What principle is being upheld in a particular decision? Taking the choice out of the context for a moment and examining it through the larger principle at stake helps give substance to the choice. In using a rule-based lens, Gary and other decision makers are asking, "What's really going on underneath each of my particular options?"

Outcome-based ethics. From a utilitarian perspective, we would look at the consequences of Gary's choices for those involved. For example, cutting the sleepover short might bring Gary short-term and long-term peace of mind. Its consequences for Sasha and Gail depend greatly on how it is handled and interpreted. If the girls experience it as appropriate and discreet boundary setting, perhaps it will help assure Gail that Gary, in putting her need for protection before his own family's interests, wants to protect her from harmful dual relationships. It may send a message to Sasha that her father has integrity and the best interests of her and her friend at heart. Alternatively, his actions could breach Gail's privacy and stigmatize her with Sasha and with anyone else Sasha tells about Gail's history at the group home. It could make Gail ashamed, unwelcome in their home, and unworthy of the kinds of activities many youth her age take for granted. At its worst, poor handling of the situation could have deleterious effects for Gail's mental health.

Rather than feeling protected, Sasha may feel embarrassed and disgusted at her father's intervention. As a result, she might cling more tightly to the friendship than she would have had he let the friendship progress naturally. Sasha might take away the message that being the recipient of mental health services is something to be ashamed of. For better or for worse, it may affect her selection of friends or her willingness to invite them home in the future.

Values. Several social work values apply in this case. In the name of social justice, social workers pledge to work to end discrimination and "promote sensitivity to and knowledge about oppression" (NASW, 2021, p. 2). In valuing the dignity and worth of the person, social workers "respect the unique worth and inherent dignity of all people and uphold human rights" (CASW, 2005a, p. 4). In acknowledging the importance of human relationships, "social workers seek to strengthen relationships among people in a purposeful effort to promote, restore, maintain, and enhance" their well-being (NASW, 2021, p. 2).

All of these values would seem to encourage Gary to be very careful in ensuring he is not treating Gail in a pejorative or stigmatizing fashion because of her prior status as a group home client. These social work values might be interpreted as supporting Gary in giving latitude to Gail's friendship with his daughter, even allowing the sleepover if that is a common element of such friendships, assuming it does not exploit or harm Gail. Of course, if Gary is concerned about Gail's history or instability, his values may place priority on protecting his family over his professional values. He may argue that it is all well and good to foster a client's relationships, but that doesn't require that it be done with the worker's own family.

Professional standards, laws and policies, ethical principles. Codes of ethics are less germane to this case in that Gary's role at the group home and Gail's former residence there seem not to fit the criteria for dual relationships. Similarly, there are no apparent laws or policies governing decisions such as Gary's, except those specific to his agency or the group home.

We can, however, examine the case through the principles of autonomy, fidelity, beneficence, and justice. How can Gary encourage the maximum level of autonomy for Gail in this case? On the one hand, allowing her to visit unfettered would seem to be in keeping with her wishes to befriend his daughter and enjoy her company. On the other hand, as a minor, Gail's capacity to judge the matter may be limited. As such, her parents' or guardians' wishes are part of the principle of autonomy, since they are empowered legally to act in her best interests. That is not to say Gail has no voice in the matter. The adults in this situation can enhance her autonomy by seeking her input, or by honestly informing her of the difficulty Gary is experiencing and the rationale for his decision.

Since Gail appears to be unaware of Gary's role at the group home or of his knowledge of her past, her trust relationship with him is linked more to his role as an adult figure and as the father of her friend. However, because of his professional role, he has a responsibility to behave in a trustworthy manner, irrespective of her relationship with him. He can uphold the principle of fidelity if he protects confidential information about her and treats her with honesty and integrity. The principle of fidelity would rule out acting deceptively to bring an end to the sleepover or using clinical information to dissuade his wife or daughter from allowing Gail to visit their home.

Gary upholds the principles of beneficence and nonmaleficence by choosing the course of action that is in Gail's best interests and that avoids causing her harm. These principles would favor those options that do not taint the friendship (irrespective of allowing the sleepover to continue) and those that support Gail's privacy.

How is justice served in this case?

- How would Gary handle any situation in which he was uncomfortable with Sasha's friends or overnight guests?
- Is it fair for him to intervene in this friendship, based solely on his knowledge of Gail's treatment history, if he has not done so in other friendships?
- Is it fair to send Gail home without spending time with her to learn more about her current circumstances and conduct? (On the other hand, is it fair to assess her if Gary never does so with Sasha's other friends?)

Practice principles. The literature on practice in rural areas provides some ideas about practice norms that may apply in Gary's case (Boisen & Bosch, 2005; Brownlee et al. 2019; Burkemper, 2005; Gumpert & Black, 2005; Halverson & Brownlee, 2010; Manning & Van Pelt, 2005; Strom-Gottfried, 2005). Essentially, these works say the same thing: it is easier for professionals to set boundaries around their own choices than around those of their offspring. Depending on the facts of the case and the appraisal of risk, practitioners should let the friendship, with all the activities normally associated with such friendships, continue or set limits on what activities the friendship can entail (no sleepovers at either home, for example) while revealing as little information about the rationale as possible (Schank & Skovholt, 1997).

Why Is a Particular Course of Action Preferable?

As alluded to in earlier sections, a theme in this case is whether Gary is acting in self-interest or in the interest of others (Gail, his daughter, his family).

Self-awareness will be essential in determining his motivations and whether they are leading to a constructive outcome.

- Is he overly averse to risk?
- Is he making unjust assumptions about Gail? Is she being unfairly exiled because he knows more about her than he does about Sasha's other friends, who might be equally worrisome?
- Does he trust his daughter's judgment in her selection of friends, and his wife's judgment in arranging get-togethers among those friends?
- Or is he naive about Gail's motivations and capacity for harm?
- Is he putting his family and career in harm's way because he is too timid to set limits around the friendship?
- Will he be comfortable telling his colleagues about the dilemma however he resolves it?

These questions help Gary put his decision to the publicity, reversibility, smell, or mom/mentor tests described in Chapter 2. The perceptions of others and the norms of the community are salient points to consider when distinguishing boundary crossings from boundary violations.

Whatever Gary decides to do in the moment, this case is ripe for discussion in supervision or consultation. Professionals who know Gary, his work, and his community can help him sort through the answers to these questions—not just for the case of Gail, but for all the future overlapping relationships that will occur as his family participates in their community over time.

How Should Gary Carry Out His Decision?

A common complaint about professional boundaries is that they convey an elitist attitude and create a unidirectional relationship in which the worker has the power to set the terms of the relationship in a fashion that marginalizes the service recipient (Lazarus, 1994). Such criticisms construe boundaries as protecting the worker from the client when in reality they protect the professional relationship and the client's interests.

Regardless of the merit of these criticisms, social workers must take care to implement boundaries in a respectful and sensitive manner. Even in his shock at seeing Gail at his house, it is important for Gary to take time to collect himself and examine his options and motivations rather than acting in a rash and fear-based manner. If, after deliberation, he decides that the best course of action is to end the sleepover, he must summon his therapeutic skills and employ them to discuss the situation with Gail and her family, being alert to Gail's responses. He should take steps to address any untoward reactions and document the experience so that he is prepared to discuss it with his supervisor when they debrief about his decision.

Even if he decides to do nothing about the sleepover, Gary should pay attention to the dynamics between the girls, in case the circumstances change in such a way that he or his wife might want to intervene to set limits on the friendship. Again, it will be helpful to talk to colleagues to review his decision making and to prepare for the conversation with his daughter and his wife, as well as with Gail or her family. Now that you have reviewed the decision-making process for one dilemma in boundary setting, take a look at the case in Box 6.5 and consider what steps you would take if you were in Lionel's shoes.

BOX 6.5

A Case for You

Lionel is active on Facebook, Twitter, and other forms of **social networking**. He appreciates the importance of firm boundaries and professionalism, and therefore he does not accept coworkers or clients as friends or followers. Mainly he uses the sites to keep up with the local music scene and share his perspectives on emerging artists. Lionel works in a residential facility, and many of the young men who leave the program do so because they have aged out of service eligibility. Few of them have stable family and social networks. A few months ago, a teen named Trae was leaving the program and asked Lionel if he was online and if he could friend him just to keep some contact instead of being "out there alone." Lionel thought carefully about the type of information he revealed about himself on social media and decided there was little risk in agreeing to Trae's request.

Tonight, after he returned home from a club, Lionel scrolled through his feeds and noticed a post by Trae from earlier in the evening. It read, "I am a worthless piece of crap and I deserve to die."

As you work though the decision-making model as it applies to this case, consider some additional points.

- This case presents both an immediate dimension (what should Lionel do now, if anything?) and a longer-term consideration about his decision to accept Trae's friend request.
- Would Lionel's decision be different if he had received a similar message from a patient listed on CaringBridge (a networking site for those involved in health-care needs)?
- What role does confidentiality play in this case?
- What are Lionel's obligations for documenting the conversation and notifying his supervisor of the situation?

Conclusion

Boundaries provide structure to the helping relationship, guiding the ways professionals and clients interact. Boundaries establish norms and set limits so that the professional roles of supervisor, teacher, caseworker, or therapist aren't confused with those of friend, business associate, or lover. They protect clients from abuses of power and place primacy on the professional relationship over all others. Sexual relationships between those in power (supervisors, instructors, counselors) and those who may be exploited by such relationships (supervisees, students, clients) are clearly unethical and in many instances, illegal. In many jurisdictions, sexual contact between workers and clients is a criminal offense. Dual relationships arise when social or business relationships are mixed simultaneously or in succession with helping relationships. While not all dual relationships are harmful, they should be avoided, if possible, since they have the capacity to confound the helping relationship. If the dual relationship cannot be avoided, it is the worker's responsibility to establish therapeutic boundaries to ensure that the client's needs and the working relationship are given priority.

Some authors have developed guidelines for weighing the risks of dual relationships (Ebert, 1997; Erickson, 2001; Gottlieb, 1994; Kitchener, 1988), and numerous resources exist to help clinicians maintain proper boundaries in complex situations (Boisen & Bosch, 2005; Brownlee et al., 2012; Burkemper, 2005; Gartrell & Sanderson, 1994; Gumpert & Black, 2005; Halverson & Brownlee, 2010; Manning & Van Pelt, 2005; Piché et al., 2015; Pugh, 2007; Reamer, 2001; Reamer, 2019a; Reamer, 2021a;

Schank & Skovholt, 1997; Strom-Gottfried, 2005). While workers in different communities and service settings may draw limits in different ways, all must be mindful of the purpose of professional boundaries and set them respectfully, forthrightly, and consistently so that the best interests of clients are maintained.

For Continuing Conversation

1. What resources can you identify to help with boundary setting around social media?
2. Friends or acquaintances may not want to see you for counseling, but they may bring up highly personal topics to get your professional input. Should you set boundaries on such conversations in your social life? How?
3. How might you handle the following situations to set clear, appropriate and culturally sensitive boundaries? What contextual factors would influence the "it depends"?

- You lead a yoga class and a client has enrolled without your knowledge.
- You called for a road service to fix a flat tire and a former client arrived driving the tow truck.
- You work on a dialysis unit and your mother's friend and neighbor is one of your patients.
- You work in a rural region and a woman and her sister are both clients of yours, though neither knows it.
- Two of your clients were formerly married to each other. You did not know this when each started service, and you don't think they know the other is seeing you.

Key Concepts

Boundary crossing. A deviation from the typical activities involved in the therapeutic relationship that does not cause harm toward or exploit the client, and is possibly supportive of the therapy itself. Examples include appropriate self-disclosure, home visits, and gifts.

Boundary violation. A deviation from the typical activities involved in the therapeutic relationship that is harmful, or potentially harmful to the client and to the therapeutic work. The therapeutic relationship becomes a means to exploit the client.

Dual relationships. A situation in which a helping professional has some connection or affiliation with the client outside the helping relationship, including but not limited to a personal relationship with the client or a personal relationship with a person closely related or connected to the client.

Norms. A standard or pattern, especially of social behavior, that is typical or expected of a group; a required standard, as of a profession.

Social networking. The use of dedicated Web sites and programs to communicate with other users who may be connected by personal or work relationships outside the social network.

CHAPTER 7

Confidentiality

Introduction

The assurance that personal information will be held in the strictest confidence is essential for the helping process. Few of us would be open with our physicians, attorneys, or clergy if we feared that those persons could not be relied upon to protect the information we entrust to them (Corey et al., 2019). Thus, our codes of ethics place a high premium on maintaining patient privacy and on requiring clinician discretion (Betteridge, 2013; E. Cohen & Cohen, 1999).

Discretion refers to expectations that the helper will not engage in fishing expeditions, seeking extraneous or tantalizing information that is beyond the bounds of the helping relationship. Even routine demographic intake information, such as a client's religion may be sensitive to the individual and superfluous to the service (Barsky, 2019). Discretion also means that staff won't seek out information or try to access records on cases for which they have no professional responsibility. Because ethical codes and individual integrity may be insufficient to protect case information from prying eyes, technology to protect records and alert administrators when access is sought by unauthorized persons is now available. With the standardization of shared electronic personal health information (ePHI), "break glass" provisions allow for emergency access to necessary information by providers who would not ordinarily have permission to see the records or who are blocked by access or authentication problems (Zerden, Cruden, et al., 2019; Yale University, 2022). Audits of these alerts serve as a line of protection from workers in large systems who may seek information on their relatives, friends, and neighbors. They also protect data in sensational or high-profile cases from curious or prying eyes.

Respect for **privacy** goes beyond what information is sought by workers to include what information is shared by them. It implies restraint on the part of the worker—not gossiping about clients, not sharing information about cases with our families or friends, and not pointing to a TV or news item and saying, "I know about that situation." **Confidentiality** requires restraint about where we discuss cases; we must ensure that conversations, even for professional purposes, do not take place in public or semiprivate places. This can be a difficult standard to uphold in some circumstances. It is challenging to create an atmosphere of privacy when offices are configured into cubicles or services are provided in shared hospital rooms or in clients' homes. Quarantines during COVID-19 escalated the use of telehealth and online classrooms creating a new challenge for protecting privacy, both in the client's home and in the worker's (Banks et al., 2020; Cooper & Zerden, 2021). Nevertheless, respect for confidentiality requires the worker to endeavor to protect clients' privacy, even under difficult circumstances. Even if it is more efficient to discuss a case in the hall or elevator on the way to a meeting, it is not ethically sound to do so.

A third feature of discretion in confidentiality is self-discipline—the notion that helpers will divulge information only for compelling professional reasons and will be vigilant in protecting written and electronic communications about clients, and cautious in responding to attempts by others to seek information, whether in the form of a subpoena, an insurance authorization form, a child custody report, or a request for case information from a fellow professional. This does not mean that helping professionals always withhold information in these cases, only that they ensure that proper consent has been obtained and that information shared doesn't exceed the purpose for which it was sought. Professional self-discipline requires social workers to be aware of ways that electronic communications can be breached and take steps to ensure systems are secure (Yonan et al., 2011). For example, not all electronic communication and service delivery platforms encrypt data and thus they present a risk for invasions of privacy (Reamer, 2021a).

As you can see, considerable attention is paid to protecting the privacy of clients, but that does not mean that direct practitioners are the only professionals responsible for maintaining confidentiality. Social workers in teaching, research, supervisory, or administrative roles must also abide by legal and ethical standards of confidentiality to guard information about or from students, employees, study participants, and supervisees (Reamer, 2016).

Box 7.1 specifies the actions needed to meet confidentiality standards.

Sometimes the respect for privacy means that professionals receive and hold information that brings them discomfort. Absent information that leads us to believe risk of harm is likely, hearing a client's abuse fantasies, criminal acts, or other troubling material may be a necessary prerequisite to helping them. Helping professionals don't have the freedom to mention these experiences to friends or family or coworkers, or to the client's friends or family or coworkers. Professionals do have the freedom to discuss them, in confidence, with their supervisors or consultants, based on the understanding that that person will maintain the client's privacy and that the information sharing is intended to ensure competent service to the client. It is not at all easy to be the repository of disturbing information, including about people with whom we reside in our communities. Many social workers seek therapeutic support as well as case consultation to manage these and other potentially traumatic implications of the profession (Posluns & Gall, 2020).

BOX 7.1

Elements of Confidentiality

- Not seeking information that is extraneous to the helping relationship.
- Respecting privacy by vigilance about what case information is shared, where or how it is shared, with whom, and for what purpose.
- Demonstrating self-discipline in guarding sensitive or difficult information shared by clients.
- Using caution in responding to others' attempts to obtain information and obtaining appropriate client consent before sharing information.
- Informing clients of duty to warn in situations where there is a risk of significant harm to the client or a third party.

As mentioned above, there are situations in which social workers are encouraged, and at times compelled, to break confidentiality (Banks & Nøhr, 2012; Barsky, 2019; Corey et al., 2019). For example, sharing case information in supervision or consultation is intended to ensure high-quality services for the benefit of the client. If a person presents a danger to themselves or others, social workers are empowered to intercede because safety takes precedence over privacy in such circumstances. **Mandatory reporting** laws require that suspicions of child or elder abuse be reported to the relevant protection agencies so that they can investigate and intercede if necessary. Some referral sources, such as employee assistance programs, or payers, such as managed care or insurance companies, may require that case information be conveyed to them as a condition of treatment. Even in these situations, though, there are limits on what providers can share and with whom they can share it. For example, if a worker suspects a child is being abused, they are not empowered to share that suspicion with the child's teacher, grandmother, or neighbor; the worker is required to report it to the local child welfare agency. Likewise, in reporting it to Child Protective Services (CPS), the worker is not obliged to share all that they know about the case, only that material necessary to carry out the responsibility for child protection.

The **duty to warn**, established in 1976 by *Tarasoff v. Regents of the University of California* (Reamer, 2018), obliges professionals to alert the intended victim of a serious threat against them or to otherwise assist that person in protecting themself (Edwards, 2012; National Conference of State Legislatures, 2018). However, it does not allow workers to talk to the media about their concerns or reveal the confidences the client has shared throughout the course of treatment. The 1991 *Wenden v. Trikha* case established a precedent in Canada for the ethical, but not legal, duty to warn third parties of threat of serious harm communicated by therapy clients (Kanani & Regehr, 2003). Social workers were deemed legally obligated to inform third parties only if "sufficient proximity" existed between the third party and the social workers; however, social workers were still bound by the mandates of the CASW *Code of Ethics* (Kanani & Regehr, 2003, p. 160).

Confidentiality is a highly charged and relatively complex area of ethics. It is influenced by laws set by various legislative bodies, by the results of civil litigation, and by regulations and policies. For example, subsequent to *Tarasoff* court cases in other jurisdictions have shaped its applications and limitations. In Canada, information sharing is regulated federally by the Office of the Privacy Commissioner of Canada (OPCC) and within each province and service sector (OPCC, 2013). The federal Privacy Act regulates information held by the government while the Personal Information Protection and Electronic Documents Act (PIPEDA) and similar provincial legislation governs the use of personal information by for-profit entities (OPCC, 2018). Provincial and territorial offices regulate the privacy protections for healthcare, nonprofit organizations, and local or regional governmental entities (OPCC, 2020).

In the United States the federal **Health Insurance Portability and Accountability Act (HIPAA)** and affiliated legislation have stipulations about the storage and sharing of patient records, and about verbal and other communications about clients (Health Information Technology for Economic and Clinical Health Act, 2009; HIPAA Medical Privacy Rule, 2003; U.S. Department of Health and Human Services, 2003a). The Family Educational Rights and Privacy Act (FERPA) "applies to public or private schools from kindergarten through universities. It gives parents (and, students, once they are 18) control over educational records allowing, them to review and correct the records and requiring consent for the disclosure of information in the record, except under exceptional circumstances" (Hepworth et al., 2022, p. 65).

In *Jaffee v. Redmond* (1996), the U.S. Supreme Court held client communications to be privileged and explicitly extended that **privilege** to licensed social workers. Disclosures about substance abuse treatment are strictly regulated in Confidentiality of Substance Use Disorder Patient Records (Legal Information Institute, n.d.). "According to these regulations, social workers and other professionals must protect records containing the identity, diagnosis, prognosis, or treatment of any client if they are maintained in connection with the performance of any drug abuse prevention function conducted, regulated, or directly or indirectly assisted by any department or agency of the United States" (Reamer, 2018, p. 121–122).

Confidentiality standards are also shaped by expectations that vary by client population and practice setting. For example, parents of minor clients typically have the legal right to know when their children appear for service and the nature of those services. However, minors' rights are protected according to age of the client, setting, and region in cases of emergency care, and when mental health services, treatment for sexually transmitted diseases, contraception, and prenatal care are sought.

Settings that take a team approach to service or involve a network of providers (such as in integrated health care or multisystemic therapy) would enlarge the network of helpers with an interest in case information and a right to be party to consultations about case progress (Franklin & Jordan, 2002; Lewers, 2019; Zerden et al., 2019).

The principle of maintaining client privacy is strongly linked to the principle of informed consent. In addition to ensuring that patients understand the pros and cons and options and limitations of various aspects of treatment, professionals must also discuss confidentiality, and inform clients about the intent to keep information private and the limitations of that intent. People have the right to understand *from the outset of service* the conditions under which their information must be shared, and they should agree to those conditions in writing. Thus, for example, a client would understand before a first appointment that using health insurance for counseling will result in a letter to the policy holder describing the services provided and explaining the insurance benefits. Or a client who describes parenting practices that raise the concern of abuse would have been aware from the beginning of services that such a disclosure would require an mandated report on child welfare.

In contemporary practice, confidentiality is also complicated by the ascendance of technology intended to lead to more efficient practice. Faxed documents, text messages, electronic records, e-mail, voice mail, video conferencing, and other tools can be used to enhance practice but can also jeopardize confidentiality by making records and other forms of stored information easier to access and disperse (Burton & van den Broek, 2009; Reamer, 2021a). Therefore, upholding the principle of confidentiality goes beyond exercising discretion. It requires vigilance so that the tools of practice are not vulnerable to misuse or misappropriation by others. It also requires new methods of tracking and destroying data when the required period for maintaining the record has lapsed.

Ethical standards for maintaining client privacy are outlined within both NASW's *Code of Ethics* (2021) and CASW's *Guidelines for Ethical Practice* (2005b):

- Both codes emphasize the social worker's responsibility to protect client information and confidentiality at all times.
- When disclosure of information is necessary for safety or mandated by regulations or a court order, social workers should disclose only enough information to achieve the desired purpose.

- Social workers are expected to inform clients in both individual and group counseling settings of confidentiality policies, and to take reasonable precautions to protect confidential information in the event of unforeseen circumstances, such as the social worker's departure from the practice.
- Social workers should avoid discussing identifying client information with students, consultants, or other professional contacts unless they have obtained consent from the client.
- Social workers must address breaches in confidentiality in an appropriate and ethical manner. (CASW, 2005b; NASW, 2021).

Innovations in electronic service delivery, social networking, search engines and other technology have given rise to guidelines about the limiting the risks to privacy in those platforms. For example, the NASW code cautions that "Social workers should avoid posting any identifying or confidential information about clients on professional websites or other forms of social media" (2021, 1.07r) and "Social workers should use applicable safeguards (such as encryption, firewalls, and passwords) when using electronic communications such as email, online posts, online chat sessions, mobile communication, and text messages" (2021, 1.07m).

The case in Box 7.2 illustrates practice that conforms to confidentiality standards.

BOX 7.2

Upholding the Standard

Althea is a school social worker who serves in several elementary schools. She has been collaborating with child protective services to offer support to Kareem, a seven-year-old boy who recently moved to the district. Kareem and his younger siblings came to the attention of CPS after their mother was hospitalized for a near fatal overdose and struggled to sufficiently care for them. Althea has been helping Kareem adjust to his new classroom and build a social network with his peers. His teacher, Ms. Lancaster, has been asking Althea for information about Kareem and his family so she can understand and help him better.

While Ms. Lancaster is a fellow professional and a potential collaborator in Kareem's care, Althea is cautious about how much

Continued

information to share with her and how the teacher will use it. In particular, she is concerned that Ms. Lancaster and some of the other faculty gossip about the families of their students. She is not comfortable with how information she might share about his case or his mother's condition will be used. Beyond these concerns, Althea has no permission from CPS or the family to share information with other professionals at the school.

After taking all this into account, Althea thanked Ms. Lancaster for her concern for Kareem. She shared with the teacher the goals they are working on, and the two discussed ways that his progress might be assisted or reinforced in the classroom. She did not share his family history or the reasons for his referral, but the two did discuss their perceptions of his strengths and struggles since arriving at the school.

Althea effectively balanced two competing priorities—to collaborate with fellow professionals who are essential members of her client's environment while protecting sensitive information about his case from misuse. While Althea may have concerns about the faculty's commitment to students' privacy, Ms. Lancaster must be regarded as an important member of Kareem's service system. As Berman-Rossi and Rossi (1990) note, "The social worker is called upon to help the child to make use of the school as well as to enable the school to become useful to the child" (p. 196). Althea's decision opens the lines of communication with Kareem's teacher while keeping the focus on service goals rather than on his personal history.

Althea's actions appear consistent with standards of the School Social Work Association of America and the Canadian Association of School Social Workers and Attendance Counsellors. Their position statement on confidentiality notes, "Information should be shared with other school personnel only on a need-to-know basis and only for compelling professional reasons. Prior to sharing confidential information, school social workers should evaluate the responsibility to and the welfare of the student. The responsibility to maintain confidentiality also must be weighed against the responsibility to the family and the school community. However, the focus should always be on what is best for the student" (Jarolmen, 2014, p. 137).

It appears that Althea did not discuss the teacher's request with Kareem's other service providers, and it is not clear whether she consulted her own supervisor or colleagues, though these discussions could have been useful in shaping her decision and developing a consistent plan for communications with school personnel. Althea might also have spoken with Kareem's parents or guardians to obtain informed consent for the information she intended to share. And, had Kareem been older, she might also have discussed with him what information he wanted the school to know or she could have redirected Ms. Lancaster to him to find out more.

Depending on her concerns and her responsibilities in relation to the school, Althea might consider acting on her observation that faculty members treat student information in an inappropriate and disrespectful manner. A school culture dominated by gossip about students not only impedes important communications, but also may reflect deeper structural issues concerning the way Kareem and others are viewed and treated. In contrast to Althea's case, the scenario in Box 7.3 illustrates the failure to keep client information confidential.

BOX 7.3

Violating the Standard

Antoine is a thirty-something single professional. He met Elise at a cocktail party and in the course of conversation told her he was a therapist. "Wow," she said, "that must be exhausting . . . listening to people's problems all day long!"

"It is," he replied. "Sometimes it's a burden, and sometimes it's amazing how messed up people are—even people who seem so put together on the outside. Sometimes I wish I didn't know so much about people I should respect."

"Like what?" she asked.

Antoine knew he should not say more, but he felt caught. He had opened the door to her question and he wanted to keep the conversation going. Besides, he was proud of his work and felt it was often misunderstood. He forged on, trying to keep his remarks general and identities vague. "Well, a man who sees me to deal with his Internet porn addiction is in the government. . . . I'm sure he's no risk as long as he can talk to me and keep those demons under control . . . but it just goes to show we never know about the people around us."

This is a particularly egregious violation of client privacy in that Antoine disclosed highly sensitive information for his own self-aggrandizement. Not only does it represent a breach of confidentiality, even without specific identifying information, but it may also signal other vulnerabilities in Jeffrey's professionalism and respect for clients. In their work on client exploitation, Epstein and Simon (1990) note that such disclosures are a form of exhibitionism, akin to excessive self-disclosure by a therapist, or seeking fame by having a well-known client. As such, it may serve as a marker for other steps along the path to boundary and other violations.

At the very least, Jeffrey's disclosure is a failure of containment, or the ability to keep to ourselves information that we know others might find scintillating. Should Antoine try to rationalize his disclosure by contending that the public official's habits render him unsuitable for office, the method he chose to share the information undermines his argument. In other words, if he had legitimate concerns that the man's addiction was placing others at risk, his first steps would be to discuss the concerns with the client and with a consultant who would also respect the client's confidentiality, not with a cocktail party acquaintance. Such conversations would help Antoine determine whom the official's behavior put at risk, and his responsibility, if any, to alert those at risk.

Passing along information that was received in the sanctity of the helping relationship is a disturbing violation of trust. And, once the information is out, Antoine is powerless to call it back, as Elise may now share it with others until it takes on a life of its own. Perhaps she knows local government officials. What if she says to one of them, "You have some pretty kinky coworkers, I hear"? Antoine has opened himself up to severe professional and civil sanctions should his acquaintance make the disclosed information public or bring it to the attention of his client.

Perhaps there are already rumors circulating about the individual's porn addiction. If so, this does not legitimize Jeffrey's actions. The source of the information differentiates confidentiality breaches from mere gossip. That is, the manner in which helping professionals come to possess information places regulations on what they are permitted to do with it. Information that is shared by clients or collateral contacts in the context of a professional relationship has special protections. Personal communications with a friend, colleague, or family member may carry the presumption of privacy, but that is mutual (expected of both parties) and less

BOX 7.4

Resolving Dilemmas in Upholding Confidentiality: Suicide and Secrets

Danielle, age sixteen, had been a client in Rebecca's private practice for approximately a month when she died in an apparent suicide from an overdose of several prescription drugs. Danielle had been referred to Rebecca by her parents, who were concerned with her declining grades and sour disposition. During the few sessions they had together, Rebecca learned that Danielle was preoccupied with her body image and sense of worth. In part this seemed to be driven by her boyfriend Antoine's criticisms of her appearance and his warnings that she shouldn't "let herself go" like her mother and sister had done.

Danielle had tentatively divulged that Antoine had been physically aggressive toward her, and that there had been one episode of forced sexual activity. When Rebecca pressed her for details, Danielle downplayed the incident, saying, "He was just trying to encourage me to be less uptight." At the time of Danielle's death, Rebecca was still trying to build trust with her client and formulate an assessment, but she suspected elements of depression, an eating disorder, and substance abuse, perhaps in order to self-medicate or lose weight.

Danielle's parents are tormented by their daughter's death and have contacted Rebecca to ask about their daughter's state of mind so they can better understand what happened.

formally articulated than the presumption of privacy in a helping relationship. Violation of a friend's privacy may cost the friendship, but it doesn't usually carry legal or ethical penalties. Although it is a fundamental concept for the helping professions, confidentiality can conflict with other ethical standards, thus creating dilemmas. An example of one such case is in Box 7.4, "Suicide and Secrets."

The death of a child is among life's most traumatic and unnatural experiences. Losses from suicide are even more challenging in that the deaths are sudden and intentional, and often violent. Suicide touches all those involved with the deceased, as peers, family, neighbors, teachers, coworkers, and others struggle to make sense of a seemingly senseless loss.

Danielle's tragic death creates a multidimensional dilemma for her therapist. On one hand, her grieving parents are seeking information ostensibly as part of their bereavement process. Because Danielle was a minor, they may have legal rights to case information. However, the ethical standards of Rebecca's profession protect a client's confidentiality, even in death. And if Rebecca shares information with the intent of bringing Danielle's parents comfort and understanding, where should she stop in revealing the girl's confidences? Finally, what role might any perceptions of culpability or liability play in Rebecca's inclination to share (or withhold) information about the case?

Applying the Six-Question Model

Who Can Be Helpful to Rebecca?

Rebecca needs several forms of assistance: interpersonal support to deal with the sudden and traumatic loss of her client, assistance in anticipating and preparing for requests for information and other examinations of her practices prior to Danielle's death, and legal and ethical advice in responding to Danielle's parents' request for information and other inquiries. Rebecca may want to turn to different resources for each of these issues.

Deaths from natural causes are less common in mental health, child welfare, and school settings than they are in fields of practice such as nursing homes or health and hospice settings. When deaths do occur in mental health and similar settings, they tend to be traumatic and un-anticipated—the result of suicide, accidents, or interpersonal violence (Strom-Gottfried & Mowbray, 2006). Deaths by suicide have a distinct impact on the professionals involved (Halligan & Corcoran, 2001). An assortment of quantitative, qualitative, and case studies indicate significant professional and personal effects following the death of a client by suicide including shock, fear of another incident, guilt, distrust, intrusive thoughts, a sense of betrayal, depression, helplessness, loss of confidence, fear, hypomania, anger, and avoidance of triggering stimuli (Chemtob et al., 1988; Cooper, 1995; Gulfi et al., 2010; Menninger, 1991; Tillman, 2008; Veilleux, 2011).

Dealing with the emotional impact of her client's death will help Rebecca's own psychosocial well-being and will ensure that she doesn't confound her ethical decision making with her grief processes. For support during this time, Rebecca may turn to her colleagues, her personal support system, her faith community, or therapeutic resources. As she processes her grief with people who are not entitled to information about the case, Rebecca should be certain that the focus of this assistance is on her and her sense of loss, rather than on Danielle or the facts of her life and death.

For the purposes of debriefing about her work on the case, conducting a **psychological autopsy**, and preparing for inquiries into the case, Rebecca should turn to her fellow professionals (Caulkins, 2019; Cavanagh et al., 2003; Sanders, et al., 2008). Hopefully she has an established system for supervision or peer consultation that she can mobilize following the death and in anticipation of the dilemmas that will likely follow. Had she sought feedback when Danielle revealed troubling information during treatment, this consultation would be a natural extension of assistance in an already complex case. If she did not, she will need to pull together people who can provide clear-headed advice in a time of crisis and ensure that she makes sound decisions in the aftermath of Danielle's death and in services to her current caseload.

Rebecca should also seek legal consultation. An attorney can advise her on Danielle's parents' rights to case information, the processes they must use to obtain access, and the legal risks and benefits in withholding case information from them. Legal consultation will also be wise should Rebecca have concerns about her liability in Danielle's death. If there is a possibility that she might face accusations of negligence in not detecting warning signs of suicide, insufficiently assessing the risk of lethality, or failing to notify Danielle's parents about risks she faced from her possible drug use and her boyfriend's abusive behavior, it would be best to know her legal rights and alternatives at the outset.

What Are Rebecca's Options?

At the two extremes, Rebecca's options are to decline to share any information with Danielle's parents or to make all case information available to them. The latter may include verbal discussions about Danielle's care and/ or Rebecca surrendering the treatment records from her services. An intermediate option would involve sharing a limited amount of information about the case, such as Rebecca's knowledge of and response to any suicide threats or the status of treatment goals at the time of Danielle's death. Families who have experienced suicide are often plagued with the question "Why?" and by feelings of responsibility for the suicide. If Rebecca believes that the parents' queries originated in these areas, she could target her response to share what she has observed or concluded in relation to these questions. The distinction here is that Rebecca is emphasizing her own impressions while sharing limited information about the case itself.

When Has Rebecca Made Similar Decisions?

While Rebecca may have never experienced the sudden death of a client or a request by survivors for case information, she has undoubtedly seen minors in her practice prior to treating Danielle. Therefore, a starting place in her decision making about what to share following Danielle's death would be what information she would ordinarily share with the parents about the teen's case. Related to this is what understanding she had with Danielle and her parents about privacy in the case. That is, while Danielle's parents may have the legal right to data on their child's care, the informed consent processes at the outset of treatment would have established the ethical limits on confidentiality.

Clinicians treating adolescent clients commonly seek agreement with the child and parents about the information to be disclosed between the two parties. This conversation helps to inform all parties about the boundaries and conditions for information sharing. It provides comfort to parents, who are rightfully concerned about their child's well-being, and it provides security to the client, who may wish to freely disclose troubling or painful material in therapy. One common standard is that the worker should share any information that would raise the parents' concerns about the safety of their child; the informed consent process elaborates on what type of information this would include in practice. If the agreement is that the youth and the clinician will give periodic updates to the parents on progress toward treatment goals, without specific information on the issues under discussion, that, too, would need to be articulated at the outset of service. The nature of Rebecca's specific understanding with Danielle and her parents would help to shape her decision in this matter. If the agreement was that information would be shared freely, Rebecca might feel entitled to share information now. If the agreement was that only a limited scope of information would be revealed, that might apply, too.

Rebecca's decision might be shaped by her actions during the course of treatment. That is, if she was faithful to the informed consent agreement in disclosing information to Danielle's parents, she would likely be less reluctant to disclose information now. However, if she failed to notify the parents about information they might have expected to learn, she might be uncomfortable disclosing it after the client's death. Rebecca should address any discomfort about possible lapses in the treatment process separately from her current dilemma. In other words, Rebecca's failure to follow the informed consent agreement during service is not a sufficient reason to continue withholding information or to share it freely now to compensate for her error.

Another precedent on which Rebecca might rely is her handling of cases where questions have been raised about the appropriateness of services rendered. If she believes that the parents' query arises out of their suspicion of malpractice or their intent to sue, and Rebecca has had similar experiences, she should consider how they would apply in this situation. Since malpractice litigation is an adversarial process, Rebecca might be very circumspect in her communications about the case and refuse to volunteer information unless a court order compels her to do so.

Where Will Ethical and Clinical Standards Lead Her?

Rule-based ethics. How would the deontological perspective view Rebecca's choices? For the option to strictly maintain Danielle's privacy, the implied rule is that the social worker should never disclose information unless the client agrees to it through informed consent, or more broadly, that no one should share another's confidences without that person's permission. This seems like a good rule for lay people and professionals. It is reflected in ethical standards and in professional practice. Following the deontological perspective would thus refer Rebecca back to the original understanding with Danielle and her parents about sharing information in the case. Danielle's original informed consent would then form the basis of Rebecca's decision about what she could ethically share (or withhold) following her client's death.

What rules are embedded in the decision to share information with the parents? Depending on the parents' motivations in seeking the information, the rules might include "It is acceptable to share information if it will help bring the family comfort" or "It is acceptable to share case information once a client is deceased" or "Parents have a right to know about the services provided to minors, so the social worker should surrender the data on request." While each of these may have merit in some cases, it is unlikely we would accept any of them as universal laws.

For the first, it may be hard to discern what will bring comfort, and the risk of revelation is that it may bring either comfort or distress at the expense of the client's privacy. The second rule would essentially overturn the promise of privacy, undermining the hallmark of the helping process. While some may argue that privacy rights are moot if the client is deceased, clients live on in the memories and relationships they leave behind. These can be irretrievably damaged if secrets are revealed without the client's consent. Last, while the third rule on parents' rights may be supported in law for many services, procedures, and jurisdictions, there are circumstances where parents are asked not to exercise that right in deference to the trust necessary for the therapeutic relationship (Corey et al., 2019).

The ethical merit of Rebecca's other choice, releasing information that is limited in some way, would depend on the basis for her decision on what to reveal. For example, disclosing information within the bounds of the informed consent agreement would be a defensible rule. Revealing information on her impressions, rather than revealing Danielle's secrets, might also be defensible. Disseminating information solely to appease the parents and forestall litigation would not be.

Outcome-based ethics. How would a utilitarian perspective view Rebecca's choices? The consequences of withholding all case information include upholding the principle of confidentiality while protecting Danielle's privacy and taking a stand for the same on behalf of other clients. It would mean not revealing Danielle's secrets and avoiding any damage they might cause to her memory. Withholding the information would place the good of the deceased person ahead of that of her living parents. A refusal to share case information might very well be troubling to Danielle's parents. It might exacerbate their distress and make them suspicious of Rebecca's motives. It might encourage them to pursue legal action for access.

Conversing about the case and sharing records would have inverse consequences. It would jeopardize the principle of confidentiality, reveal Danielle's secrets, and perhaps lead to mistrust among current and future clients. While it might placate Danielle's parents, there is no guarantee that would be the case. In fact, learning disturbing information might exacerbate the parents' grief. A further consequence for Rebecca is that it could be construed as a violation of her ethical responsibilities. As such, it might result in a complaint to her licensure board or professional association. If the breach were deemed to have violated HIPAA, there might be additional penalties and perhaps even a lawsuit or licensure action for breach of privacy.

Values. The primary social work value at play in this case is that of integrity—the social worker must behave in a trustworthy fashion. Embracing that value would mean declining to release unauthorized case information to Danielle's parents. Because social workers also value service to others and supporting relationships, it may be difficult for Rebecca to refuse the parents' request. However, Rebecca's greatest responsibility is to her client and to acting in accord with Danielle's expectations when they commenced treatment.

Professional standards. The ethical standards in this case are fairly straightforward. As noted at the outset of this chapter, NASW standards permit communications for compelling professional reasons and to prevent harmful acts. However, both the NASW and CASW codes also explicitly state, "Social workers should protect the confidentiality of deceased clients consistent with the preceding standards" (CASW, 2005b, 1.5.11; NASW, 2021, 1.07r). The CASW guidelines also require that the social worker discuss policies regarding confidentiality and minors with the parents prior to the first session with a child, and that confidential information be disclosed "when such disclosure is in the best interest of the child" (CASW, 2005b, 1.5.5).

Ethical principles. The principles of autonomy, fidelity, and nonmaleficence are all relevant to the case. Of Rebecca's choices, the decision to withhold case information best honors Danielle's right to make her own decisions about what she wanted others to know or not know about her life. That option also demonstrates Rebecca's honesty in that she would be acting in good faith to assure that Danielle's privacy is protected. Discretion in information sharing also meets the principle of nonmaleficence if it best protects Danielle's legacy. Some might argue that Danielle's legacy is not the real Danielle unless people better understand the struggles and events she experienced when she was alive. While authenticity and honesty are valid concepts, the principle of autonomy grants every person the right to keep her thoughts and experiences private. If Danielle chose to present a different face to the world than the one she was experiencing in her innermost thoughts, it is not Rebecca's duty or right to undermine that choice.

Laws and policies. Seeking legal consultation would be essential for Rebecca to weigh her choices according to relevant laws which may specify parental rights to information during treatment and following a minor's death. They would also specify the penalties for professionals who disclose of client records without proper authorization. HIPAA or PIPEDA and related acts might also be relevant in this decision, as would the confidentiality provisions in various jurisdictions, if they are more stringent or specific. Because the language in these statutes presumes the client is living, the applicability to Danielle's case may be open to interpretation. For example, some states may forbid disclosure of minors' protected health information including information concerning past treatment. In states that permit or require disclosure, or those that have no law, the professional may release information unless he or she deems such disclosure would be an invasion of the minor's privacy, endanger or cause harm to the client, or otherwise not be in the best interest of the client (Stefan, n.d.).

Practice principles. The practical expectations concerning confidentiality are congruent with the ethical standards. Clinicians go to great lengths to protect the privacy of their clients, revealing information in only a narrow range of circumstances, typically with the client's permission or when compelled to do so to prevent harm such as child maltreatment. This case offers no potential for prevention and no capacity by which Rebecca can obtain her client's guidance or permission. She may use previous conversations around informed consent as a guide to the client's wishes, but those will provide only an approximation of permission, since at the outset of therapy neither Rebecca nor Danielle likely anticipated the issues that would arise.

Entities that wish to compel clinicians to surrender case information have processes at their disposal to do so. Agencies and individuals can issue subpoenas for testimony or records regarding a case. Should the professional object to the disclosure, the court can review the merits of the request and the refusal and issue an order for compliance if it so chooses. If the disclosure is ordered by the court but the client refuses, the worker faces a double bind where sanctions may arise from honoring either party over the other. However, in Rebecca's dilemma, those who are likely to petition for the information are probably the same people representing the client's estate. As a result, if presented with a court order to surrender information in the case, Rebecca might feel disloyal to Danielle, but she should be secure in the knowledge that she did not surrender her client's confidences carelessly and without due process.

Case information. The discussion of subpoenas and court orders reminds us that ethical decision making involves consideration of the facts of the case. We do not know the nature of Danielle's despair or suicidal ideation prior to her death. Furthermore, we do not have information about Danielle's maturity at the time of her disclosures to Rebecca or when she assented to treatment. We do not know about the veracity of her accounts of abuse by Antoine. We do not know Rebecca's liability in the case, or what Danielle's parents intend in seeking information. If there was no indication of suicidal intent during treatment, if Rebecca's clinical practices were sound, and if Danielle's parents simply want assurance that they were not at fault for her death, Rebecca could probably respond to their queries without violating the confidentiality her client had been led to expect. If the parents simply want an opportunity to talk about their daughter and her struggles with a safe person outside the family, such a meeting would require little disclosure on Rebecca's part. Shifts in the facts of the case, however, might lead in another direction, as the decision-making schema clearly supports Rebecca in withholding information on the case unless she is compelled to release it (Pinals, 2019).

Why Is Rebecca Selecting a Particular Course of Action?

Any given resolution to an ethical dilemma can be rendered inappropriate if it is selected for the wrong reasons. Therefore, it is vital for helping professionals to examine their motivations in favoring one resolution strategy over another.

Earlier in this chapter we alluded to possible treatment errors that can take on greater significance in light of the client's sudden death. Failing to establish clear guidelines for sharing information with the minor's parents, failing to follow through on information-sharing agreements that were made, or negligently addressing the client's risks to herself or others are just some examples of possible errors. If she did make errors in practice, Rebecca may be tempted to withhold information from the parents because of her own liability. In fact, she may even receive legal advice to do so. While there may be valid reasons to withhold information in the case, from an ethical perspective, doing so to obscure her own errors would place Rebecca's interests over the interests of the parents, and potentially Danielle's interests. It might also be strategically unwise, in that attempts to hide errors can exasperate the other parties and exacerbate the errors themselves.

Rebecca may also perceive confidentiality as an all-or-nothing proposition. This stance would push her to the tell-or-don't-tell extremes among her options. In doing so, she may overlook valid options of limited, discreet disclosures that could contribute to the parents' peace of mind without revealing information that would taint the memory of their daughter, violate her privacy, or indict those, like her boyfriend Antoine, who are still living.

The principle of publicity might favor any of the choices, depending on Rebecca's rationale for employing a given choice. Fellow professionals and other teen clients would likely understand and respect Rebecca's strict adherence to patient privacy to support the sanctity of the therapeutic relationship. However, other parents and the court of public opinion might find that stance irrelevant in light of the patient's death, and heartless in light of the parents' despair. Should she decide to share information, the positions of these stakeholders would probably be reversed. Withholding information only to serve her own interests or to stonewall investigation of the case would probably be condemned by a variety of observers and violate the smell test.

What happens when Rebecca puts herself in others' shoes? If she were the parent, Rebecca would no doubt have the same questions and expectations as Danielle's parents. What if she were Danielle? Based on her knowledge of the teen, what does Rebecca believe she would want? Perhaps she would wish to keep her relationship with Antoine and her substance use concealed. But would she permit certain information to be shared if it brought comfort to her parents and facilitated their mourning? Reversibility always requires speculation as the social worker endeavors to view the choices from another's point of view. In this case it may help Rebecca to be faithful to her client's wishes and the spirit of patient privacy while protecting the parents (and Danielle's memory) from hurtful and unhelpful information.

In meeting the mom or mentor test, Rebecca need not rely on her imagination about what people she respects might do in this situation. As part of her decision making in the case, she can call on her mentors for input about her choices without sharing identifying case information. Like all consultation, these conversations may lead her to different conclusions, but in doing so they will ensure that she has evaluated the case from a variety of angles.

How Should Rebecca Carry Out Her Decision?

While some risk management practices would suggest that professionals avoid contact with the aggrieved and bereaved family of a client who has died by suicide, clinical wisdom and practical experiences seem to suggest otherwise (Jordan, 2008; Jordan & McIntosh, 2011; Pearlman, 1992; Schacht, 1992). That is, while social workers may be reluctant to reach out to a family and express their sadness at the death for fear that it will open them up to questions and condemnation, such an authentic expression of shared loss is usually viewed positively by the family as a sign of caring (Kleepsies et al., 1993). Conversely, avoiding such contact or staying away from the funeral or visiting hours may be interpreted as cold and heartless and may exacerbate the family's distrust and anger at the worker (Wurst et al., 2010).

The conversations Rebecca has with the parents immediately following the loss will set the stage for her approach to them at a later point. Those encounters will be an opportunity for Rebecca to demonstrate sensitivity and professionalism and gauge the parents' concern. Rebecca should defer substantive discussions about Danielle's state of mind or the parents' requests for information to another time and setting. In addition to allowing them to find a more appropriate venue and context for the conversation, addressing their concerns at a later point will allow Rebecca to plan her strategy and allow all parties to meet when they are no longer experiencing the disorientation that immediately follows a traumatic loss.

When the meeting is arranged, Rebecca should establish the scope of the conversation so that the parents do not arrive with unrealistic expectations. Rebecca must manage several tensions in the meeting. She must be sensitive to the parents' pain and allow them to express their grief without taking an ongoing role as their therapist. She must also be clear about the confidentiality limits she will follow and the rationale behind them, while being sensitive to their needs and sympathetic to their request.

Rebecca should expect an emotional and delicate conversation. She should be well prepared for it in advance, anticipating what she wants to say and the ways in which she will address various rejoinders, pleas, or queries from the parents. She should also anticipate her own feelings that may come up in the session and use her consultation to prepare for them. She should make use of her professional support system to debrief after the meeting and prepare for next steps as needed. Rebecca should have kept a record of her actions throughout the duration of the case, and she must be certain to document the content, flow, and conclusions reached in the meeting with Danielle's parents as well (Corey et al., 2019; Kane et al., 2002; Reamer, 2018).

This case reflects the complex and emotionally trying aspects of decision making about confidentiality. Having worked through the 6Q steps on that case, it is time to try your skills on another privacy dilemma in Box 7.5.

BOX 7.5

A Case for You

Donna's field placement is with a large child welfare unit. Because most of the investigations take place in schools, client's homes, courthouses, and police stations, none of the workers has a private office. Instead, the staff members have cubicles in a large room, from which they can do paperwork, make phone calls, and have video-calls with earphones. A conference room is available for confidential meetings.

In her first two weeks, Donna observed a lot of cross-cubicle conversations, where one worker would pop up and ask another the status of a case. In addition to creating a noisy environment as a background for phone calls, it also let everyone hear about families that were not part of their own caseload. She also noticed that workers often left their case information open on their desks or computer screens. When she asked about it, her colleagues assured her, "Access to this suite is protected by name badges, so clients could never get back here."

Today, Donna's supervisor stopped by and apologized for not setting aside regular supervision time. "Let's go to the café and get a bite to eat—we can talk over lunch."

These experiences conflicted with what Donna had learned about confidentiality, but she wondered if she was being overly sensitive as a newcomer. Perhaps the material in her books and classes was not realistic for settings such as her placement? Not all of the child welfare workers had social work degrees or licenses, so maybe the standards didn't apply to them?

As you process this case, it might help to recall the earlier discussion of integrity and the premises of virtue ethics. Are there ethical concerns at stake? If so, should Donna act? And how?

Conclusion

Confidentiality is the cornerstone of the helping process. The assurance of privacy creates a climate in which an individual's most intimate acts, thoughts, and emotions can be revealed and addressed. Requests for case information can be fulfilled with waivers signed by the client or duly issued subpoenas or court orders. While there are many legal and ethical protections for privacy, the right is limited for certain populations (minors), and for certain acts (child abuse) and actions (danger to oneself or others). Privacy may also be limited as a condition of treatment. For example, clients in involuntary or correctional settings may have to agree to certain forms of information sharing, and clients who use insurance for services will find that some information is shared with the payer in order to secure reimbursement. Ethical standards about confidentiality require that people be informed up front about the limits on privacy. Such informed consent protects both the social worker and the client should circumstances arise that require disclosures to be made.

Even with proper informed consent and permission to make disclosures, professionals are expected to exercise discretion in the amount of information they seek and in the amount they share. They must safeguard data by treating records and electronic communications with care and avoid discussing cases in nonsecure settings, such as lobbies, elevators, or restaurants. Communications about cases should be in the clients' interests, not for the comfort of the worker, the amusement of friends, or the satisfaction of family members.

For Continuing Conversation

1. The NASW Code of Ethics states, "Social workers should avoid searching or gathering client information electronically unless there are compelling professional reasons, and when appropriate, with the client's informed consent" (2021, 1.07q). In what situations would it be ethical to do online searches for information about clients or prospective clients?

2. Have you ever been tempted to tell a friend or family member about one of your cases? What led to that impulse? How did you handle it? What advice could you give colleagues about avoiding that temptation?
3. If a client told you she had committed a crime in the past, what factors would you consider in deciding whether to breach the client's privacy?

Key Concepts

Confidentiality. The professional responsibility to safeguard private information solicited from or collected about clients. Exceptions to confidentiality occur when there is a conflict with the therapist's duty to warn or duty to protect.

Duty to warn. The professional responsibility to balance respect for client privacy and autonomy with the risk to others. Standards and statutes based on duty to warn require professionals to warn potential victims and/or law enforcement authorities if there is reason to suspect an imminent danger of a client harming themselves or others. Sometimes known as the duty to protect.

Health Insurance Portability and Accountability Act (HIPAA). A 1996 U.S. federal law that restricts access to individuals' private medical information.

Mandatory reporting. The requirement of certain professionals who have regular contact with vulnerable individuals such as children, persons with disabilities, and older adults to report abuse, whether observed or suspected. Types of abuse that must be reported vary by profession, and may include neglect, or financial, physical, and sexual abuse.

Privacy. The ability of a person, family, or group to suppress information, prevent observation, or avoid interference.

Privilege. The right of a social worker, lawyer, or other professional to refuse to divulge confidential information regarding their cases.

Psychological autopsy. The thorough collection of information that is likely to help reconstruct the psychosocial environment of individuals who have died by suicide. It may include interviews with family and friends, health records, and other available data, to better understand the circumstances of the individual's death.

CHAPTER 8

Competence

Introduction

According to the principle of **competence**, people we are serving must be able to trust that we are qualified to care for them, and that we will do so to the best of our abilities. This means that a social worker is ethical, unbiased, has the knowledge and experience necessary to address clients' needs, and uses resources such as **supervision** and continuing education to ensure ongoing effectiveness. Competence also implies that professionals will be self-regulating—that they will refer cases when they do not have the requisite abilities, engage in self-care, seek help if personal problems or addictions impair their work, and pursue additional knowledge, training, or **consultation** to maintain and advance their skills. Competent practice means professionals know their limits and take action themselves to address these limits, instead of waiting for someone else to tell them they are in over their heads (British Columbia Association of Social Workers, 2011). A crucial element of competence is the capacity to work across differences such as race, age, ability, socioeconomic status, and language fluency. Cultural competence, nondiscrimination, and anti-oppressive responsibilities are addressed in Chapter 10.

Competence is related to the principles of beneficence and nonmaleficence in that competent practice involves doing good and not doing harm. It is applies to other standards such as informed consent, in that clients have a right to know about the worker's ability to help them with the needs that they present. In situations where the worker must still deliver services despite minimal competence (for example, in regions with scarce resources or using a new intervention), good practice demands that clients understand the relative risks and benefits of seeking treatment under these circumstances and that clinicians do whatever they can to bolster their competence, including getting extra training, reviewing available literature, seeking specialized supervision, and carefully evaluating the services rendered.

Elements of competence are as follows:

- Knowledge, experience, and skills necessary to address clients' needs
- Use of supervision and consultation and other resources to ensure effective practice
- Engagement in self-care to maintain physical, spiritual, and psychological health
- Freedom from impairments that may diminish effective caring
- **Self-regulation** and self-awareness—being ready and willing to refer cases when necessary and to seek help when impaired, burned out, or not competent
- Continuing education and training to maintain and advance knowledge and skills

Social work provisions related to competence state that

- "Social workers should provide services and represent themselves as competent only within the boundaries of their education, training, license, certification, consultation received, supervised experience, or other relevant professional experience." (NASW, 2021, 1.04a)
- "Professional self-care is paramount for competent and ethical social work practice. Professional demands, challenging workplace climates, and exposure to trauma warrant that social workers maintain personal and professional health, safety, and integrity. Social work organizations, agencies, and educational institutions are encouraged to promote organizational policies, practices, and materials to support social workers' self-care." (NASW, 2021, p. 2)
- [Social workers should not accept employment, provide services, or use unfamiliar interventions without] "appropriate study, training, consultation, and supervision from people who are competent in those interventions or techniques." (NASW, 2021, 1.04b)

- [In the absence of recognized standards on an] "emerging area of practice, social workers should exercise careful judgment and take responsible steps (including appropriate education, research, training, consultation, and supervision) to ensure the competence of their work and to protect clients from harm." (NASW, 2021, 1.04c)
- [More generally,] "social workers should seek the advice and counsel of colleagues whenever such consultation is in the best interests of clients." (NASW, 2021, 2.05a)

And, social workers who provide supervision, consultation, or instruction should do so only within their areas of knowledge and competence, and they are expected to stay abreast of current developments in the field.

- "Social workers do not claim formal social work education in an area of expertise or training solely by attending a lecture, demonstration, conference, workshop or similar teaching presentation." (CASW, 2005b, 7.1.4)
- "Social workers uphold provincial and territorial regulations for continuing professional education, where such regulations exist." (CASW, 2005b, 7.1.5).

The case in Box 8.1 demonstrates the strategies for upholding standards of competence.

BOX 8.1

Upholding the Standard

Liu has recently opened a full-time private practice after five years in an agency setting. She is awaiting designation as an approved provider for several insurance companies and in the meantime is finding it difficult to sustain her cash flow with self-paid clients.

Today Liu received a call from a woman whom she had seen in counseling for several months the year before. The woman and her husband recently adopted a baby from China and are concerned about the child's development and capacity for attachment. Because she had been happy with Liu's care in the past, she felt confident in Liu's ability to help with this new issue.

Liu was in a quandary. As a Chinese woman, she might be well positioned to help the client and her husband understand the child and the issues she presents. She had already forged a trusting relationship with the parents and might be of further help to them. On the other hand, Liu had never worked with children, had no expertise in adoption, and was not familiar with the literature on bonding and attachment. While she desperately wanted to take the case, she decided that she did not have the requisite expertise to help with such a crucial issue.

Liu met with the couple once to observe the child and talk with the parents about their needs, observations, and expectations. She then facilitated a referral to colleagues at her former workplace with expertise in early childhood disorders. She offered to be available to the couple and the receiving therapist if her cultural and family therapy expertise would be beneficial to the case.

Liu's decision represents professional maturity and ethical sophistication in putting the clients' best interests before her own financial needs. While she could have rationalized agreeing to work with the family, her understanding of the dynamic issues in the case led her to exercise restraint and refer the family to someone better prepared to help. Liu's actions were in keeping with standards in the NASW *Code of Ethics* that "social workers should refer clients to other professionals when the other professionals' specialized knowledge or expertise is needed to serve clients fully" (NASW, 2021, 1.16a).

In exercising **self-awareness** and self-restraint, Liu shows that she is practicing within her area of competence and upholds her fiduciary responsibility to her clients, who must rely on her ability and judgments. In declining the case, Liu furthers the respect and trust that were built in the previous episode of treatment. In the long run, her demonstrated concern for their well-being and her strong sense of self may encourage the couple to return to her in the future should they have needs in areas where she can be of help.

Box 8.2 illustrates the hazards when social workers fail to adhere to standards on competence.

Kerry's willingness to speak up about her observations of Jeb's behavior demonstrates moral courage. In contrast, Nancy's decision to overlook

BOX 8.2

Violating the Standard

Jeb has worked at a mental health center for more than twenty years. Since his wife left him last year, Jeb has poured himself into his work, taking on the most difficult cases, working long hours, becoming exceptionally distressed when clients struggle or withdraw from treatment. Kerry, the administrative assistant in his unit, has observed other changes in Jeb's behavior. He disappears from the office during the day for hours at a time and appears giddy and incoherent when he returns. His documentation is months behind, and he is often forgetful, missing meetings and repeating himself in conversations.

Kerry was reluctant to approach Jeb directly, so she raised her concerns with Jeb's supervisor, Nancy. Nancy suggested Kerry mind her own business. "Jeb's going through a rough time right now. I don't want to make him feel worse when work is all he has these days. I'm not going to confront him with such vague accusations when he's carrying half the cases for the unit."

Jeb's impairment is a disservice to him and his clients. It also puts Nancy at risk for enabling his negligent practice. While Jeb's coworkers may be reluctant to assume that he is drinking while out of the office or experiencing loss or depression, they don't need to *determine why* he is acting as he is, but they do need to *describe what* they have observed. Kerry, Nancy, and other workers can substantiate a pattern of problematic behavior including, at the very least, errant recordkeeping, extreme reactions to client difficulties, and missed appointments. Like other professions, social work's ethics codes have standards that speak to this situation:

> "Social workers who have direct knowledge of a social work colleague's impairment that is due to personal problems, psychosocial distress, substance abuse, or mental health difficulties and that interferes with practice effectiveness should consult with that colleague when feasible and assist the colleague in taking remedial action." (NASW, 2021, 2.09a)

> "Social workers who believe that a social work colleague's impairment interferes with practice effectiveness and that the colleague

has not taken adequate steps to address the impairment should take action through appropriate channels established by employers, agencies, NASW, licensing and regulatory bodies, and other professional organizations." (NASW, 2021, 2.09b).

"Social workers take appropriate action where a breach of professional practice and professional ethics occur, conducting themselves in a manner that is consistent with the Code of Ethics and Guidelines for Ethical Practice, and standards of their regulatory body." (CASW, 2005b, 7.2.1)

In keeping with their codes, the professionals who are Jeb's colleagues should speak with him to share their concerns and their willingness to assist him to get the help he needs. The organization's human resource department will be an important resource for such a meeting, particularly if it is conducted as a supervisory intervention. Koocher and Keith-Spiegel (2008) suggest that workers prep carefully for such a meeting, holding it in a private and business-like environment, alerting the worker to the purpose of the session when arranging the meeting time ("I want to share some observations with you," "I need to speak with you about my concerns"), remaining calm and confident in the session, staying mindful of the personal and organizational interests at play in the conversation, and approaching the individual in a factual and nonjudgmental manner. Box 8.3 summarizes the elements to consider when approaching colleagues about competence concerns.

Role and goal clarity are important here. The person raising the concerns, whether a supervisor, subordinate, or peer, should avoid the roles

BOX 8.3

Six Considerations for Sharing Concerns with a Colleague

1. Make careful preparations
2. Consider meeting environment
3. Communicate purpose
4. Remain calm and confident
5. Stay mindful of personal and organizational interests
6. Approach the individual as an ally who will work with them to address the concerns

Source: Koocher & Keith-Spiegel, 2008.

of detective, confessor, or therapist, and should focus instead on helping the **impaired worker** to develop a mutually satisfactory plan for change. That agreement may include a self-referral for counseling, referral to an employee assistance program or other service, notification of other individuals or entities about the concerns, and/or a corrective action plan with specific consequences for future transgressions.

Clearly this is not an easy conversation for either party. Empathy for the impaired worker and the skillful application of communication strategies are essential for successfully navigating this "crucial conversation" (Patterson et al., 2002, p. 1). Koocher and Keith-Spiegel (2008) recommend that the person raising the issue debrief with a colleague, and mentally organize the information that comes up in the conversation before documenting the discussion. Organizational policies may, of course, structure the worker's options by dictating the type of follow-up that must take place.

Kerry may not be a social worker, but she clearly has ethics on her side. She should not be deterred by Nancy's reluctance to intervene with Jeb. Kerry and others who have observed Jeb's difficulties should report this information to the agency administration. This is not a matter of being disloyal to Jeb: a confrontation may be an opening for the help he needs to stop a dangerous, destructive spiral. And the coworkers' actions are in service of his clients and other vulnerable people who need and deserve the very best services available. They may have organizational and personnel policies on their side as well. And, for some workers, intervening to stop professional impairment or incompetence may be a condition of their license, such that in acting to limit a coworker's liability they are also mitigating their own.

In "The Case of the Shirking Violet" (Box 8.4), you have the opportunity to follow the ethical decision-making process through a dilemma involving professional competence.

BOX 8.4

Resolving Dilemmas in Competence: The Case of the Shirking Violet

Violet is a new employee at a mental health center in a rural area. Her employer recently received a state contract to provide mental health services to children in the area who have been victims of sexual abuse. Violet took courses in child psychopathology and family violence in her graduate program, but she has never provided therapy to children and knows very little about trauma or sexual abuse. She has been asked by the agency's director to lead the treatment team for this new program, and she protested that she felt unprepared to do so. The director replied, "Violet, I thought you were a generalist practitioner. In small towns like ours, we all have to stretch ourselves a bit. Now, I expect you to develop a can-do attitude and take on this project, or I'll find someone who will."

Applying the Six-Question Model

Who Can Help Violet?

Violet needs two types of assistance with her dilemma: someone who can assist her with the pressure she is experiencing to practice outside her ability, and someone who can help enhance her competence. It would be appropriate for Violet first to approach her supervisor with both concerns. While she may be concerned that the supervisor is already on the side of the director on this issue, approaching the supervisor first serves several functions. It clarifies the supervisor's stance and allows Violet a chance to articulate her concerns and learn what plans, if any, exist to help her develop the skills necessary to take on the new project. Does the supervisor understand and appreciate Violet's apprehensions? Can the supervisor envision the risks involved if the agency embarks on an ambitious new initiative with someone at the helm who is unprepared?

If the supervisor agrees with Violet's concerns, does she have the expertise necessary to prepare and guide Violet in her new role? Can she intercede with the director to set a less ambitious timeline to ensure that the agency can properly meet its obligations to the funding source? Can the supervisor develop a learning plan that will prove satisfactory to the director and to Violet?

Consulting with the supervisor will also provide a valuable check for Violet about the validity of her concerns. For example, if she is perennially timid about taking on new assignments, is resistant to change, or is inclined to underestimate her skills, her supervisor will need to address these issues as part of a larger pattern of behavior. If the proposed new role is primarily one of program planning rather than clinical services, has she had experiences that may help prepare her for this next level of practice? Are there areas of her current work that transfer readily to these new services? A person who has been providing good supervision can nondefensively help Violet examine her concerns and her competence for the new position.

On the other hand, Violet's agency may not be competent. It could be characterized by rash administrative decisions, lax supervision, high turnover, and laissez faire employees. Who can Violet turn to if this is the case? One hopes that in her professional preparation she had faculty or field instructors whose opinions she values, and that she discusses the situation with them. Alternatively, perhaps she has colleagues inside or outside her current agency to whom she can turn. The key is to seek out those people who can hear her concerns, provide feedback, and help her weigh her options. Sometimes people in situations like Violet's are reluctant to pursue consultation because they are ashamed of their situation, or because they are reluctant to air the agency's dirty laundry to the community. Violet should keep in mind that her purpose in talking with others has a constructive intent. It is not to demean the agency or reveal her vulnerabilities, but rather to ensure that she has the skills needed to respond to the demands of her workplace and adequately serve the clientele. Outside coaching or consultation from her professional association may also help Violet strategize about how to respond effectively to the director's orders. Violet may also use these resources as a sounding board to determine if the situation is so untenable that she should resign.

If Violet decides that she should take on the new role, she should seek assistance in evaluating what knowledge and skills it will demand that she doesn't currently possess. Then, with the help of her supervisor, a mentor, or peer consultant she should develop a plan to address those areas of weakness. Following the plan, Violet can enhance her competence through readings, case discussions, online classes or continuing education programs, and sessions with an expert in that subject area.

What Are Violet's Options?

In examining the options, let us assume that Violet is accurate in her appraisal that she is not competent to take on the new role, and that her supervisor is not able or willing to intercede with the director on Violet's behalf. Under these conditions, three options remain. Violet can take the position, she can decline it and attempt to stay at the agency, or she can resign.

When Has She Made Similar Decisions?

In considering the experiences Violet can draw on in this dilemma, it would be helpful for us to know her history in dealing with authority figures and in successfully advocating for herself and others.

- Is it her pattern to leave when adversity arises?
- Is she known for her complaints and inflexibility? Or has she been able to seek constructive solutions to disputes in the past?
- Does she have allies at the agency who might share her concerns about the agency's readiness for the new program?

Despite her short tenure at the agency, she may have a reservoir of personal or professional experiences that are relevant for addressing the pressures the director has placed on her.

What about experiences in practicing in areas of low competence? As a student intern and as a new employee, how has she been able to achieve a level of comfort with the demands of roles? How might she apply those experiences to this case? If observation has been a useful learning method, can she strive to build that into her request for staff development in children's services?

Violet must decide if she can develop a proper level of competence in keeping with the agency's changes, slow or stop those changes, or remove herself from the agency. We hope that Violet brings to this decision a history of successful decisions and actions that can serve as a foundation for her choice in the current dilemma. A history of poor, deferred, or unexamined decisions will mean a weaker set of precedents from which she can draw.

Where Do Ethical and Clinical Guidelines Lead Her?

Rule-based ethics. What are the rules embedded in Violet's choices? In choosing to leave or resist the pressure to take on a role for which she is unqualified, the rule might be "Refuse to accept tasks for which you are incompetent." The same rule might also be embedded in the choice to accommodate the director's plan and develop competence. An alternative rule for that choice might be "In some circumstances (few resources, demanding boss, plan to improve skills), it is okay to practice outside one's competence." Would these rules be desirable if they were to apply to everyone?

We can probably agree that full competence is an important and expected paradigm for care in the health and social services, but we can also acknowledge that it is not standard procedure or a universal rule. All practitioners in training are practicing outside their competence in order to develop an acceptable level of skills, and the supervision provided in internships and residencies is a necessary but perhaps insufficient effort at ensuring competent care. The second rule (allowing exceptions for less-than-full-competence) may be more realistic and universalizable, but it also opens the door for greater misuse, in that there will always be a rationale for not meeting the competence standard and the spectrum between incompetence and competence can be huge.

When we look at Violet's choices though a deontological perspective, the rule that states people should not practice beyond their competence is likely the one we would prefer to have as a universal law. Each of Violet's choices could be in keeping with this rule.

Outcome-based ethics. The utilitarian perspective requires us to consider the consequences of Violet's choices. Choosing to get proper training and accommodate the director's demands would help Violet keep her job, and it would ensure that the new program goes forward and that services are provided to clients in need. The quality of those services, at least at first, is questionable, so we must consider the potential for harm from Violet and other ill-equipped clinicians. On the other hand, perhaps substandard but attentive and caring services are the only alternative to an absence of such services. For children desperately in need of these services, Violet's decision to stay and work on her skills would be a positive consequence.

What are the consequences of resisting the director's appointment of Violet to the new role? Someone else may take the position, with no guarantee of better preparedness than Violet or a comparable dedication to quality. If no one is able to take the job and the agency loses its contract, children may lose needed services, and the agency may be put at risk in both the short and long terms. If she is branded uncooperative due to her resistance, Violet may lose her job, to both her personal detriment and that of her clients. If she decides to resign rather than take on a task she is ill prepared for, she and her clients will be harmed, and her prospects for getting a new job may be damaged by the circumstances under which she left this one. On the other hand, a consequence of resigning may be freedom from a problematic practice environment where staff members are forced to take on duties they are not competent to do thus putting the agency and clients at risk.

Values. Social work values appear to support Violet's choices, in that each of her options is a different route to ensuring quality practice. Competence is one of the six core values of the profession, according to NASW and CASW. It appears that her personal values are in harmony with the profession's values, though they are in tension with those of the director, who apparently values cooperation and organizational growth over worker proficiency. If Violet is mindful of the director's values, however, she may attempt to craft a response that is congruent with his beliefs and imperatives.

Professional standards. The tenets of the social work codes cited at the beginning of this chapter support Violet's concerns and her intention not to take the position without proper preparation. Other ethical standards may relate to how she carries out her decision. For example, NASW standards caution clinicians not to abandon clients, and to withdraw "services precipitously only under unusual circumstances, giving careful consideration to all factors in the situation and taking care to minimize possible adverse effects" (NASW, 2021, 1.17b). Should Violet decide that a resignation is in order, she should be mindful of her clients in the way that she times and carries out her departure.

Violet's choices might be affected by ethics standards about workers' obligations to their employers. The standards state that social workers should "adhere to commitments made to employers and employing organizations" (NASW, 2021, 3.09a), "strive to carry out the stated aims and objectives of their employing organization" (CASW, 2005b, 4.1.1), and "work to improve employing agencies' policies and procedures and the efficiency and effectiveness of their services" (NASW, 2021, 3.09b). Social workers are also expected to "take reasonable steps to ensure that employers are aware of social workers' ethical obligations" (NASW, 2021, 3.09c), "endeavour to effect change through consultation using appropriate and established organizational channels" (CASW, 2005b, 4.1.5), and "not allow an employing organization's policies, procedures, regulations, or administrative orders to interfere with their ethical practice of social work" (NASW, 2021, 3.09d).

These provisions would support Violet's efforts to educate the director about her concerns and their basis in ethics. They would also seem to encourage her to try to make her situation work at the agency but resist being forced into a role without preparation or support.

Two other standards apply to the director and may be useful to Violet as she makes a case for delaying the program or securing staff development:

- "Social work administrators should take reasonable steps to ensure that the working environment for which they are responsible is consistent with and encourages compliance with the NASW Code of Ethics and ... eliminate any conditions in their organizations that violate, interfere with, or discourage compliance with the Code." (NASW, 2021, 3.07d)
- "Social work administrators and supervisors should take reasonable steps to provide or arrange for continuing education and staff development for all staff for whom they are responsible. Continuing education and staff development should address current knowledge and emerging developments related to social work practice and ethics." (NASW, 2021, 3.08)
- "Social workers strive to facilitate access for staff under their direction to ongoing training and professional education, and advocate for adequate resources to meet staff development needs." (CASW, 2005b, 4.3.5).

Ethical principles. The ethical principles of fidelity and beneficence are also useful in considering Violet's dilemma. Violet should behave in a trustworthy manner toward her director, being forthright about her concerns and constructive in her pursuit of a mutually satisfactory solution. Her concern about whether she can ethically deliver the new service, and her honesty regarding her preparedness to work in the new program, are hallmarks of fidelity. Violet's ultimate decision should uphold the principle of beneficence in promoting the well-being of others and avoiding harm. As such, her efforts to develop skills for effective services or avoid the provision of poor services are preferable to simply leaving in order to remove herself from an untenable situation while allowing poor practices to take place.

Practice principles. Beyond ethical standards, practical and clinical standards would also support Violet's contention that mental health practice with children and trauma survivors requires intentional training and experience (George et al., n.d.; Levenson, 2017). For example, the *NASW Standards for Social Work Practice in Child Welfare* (NASW, 2013), the *NASW Standards for the Practice of Social Work with Adolescents* (NASW, 2000), and the *Child Welfare League of America's Standards of Excellence for Services for Abused or Neglected Children and their Families* (CWLA, 1999) describe specific areas of knowledge and practice competence that should be held by an individual working with this population. Resources for Canadian mental health practitioners working with child abuse include the Child Welfare League of Canada's *Children in Care in Canada* (Farris-Manning & Zandstra, 2003) and CASW's *Social Work Practice in Child Welfare* (CASW, 2005c).

It appears that the director not only wants Violet to provide services to children in trauma, but also to lead the team, which means that others would be looking to her for advice in developing their skills and knowledge. Even if she developed comfort with her own skills, would she feel adequately prepared to provide clinical expertise to others?

Why Is She Selecting a Particular Course of Action?

As Violet narrows her options, she will need to examine her motivations in selecting one over the others. For example, is her decision to leave the agency principled in light of her inability to ensure competent services, or is it a more self-serving choice to avoid conflict or the effort change requires? If she decides to stay without taking on the new role, is she comfortable with the quality of services others will provide; is she deferring inappropriately to the director's position; or is she reasoning that as long as she's not involved, no ethical dilemma exists?

If she decides to take the job and develop the proper credentials for serving children, is she confident that colleagues and mentors will see the wisdom in her decision? Can she deliver the services in such a way that she would be comfortable if she were in the clients' shoes?

How Should Violet Carry Out Her Decision?

As Violet considers her options, it would be helpful for her to know what commitments the agency made in the proposal funding the new program and what stipulations were in place when the contract was awarded.

- In the agency's application, did the director accurately represent the agency's capacity to serve this new cohort of clients?
- Was the funding agency aware of the training and infrastructure needs that the service requires?
- Are there state regulations or other policies that might support Violet in her quest for developing competence in children's services?

Affirmative answers to these questions will help Violet get concessions from the director to ensure that the agency provides quality services. In contrast, negative answers, or indications that the director misled the funder about the agency in order to secure the contract, will not bode as well for Violet's prospects as a change agent.

In the absence of others who can competently assume the role the director is envisioning for Violet, the most ethically and clinically sound option is for her to get the training needed to develop competence in practice with abused children. To effectively carry out this decision, she must consider her director's needs and those of her clients.

Through consultation, self-examination, and research, Violet should determine precisely what resources are necessary for her and other staff members to develop competence. She should be prepared with the costs associated with developing competence and the time it will require. Also, if there are accommodations that will be needed (reduced caseloads, triaging of cases so that more difficult cases are referred out early on), she should incorporate those elements into her plan. Concurrent with this research, Violet should confer with her colleagues to determine what their needs are and where they stand in relation to her concerns about the new program. In essence, she wants to conduct a force-field analysis (Brager & Holloway, 1992; Hardcastle & Powers, 2004; Heward et al., 2007) to specify the factors and personnel who will support her position and those who will resist it.

Whatever the analysis reveals, it is likely that the director will be a key in successfully securing the time and resources for the staff to develop necessary skills. If another staff member has a positive history with the director and is able and willing to present the plan to him, that individual may be a more appropriate choice than Violet, a new employee who has already revealed her reservations about the new services. Whoever presents the proposal to the director should employ communication skills, listening, and empathy to try to understand the director's position and the nature of his resistance, if any, to the plan. They should present the concerns in a straightforward manner, supporting the request with data on the risks for individuals and the organization if the children's services contract is not carried out with competence. Having anticipated the nature of the director's resistance, the envoy should structure the proposal to mitigate the director's concerns and make it congruent with his values and responsibilities. Uniting his substantive interests with those of the staff will increase the likelihood that all parties can come to a mutually satisfactory agreement (Fisher et al., 1991). Although Violet and the staff may have grave concerns about the consequences if the staff development proposal is not accepted, resorting to dire predictions and threats at this point will not improve their prospects for successful negotiation. This does not mean that they should avoid mentioning their concerns—only that they should be mindful of the timing and way in which they present the possible risks.

If the director agrees to the proposal, he should specify the plan in writing and circulate it to those who will be responsible for carrying it out, including the business office or financial manager and supervisors. The implementation phase is sometimes an unexpectedly difficult period for change proposals in that the gains of the change have not been felt, but the costs have; after the initial enthusiasm for change wears off, staff and administrators may renege on their agreements (Brager & Holloway, 2002). Therefore Violet and her colleagues should be vigilant in pursuing and evaluating the elements of the staff development plan.

When implementing her decision with her clients, Violet should consider what her clients should know about her clinical competence with children and the degree to which that should be part of her informed consent processes. On one hand, clients have a right to know that she is in the process of developing skills in that area so that they can elect not to see her under those circumstances if they wish. On the other hand, too much information may divert the attention inappropriately from the clients' conditions and needs and may unnecessarily undermine their confidence in her. Striking the right balance in the way that conversation is phrased will respect their autonomy and demonstrate trustworthiness while creating a solid foundation for services.

The case in Box 8.5 offers you the opportunity to try your decision-making skills on a dilemma involving competence standards.

BOX 8.5

A Case for You

Christopher is a new employee at a veterans' services center. His caseload consists primarily of individuals with substance addictions. He has worked hard to keep up with changes in the field, including new research on neurobiology, and is incorporating trauma-informed practices in his work, as well as motivational interviewing, medication-assisted, and harm-reduction approaches. Through case staffing meetings and client reports, Christopher has come to realize that several of his colleagues still subscribe to confrontational techniques and insist that twelve-step programs are the only real form of recovery. Christopher has tried to broach the subject of alternative approaches and the evidence for them with his supervisor and coworkers but they have shut him down. His supervisor advised him, "A lot of these guys are in recovery themselves, and they know what worked for them. That's all the evidence they need," and "We have a very trusting, autonomous practice here. We don't try to dictate what theories or approaches workers use."

While Christopher appreciates these sentiments, he contends that his work is affected by ways his clients have been treated by other providers in the past. He believes it is confusing to them to switch approaches, and he is confident that his approaches are superior to the other methods. Christopher is also concerned about the interns at the agency: What kind of messages and training are they receiving?

As you work through the decision-making model, consider the following points:

- Are Christopher's concerns valid?
- Are the differences between the workers a matter of style and preference or of incompetence? What is the distinction?
- What responsibilities do organizations have for the ongoing competence of their workers?
- How can professionals determine whether a new approach is an improvement over traditional methods or simply a fad?
- Is it unethical for providers to refuse to learn new developments in the field?

Conclusion

Professional competence is a journey, not a destination. While social workers must have an acceptable level of skill and knowledge to address the needs of their clients and service settings, they must also constantly strive to improve those skills to keep pace with workplace demands and the changing knowledge base of the profession. Competent workers are self-aware, they know where their strengths and limits lie, and they ensure that clients and services are not compromised by substandard care. Professionals must also be alert to their own physical and mental health, ensuring that they get assistance with personal difficulties so their clients are not harmed by worker impairment. And social workers take responsibility for encouraging others to practice with competence. This may mean intervening when colleagues are impaired or behaving unethically. It may also require creating professional development opportunities so that staff can get assistance in addressing areas of incompetence.

For Continuing Conversation

1. How would you be able to detect an organization where incompetence is the norm before taking a job there or referring clients there?
2. How can busy professionals stay current with **evidence-based practices** in order to maintain their competence?
3. The codes of ethics don't specify how much training is required to achieve competence. What signs would you use to identify adequate or inadequate competence in your own practice?

Key Concepts

Competence. The ability of an individual to do a job properly. It involves a combination of practical and theoretical knowledge, cognitive skills, behaviors, and values necessary to perform job duties well.

Consultation. Interpersonal relationships between individuals or agencies possessing special expertise. Clinicians may use consultation as a problem-solving process specific to a particular goal or situation, unlike supervision, which is more ongoing and broadly focused.

Evidence-based practices. Approaches to prevention or treatment that are validated by some form of documented scientific evidence, including but not limited to controlled clinical studies.

Impaired worker. A clinician whose ability to deliver care effectively has been compromised or diminished due to personal circumstances, psychological distress, substance use, or mental health issues.

Self-awareness. Conscious knowledge of one's own character, feelings, motives, and desires.

Self-regulation. Ability to control or manage oneself without intervention from external individuals or action, including self-knowledge of when one is impaired from performing job duties effectively.

Supervision. An administrative or educational process used to help clinicians to further develop and refine their skills, ensure quality of care delivered to clients, increase clinicians' self-awareness, or better understand clinical philosophy or agency policy.

CHAPTER 9

Professionalism and Integrity

Introduction

The principles of **professionalism** and **integrity** refer to people's responsibilities to be truthful, to keep their promises, to treat each other fairly, and to behave in a consistent and trustworthy manner. In practice, this means that practitioners will avoid dishonesty, including lying, presenting information in vague or misleading ways (as in distorting research findings), engaging in false advertising, or misrepresenting competence. Lapses in integrity include telling half-truths by selectively presenting the relevant facts; leaving false impressions by failing to correct someone's misunderstanding; stealing time, supplies, or money; engaging in fraud; and being "disingenuous, inauthentic or insincere" (E. Cohen & Cohen, 1999, p. 75). Integrity also refers to how professionals are expected to treat each other. It means demonstrating respect, using proper channels and processes to resolve disputes, sharing credit and taking responsibility as appropriate, being fair in appraisals of others, and using discretion in the ways that one characterizes one's colleagues. Box 9.1 lists the components of professional integrity.

Professionalism is a broader concept than integrity. It implies possession of the characteristics that are expected of a professional, including integrity, but also including a worker's credibility and conduct. There was widespread public scorn when online postings showed medical students posing with "their cadavers," and when an obstetrician lamented a patient's tardiness on Facebook and mused about showing up late for the delivery (Beck, 2013; Heyboer, 2010). The uproar over these posts wasn't merely for the sentiments they contained, but also because they reflected

BOX 9.1

Elements of Integrity

- Refraining from dishonesty or lying, presenting vague or misleading information, false advertising, or misrepresenting one's professional competence
- Correcting misinformation or misunderstandings
- Respecting colleagues, being fair when acknowledging success and when taking responsibility for failures
- Resolving disputes with colleagues appropriately and using discretion in negative critiques or judgments

negatively on the professions involved. Think of a situation when someone's actions or statements made you cringe. Imagine that person was a colleague, teacher, physician, or community leader. You may even have thought, "That's unprofessional." In doing so, you're on the right track in understanding the specifiable and subtle elements of this principle (Decker, 2012).

Standards for these principles state that social workers

- Should not "use derogatory language in their written, verbal, or electronic communications to or about clients." (NASW, 2021, 1.12)
- Should not "exploit clients in disputes with colleagues or engage clients in any inappropriate discussion of conflicts between social workers and their colleagues." (NASW, 2021, 2.04b)
- Should not solicit "testimonial endorsements (including solicitation of consent to use a client's prior statement as a testimonial endorsement) from current clients or from other people who, because of their particular circumstances, are vulnerable to undue influence." (NASW, 2021, 4.07b)
- Should not "take unfair advantage of any professional relationship or exploit others to further their personal, religious, political or business interests." (CASW, 2005b , 2.2.2)
- "Should ensure that their representations to clients, agencies, and the public of professional qualifications, credentials, education, competence, affiliations, services provided, or results to be achieved are accurate . . . claim only those relevant professional

credentials they actually possess and take steps to correct any inaccuracies or misrepresentations of their credentials by others." (NASW, 2021, 4.06c)

- "Do not make false, misleading, or exaggerated claims of efficacy regarding past or anticipated achievements regarding their professional services." (CASW, 2005b , 7.1.6)
- "Should protect, enhance, and improve the integrity of the profession through appropriate study and research, active discussion, and responsible criticism of the profession." (NASW, 2021, 5.01b)
- Should "uphold the dignity . . . of the profession and inform their practice from a recognized social work knowledge base." (CASW, 2005b, 7.1.2)

These standards and examples focus on integrity as a matter of conduct. Banks (2010b) suggests, however, that integrity is manifested in three ways: (1) through morally good or correct conduct, (2) by commitment to and identification with a set of professional ideals or principles, and (3) by "reliable accountability" (p. 2177) through reflection, refinement, and renewal of our capacities. The latter two categories indicate the importance of dedication to the fundamental values of the profession and to navigating personal and professional challenges, so they are grounded in integrity.

The case in Box 9.2 describes a social worker acting with professionalism and integrity.

BOX 9.2

Upholding the Standard

Elaine's student Nat wrote an excellent analysis of the Medicare prescription drug program for his final paper in her policy class. Elaine suggested that Nat consider submitting it to a social work journal for publication. She met with him to discuss the specifications for journal publication and the changes he might make to meet those criteria. When he had revised the paper, she reviewed it and gave him feedback. When a colleague heard of their collaboration, she asked Elaine if she planned to be first or second author on the article. "Neither," Elaine replied. "The paper is entirely Nat's. My work with him on it was to help him learn about writing for publication. I was his teacher and editor, not his coauthor."

Elaine's colleagues may rationalize that her inclusion as an author is justified by the time she spent helping the student and the pressure on faculty members to acquire publication credits. From the student's point of view, coauthorship credit may duly reflect the faculty member's assistance. It may also seem a small price to pay for the professor's continuing support as a mentor and colleague. Even if students determines that the coauthorship is unwarranted, they may ultimately feel powerless to resist a professor or supervisor's insistence on inclusion.

Professionals who wish to act with integrity *and* get proper credit for particular activities have several avenues of assistance. Individuals in academia can refer to guidelines on authorship, which specify the nature of the roles that qualify for different levels of credit (APA, 2019; National Institutes of Health, 2021). Similar resources surely exist for other settings and scenarios. Those with the greatest power in the transaction must be mindful of the fair use of that power and the potential for conflicts of interest.

The NASW *Code of Ethics* (2021) and the CASW *Guidelines for Ethical Practice* (2005b) state, "Social workers should take responsibility and credit, including authorship credit, only for work they have actually performed and to which they have contributed" (CASW, 2005b, 3.2.4; NASW, 2021, 4.08a). Elaine's interpretation of her role and her refusal to be listed as a coauthor were in keeping with this standard. The codes go on to state, "Social workers should honestly acknowledge the work of and the contributions made by others" (CASW, 2005b, 3.2.5; NASW, 2021, 4.08b), so Nat should credit Elaine's assistance in his author's acknowledgments and in his conversations about the work.

Sometimes the role distinctions are less clear than they are in Nat and Elaine's case. If, for example, a faculty member's grant or an organization's intake system led to the creation of a large database from which a student created a study, should the faculty member or data manager be listed as coauthors on articles, reports, or presentations that come out of study? Is the original effort in gathering, organizing, and storing the data the type of contribution the code intends?

For all professionals striving to uphold the standard of integrity, consultation with colleagues will help discern how the field's norms would apply to a particular case. And the tests of right and wrong (publicity, reversibility, smell, and mom/mentor tests) can also be employed to encourage ethical decision making. The failure to act with caution and professionalism is demonstrated in Box 9.3.

BOX 9.3

Violating the Standard

Alden worked for a community mental health center for ten years. While he ostensibly resigned from his position to start his own private practice, the timing of his departure was influenced by his increasing dissatisfaction with the agency's philosophy. Alden was interested in alternative approaches to physical and mental well-being such as energy-field work, mind-body practices, acupuncture, and microbiome wellness. He had taken extensive coursework on these topics, and the more he studied, the more concerned he became with the mental health agency's primary emphasis on psychotropic medication. His efforts to encourage his colleagues and the administration to consider other methodologies that they might suggest to their clients were met with derision. Finally, he decided that it was best to start his own practice as part of a comprehensive wellness collaborative.

Last week, one of his former clients asked her new case manager about Alden's whereabouts and wondered about getting a referral to see him. Cheri, the case manager, replied, "I don't think that's wise. From what I hear, he was let go. His new practice is a lot of crystals-and-incense nonsense."

Cheri's conversation with the client was both inaccurate and inappropriate. She misconstrues the nature of Alden's departure from the agency, condemns his practice interests, and fails to address the client's request for a referral. The NASW and CASW codes address Cheri's actions in the following standards:

- "Social workers should treat colleagues with respect and should represent accurately and fairly the qualifications, views, and obligations of colleagues." (NASW, 2021, 2.01a)
- "Social workers relate to both social work colleagues and colleagues from other disciplines with respect, integrity and courtesy and seek to understand differences in viewpoints and practice." (CASW, 2005a, 3.1)
- "Social workers should avoid unwarranted negative criticism of colleagues in verbal, written, and electronic communications with

clients or with other professionals. Unwarranted negative criticism may include demeaning comments that refer to colleagues' level of competence or to individuals' attributes such as race, ethnicity, national origin, color, sex, sexual orientation, gender identity or expression, age, marital status, political belief, religion, immigration status, and mental or physical disability." (NASW, 2021, 2.01b)

If Cheri has concerns about the appropriateness of a referral for that particular client or the suitability of Alden's approaches, there are other methods she can use to convey her opinions in a more professional manner. For example, she might forthrightly describe Alden's new workplace and ask the client what interests her about that service. She might provide the web address for the practice and offer to discuss the client's reactions and interest. Based on the client's reasons for wanting the referral, she should provide the contact information, as well as that of other resources that might address the interests the client expressed. Cheri might also talk with the client about the outcomes she is seeking in treatment and help her identify some of the signs she can look for in effective services, with Alden or anyone else. If Cheri has serious reservations about the efficacy of Alden's approach or the appropriateness of that approach for this particular client, she should have a sound basis for those opinions and present them with the client's interests in mind. Finally, she should take care to construe her opinions as opinions, in recognition of the client's right to select services anywhere and out of respect for Alden's status as a fellow professional. As indicated at the outset of this book, ethical dilemmas arise when there are not clear answers to vexing problems. In the case in Box 9.4 the social worker is trapped "between a rock and a hard place" in trying to maintain his integrity.

When welfare reform was enacted in the United States in 1996, the changes were intended to reduce the number of people on welfare by employing a combination of penalties and incentives to encourage recipients to move into the workforce. Similar restrictions, such as work requirements and diversion strategies, were put in place under Canada's welfare reform policies, and led to a 21% decrease in welfare participation between 1994 and 2005 (Berg & Todd, 2010). Under welfare reform, each state and province created different mechanisms and definitions to meet the federal mandate. For example, some states in the United States defined education broadly and included those activities in work definitions. Conditions

BOX 9.4

Resolving Dilemmas in Professionalism:
A Rock and a Hard Place

Angela has one child and is seven months pregnant. The father of her children is an undocumented laborer whose whereabouts are unknown, though he is being sought by child support enforcement authorities. Angela works six days a week as a housekeeper for a hotel chain. Vernon is her case manager in a welfare-to-work program. In implementing federal welfare reform, the program has high expectations for participants, and it has stiff penalties for those who fail to maintain employment. Because Angela was reported last year for child neglect, she also has a worker in child protective services (CPS), and a case plan she must follow to maintain custody of her child.

At this week's appointment, Angela reported to Vernon that she had lost her job. When pressed to explain, she said that she had been late for work on several occasions due to appointments and parenting classes related to her CPS case plan. The final straw for her boss was when she objected to lifting heavy objects and moving furniture because of her pregnancy. Vernon knows it will be difficult for her to find employment so close to her delivery date, yet he also knows that she will be ineligible for benefits when she stops working. Meanwhile the clock on her lifetime cap for receiving welfare will continue to tick.

Should Vernon record her loss of employment?

such as pregnancy were treated differently by each state. Some states made it an exclusionary criterion for work requirements, while most did not. Proponents of welfare reform note the program's success in reducing welfare rolls by 57% (Jansen, 2006). Critics note that many welfare recipients have moved into low-wage or part-time jobs that leave them without health care or a living wage (Guzman et al., 2013).

Angela's difficulties stem from a variety of causes, the most recent of which involves the welfare-to-work provisions. She is a single parent who is unlikely to receive sufficient and consistent child support from the father of her children. Safe and adequate child care is scarce and expensive, particularly for people with multiple children who make a minimum wage, work odd service-sector schedules, and lack reliable transportation. Angela's involvement with CPS means that she has additional obligations to fulfill in meeting the expectations of the service plan for neglect. While CPS can help Angela access needed resources, it may also put an undue burden if her CPS worker takes a kitchen sink approach to developing case objectives (Hepworth et al., 2022). For example, if the charge of neglect stemmed from her need to work irregular hours, resulting in substandard childcare arrangements, are parenting classes and regular caseworker meetings a just or appropriate way to address the problem?

The neglect charge may simply be a symptom of the irreconcilable structural demands placed on Angela and other people with few social supports and financial resources. Sometimes the demands of work and family collide, and low-wage workers rarely have the capacity to meet those demands when, for example, a child is sick, a babysitter quits, bus schedules are suspended for a holiday, or an employer requires overtime work. These dilemmas proliferated when the COVID-19 pandemic closed or reduced some public services while forcing other workers deemed essential to continue reporting for work (Banks et al., 2020). As a welfare-to-work participant, Angela's success on the job takes on greater importance (Toft, 2010). As a parent under CPS supervision, she must also place a priority on the care of her child. As a pregnant woman, she is dedicated to her own health and that of her baby. But pregnant women, on welfare or not, are often the subject of workplace discrimination. While it is illegal to discriminate, it is also difficult to prove that discrimination has taken place.

Often, these competing and seemingly irreconcilable obligations are invisible to all but the client, who must try to conform to them. Angela is fortunate to have Vernon's interest and attention in the matter. Vernon's dilemma arises from his role in her double bind. He must hold her accountable for her failure to work even if he believes that she was wrongfully terminated because of her pregnancy or unfairly terminated because she couldn't reconcile CPS's demands with her job.

Vernon's interpretation of the events also figures into his dilemma. First, he understands that discriminatory systemic factors are at play in her case. He also believes in the legitimacy of her actions. That is, he believes that Angela made a concerted effort to comply with the demands placed on her, and that she was right to avoid tasks at work that would jeopardize her pregnancy. Had he taken a derogatory view of her or her decisions on the job, he might be less sympathetic to her predicament, but also less conflicted. What can he do now to treat his client with integrity and carry out his professional obligations? If he can't help Angela, will he act to address the structural factors that created this cruel double bind?

Applying the Six-Question Model

Who Can Serve as a Resource to Vernon?

In all likelihood, the dilemmas Angela's case presents are not unique, which means that there should be multiple avenues for consultation and action. Vernon's supervisor and colleagues at the agency will be first lines of assistance, as they are most familiar with the interpretation of welfare-to-work policies in their region. They will be able to share information on precedents from other cases and the options available to Vernon and Angela. The agency attorney may help Vernon understand the legal limits of his choices. Furthermore, the attorney could address the implications of Angela's termination from the hotel job and any recourse she may have in filing her allegation of pregnancy discrimination. Angela's CPS caseworker will be an important contact and a potential ally in ensuring that the units work cooperatively for the best interests of the family.

Vernon might also research welfare rights groups, legal aid, and other organizations to which he could refer Angela for assistance. A consequence, however, might be that some of the resulting advocacy would be directed at him or his employer. Fear of activism should not deter Vernon from letting Angela know about helpful resources—in fact, it may be just the leverage needed to bring attention to problematic agency practices. Vernon should be mindful of the risks and be prepared for resistance or backlash directed at him or his agency.

If Vernon takes on the laws and policies that gave rise to this dilemma, he has multiple resources. These include national organizations that are concerned with welfare policies, including NASW and CASW; the National Welfare Rights Organization; the National Women's Law Center; the National Association for the Advancement of Colored People; the National Partnership for Women and Families; the Canadian Research Institute for the Advancement of Women. Vernon may also find that local social justice, antipoverty, or women's rights groups in his region offer perspectives and advocacy on the issues Angela is facing.

Vernon might ask key decision makers, such as legislators and the officials in his state who are responsible for welfare policies, to respond to a composite case like Angela's in order to educate them about the deleterious effects of particular policies and seek their assistance in making constructive changes (Mizrahi, 2022). Social workers are expected to challenge injustice and they have important roles to play in putting a personal face on often impersonal policy decisions. However, all workers must be mindful of their role in speaking out about such matters. While all are entitled to engage in public discourse as private citizens, professionalism requires social workers to respect their employers' resources and positions when pursuing social change efforts. Direct action, boycotts, and other forms of community organizing may be commonplace in some social work jobs, but in roles like Vernon's they can incur political and financial repercussions. As such, the methods for seeking justice may vary depending on the setting and role where a social worker is employed. Professionalism also requires social workers to ensure the client's confidentiality and wellbeing are protected as the worker moves from case advocacy to cause advocacy. This means being alert to the risks of privacy intrusions, retaliation, or other complications of becoming an exemplar or test case in policy change.

Organizations and individuals who share Vernon's concerns can inform him of existing efforts to help clients like Angela and of initiatives to improve policies and practices. Vernon can use this information to assist his client and to determine the ways that he can contribute to change efforts. Written resources can help him develop effective strategies for leveraging change within his agency (Hardcastle & Powers, 2004; Hemmelgarn et al., 2010).

What Are Vernon's Options?

Vernon has several alternatives that can be exercised individually or in combination regarding Angela's immediate bind. He can

- adhere to the policy and count her months of unemployment against her, despite his sensitivity to her plight;
- seek and pursue options to stop the clock while she maintains unemployment for the duration of her pregnancy;
- appeal her termination from the hotel or encourage her to seek other work immediately; or
- subvert the policy and falsify documentation that she is working, although she is not.

Whichever action Vernon chooses for Angela's case, he should also pursue systemic changes to address the structural conditions that created the dilemma, though that alternative won't be weighed as part of the decision-making process.

When Has Vernon Faced Similar Dilemmas?

At the heart of this dilemma are two themes: reconciling the needs of clients with bureaucratic limitations and reconciling workers' personal beliefs with the standards of the system within which they work. The case evokes both the perspective of virtue ethics and the concept of integrity in its broadest form. The dilemma is characterized by competing interests: those of the client, the system, and the worker. Vernon's understanding of the essence of the dilemma will help him identify the precedents he can draw on in deciding how to act in this case. It will also help him to decide which responsibilities he will honor over others; as Banks states, "How can I be caring, courageous or just as a professional practitioner?" (2010a, p. 124).

- Have there been situations in which he took a stand for a client against his employer or another institution? Was that effective? Was it a stance he's proud of?
- Have there been situations in which he went the extra mile for clients, helping them to access information or resources when his role required much less? Were these efforts fruitful? Did he believe he had done the right thing, professionally and personally?
- Or, conversely, has it been his habit to draw limits around his responsibilities, even when individual scenarios required more? Has that stance worked for him, perhaps by helping him maintain balance in his professional roles and avoiding burnout?
- Is Vernon inclined to side with the underdogs, looking for opportunities to give voice to that person's needs, even at the risk of his job or well-being? Does Vernon view adverse organizational decisions as symptoms of injustice, oppression, and implicit bias?
- Does he have a grudge against his organization, such that he's looking for an opportunity to use clients to advance his cause, perhaps in his own interests, rather than theirs?
- Have there been instances in Vernon's personal or professional life where he has been willing to lie for what he perceived to be a greater good? Do these instances constitute civil disobedience or fraud?

These questions enable self-reflection that will help Vernon identify instances in the past that can guide him today. They also encourage him to examine his motivations in selecting a particular course of action and ensure he is doing the right thing in the right way and for the right reason. Maybe the evaluation will help reveal other needed changes beyond those in Angela's case or the policies that affect her. That is, if Vernon is perennially disenchanted with his agency and eager to take on its policies in the name of client empowerment, an additional ethical question will involve his decision to remain employed by an agency whose policies he abhors. Or if he simply finds himself distressed at the decisions he is required to make on a daily basis, perhaps another social work role is more suitable for him. Understanding the dilemmas that Angela's particular case symbolizes will help strengthen Vernon's decision making.

Where Will Ethical and Clinical Guidelines Lead Him?

Let's collapse Vernon's choices into two: he can follow the policy (thereby reducing Angela's benefits and running down her clock while encouraging her to find work or while seeking a formal exception in light of her pregnancy), or he can keep her listed as working, while also encouraging her to regain employment or seeking an exception. The core difference between the two approaches is whether Vernon follows the rule about work requirements or not.

Rule-based ethics. Deontology, with its emphasis on universal laws, would endorse rule-following over rule-breaking. Imagine it as a choice between requiring people to comply with laws, even unfair or illegitimate laws, versus allowing people to comply only with those they support, and you see where the deontological stance comes down.

Outcome-based ethics. Utilitarianism, with its emphasis on effects, might support another choice, depending on which consequences are emphasized. Among the outcomes of enforcing the policy are short-term and long-term financial hardships for Angela. Unless she can find a cooperative employer at this late stage in her pregnancy, or an exception to the stated policy, she will face a reduction in benefits, diminished time on her welfare clock, and significant pressure to return to the workforce immediately following the birth of her baby. Each of these is a troubling consequence in and of itself, and a trigger for other potential problems. For example, under pressure to return to work, might Angela take a job that puts her health and ability to care for her children at risk? Might her reduced income or haphazard child-care arrangements also jeopardize her children?

Against these scenarios, following the policy also has positive consequences. Complying with the established rules means that Vernon is fulfilling the expectations and trust placed in him by his employer and, in extension, by society, for the measured use of public resources. Compliance means that Angela is being held to the same standard as other welfare recipients in her jurisdiction. Following the rules means that the system is not undermined by individual whims, favoritism, or subversion.

What are the consequences of Vernon lying about Angela's work status? It may save her and her children from perilous financial consequences and may keep her from putting herself at risk by taking undesirable jobs late in her pregnancy or soon after delivering. Marking Angela as working when she is not may let her know that she will not be punished for doing the right thing in standing up for her health at the hotel or trying to comply with the CPS mandates. On the other hand, it may also send a message that it is acceptable to defraud the welfare system. Vernon's collusion with that lie makes that message more destructive, as it puts his integrity (and that of his profession) in question. It may undermine Vernon's authority with Angela and put him at risk of blackmail should she threaten to reveal their secret. Lying at this point may remove Angela's motivation and Vernon's leverage to have her return to work when she is able.

If the lie is revealed, the act of fraud may also result in severe legal penalties for Vernon and his client. Vernon may consider his choice an act of civil disobedience, a necessary evil in calling attention to a flawed system. However, there is no guarantee that his actions will engender the sympathy he hopes for—many citizens scoff at the struggles of people who receive government assistance even while they, too, benefit from social programs. And, although Vernon may be willing to endure the consequences of his actions for a greater good, the same may not be true of his client. What voice will/should Angela have in the decision not to follow the welfare guidelines?

Even if the plan works and Angela is spared deleterious consequences, Vernon's actions have done nothing to remedy the larger problem. Choosing a more forthright method of addressing the policy would benefit not just one client, but all who share her circumstances now and in the future.

Values. The personal values that might drive Vernon's feelings in the case can be revealed through the process of self-reflection described earlier. Concerns for fairness, loyalty, trustworthiness, empowerment, and righteousness may all come into play as he considers his alternatives.

Social work values present a mixed picture. The value of social justice inspires social workers to strive for social change, specifically in areas of "poverty, unemployment, discrimination, and other forms of social injustice" (NASW, 2021, p. 5). However, the value placed on dignity and worth suggests that while social workers must enhance clients' capacities and opportunities, they must be "cognizant of their dual responsibility to clients and to the broader society. They seek to resolve conflicts between clients' interests and the broader society's interests in a socially responsible manner consistent with the values, ethical principles, and ethical standards of the profession" (NASW, 2021, pp. 5–6). This value suggests that the method Vernon is considering for reconciling his client's situation with agency policies is unacceptable. The value of integrity affirms this conclusion. "Social workers take all reasonable steps to uphold their ethical values, principles and responsibilities even though employers' policies or official orders may not be compatible with its provisions" (CASW, 2005b, 4.1.7) and "social workers act honestly and responsibly and promote ethical practices on the part of the organizations with which they are affiliated" (NASW, 2021, p. 6).

Professional standards. The CASW guidelines acknowledge the tension between client interests and societal responsibilities in the following standard: "In performing their responsibilities to society, social workers frequently must balance individual rights to self-determination with protection of vulnerable members of society from harm. These dual ethical responsibilities are the hallmark of the social work profession and require well-developed and complex professional skills" (CASW, 2005b, 8.0). The NASW *Code of Ethics* further explains this balance: "Social workers' primary responsibility is to promote the well-being of clients. In general, clients' interests are primary. However, social workers' responsibility to the larger society or specific legal obligations may on limited occasions supersede the loyalty owed clients, and clients should be so advised" (NASW, 2021, 1.01).

In reconciling those tensions, the ethical standards endorse truthfulness and trustworthiness, stipulating that social workers

- "Should not participate in, condone, or be associated with dishonesty, fraud, or deception." (NASW, 2021, 4.04)
- "Generally should adhere to commitments made to employers and employing organizations." (NASW, 2021, 3.09a)
- Should "work toward the maintenance and promotion of high standards of practice." (NASW, 2021, 5.01a)
- Should "uphold the dignity and integrity of the profession and inform their practice from a recognized social work knowledge base." (CASW, 2005b , 7.1.2)
- Should "promote excellence in the social work profession." (CASW, 2005b, 7.1.1)
- Should "uphold and advance the values, ethics, knowledge, and mission of the profession . . . protect, enhance, and improve the integrity of the profession through appropriate study and research, active discussion, and responsible criticism." (NASW, 2021, 5.01b)
- Should "strive to promote the profession of social work, its processes and outcomes and defend the profession against unjust criticism." (CASW, 2005b , 7.1.7).

Several standards also offer guidance on addressing troubling organizational practices. Social workers should

- "Work toward the best possible standards of service provision and are accountable for their practice." (CASW, 2005b, 4.1.2)
- "Work to improve employing agencies' policies and procedures and the efficiency and effectiveness of their services." (NASW, 2021, 3.09b)
- "Take reasonable steps to ensure that employers are aware of social workers' ethical obligations . . ." (NASW, 2021, 3.09c)
- "Take all reasonable steps to uphold their ethical values, principles and responsibilities even though employers' policies or official orders may not be compatible with its provisions." (CASW, 2005b, 4.1.7)
- Should "not allow an employing organization's policies, procedures, regulations, or administrative orders to interfere with their ethical practice of social work . . . take reasonable steps to ensure that their employing organizations' practices are consistent with the NASW Code of Ethics." (NASW, 2021, 3.09d)

- "Should be diligent stewards of the resources of their employing organizations, wisely conserving funds where appropriate and never misappropriating funds or using them for unintended purposes." (NASW, 2021, 3.09g)

While the codes of ethics could be interpreted as supporting Vernon's concerns, they clearly do not endorse any method of rectifying them that involves dishonesty. They would support Vernon in raising his concerns and working through available appeals mechanisms on Angela's behalf and through established channels for longer-term policy change.

Ethical principles. An examination of ethical principles lends further support to Vernon in upholding the agency's policy. Fraudulent practices, even with good intentions, violate the position of trust that society has given Vernon, misuse scarce resources, and run the risk of doing serious harm to the worker and his client. Putting Angela at risk through fraud, even if it is for short-term benefit, diminishes her autonomy and long-term opportunities.

Laws and policies. Falsely reporting Angela's work status is probably illegal and certainly a violation of agency regulations. Beyond the right-wrong aspect of his choices, are there laws or policies that might allow Vernon to ethically excuse Angela from the work requirements? For example, if Angela's termination from the hotel was, in fact, a violation of the U.S. Pregnancy Discrimination Act, or Canada's federal Employment Insurance Act, does that protect her from penalties under the welfare-to-work program? Women who are pregnant must be treated like any other employee with a temporary medical condition (Strom, 2021). Therefore, if the hotel manager allowed a worker with a broken ankle to reduce their activity, then Angela is entitled to the same benefit. If it is determined that the employer at the hotel discriminated against Angela, that may indeed constitute good cause for not meeting the work requirements of the welfare program, and she would be allowed to retain her benefits.

Might her pregnancy alone constitute a good cause for her to be exempt from penalties for not working until after she delivers the baby? While different locales have different expectations for pregnant women, some jurisdictions excuse those in the final trimester from the work requirement. Vernon should be conversant with the policy in his area and pursue the exception if it applies to Angela. He might also explore whether there are policies in force in CPS that might be brought to bear on Angela's welfare status at this stage of the pregnancy. Advocates for healthy babies emphasize the importance of prenatal care, so it would seem there should be allies for Angela's opposition to onerous lifting at her job. Perhaps there are alternative definitions of work (educational programs, for example) for which Angela might qualify, rather than being deprived of support for not having a job at this time.

Why Has Vernon Selected a Particular Option?

As noted throughout this section, it is important for Vernon to consider the motives behind his choices for resolving the dilemma. While it is clearly wrong to commit welfare fraud, he might justify his actions through a variety of flawed principles. For example, he might use all-or-nothing reasoning, focusing on the financial losses that Angela will endure in not working, while losing sight of the other risks that will accrue for her if he subverts the policy.

Vernon may contend that he is simply acting in his client's best interests, misapplying that concept by focusing only on an individual client, versus the universe of clients in need of just policies and adequate welfare funds, and focusing only on her financial interest instead of her need to act lawfully, be treated in a trustworthy manner, and so forth. He may rationalize that his actions follow the spirit, if not the letter, of the law since Angela wants to work and would be working if she hadn't been mistreated by the hotel manager or the CPS bureaucracy. Such justifications are an invitation to use the publicity, reversibility, smell, and mom/mentor tests, since it is unlikely that the public, Vernon's colleagues, or even a loving parent would accept that rationale for deceptive actions. Using the test of reversibility and putting himself in Angela's shoes, Vernon might be grateful for the break from rigid welfare rules, but not likely at the risk that fraud would create.

Rather than fraudulently record Angela's status, if Vernon decided to inform his supervisor of the issues and fight for an exception for her, openly documenting his choices at each step of the process, he would still need to consider his motives. A particular concern would to be certain his decision to take on the system is in Angela's best interest and with her consent, not an opportunity to act out on behalf of his disagreement with the policy.

How Should Vernon Carry Out His Decision?

While it may be tempting to overlook Angela's change in work status and fail to document it, such actions are clearly not an ethical avenue for addressing what Vernon perceives to be unfair policies. Vernon must uphold the policy while pursuing options to mitigate the damage. A first step will be to inform Angela of the implications of not working and determine her plans and preferences for responding to the change in status. Vernon may offer to intervene on Angela's behalf with her former employer and/or assist her in securing legal assistance for an Equal Employment Opportunity Commission claim for pregnancy discrimination.

Vernon should secure Angela's permission, if he hasn't done so already, to speak with her CPS worker so that their interventions can be coordinated, and incompatible expectations reconciled. The CPS worker may be an ally in any appeals concerning Angela's work status with the welfare program. They may also be able to provide funds or resources to supplement the benefits and wages lost while Angela is unemployed.

Vernon should seek the support of his supervisor in temporarily exempting Angela from the penalties of job loss, using whatever appeal or exclusionary criteria exist within their system. Vernon's careful documentation and clear articulation of Angela's history and circumstances may help to make the case for a good-cause exception if any such opportunities exist. He will need to think strategically about his actions so that the exemption is pursued in a timely manner and is not negatively affected by any discrimination claims.

If his efforts are not successful, Vernon can be confident that he acted with integrity and did everything in his power to advocate ethically for his client within the system they have. This may be of little comfort if Vernon believes the social service system is failing people like Angela through policies that couple unreasonable demands with little opportunity for success. Vernon may find some solace in targeting his interventions at the system rather than at the individual client. There may be positions or roles within his agency where he can formally intervene, for example as a legislative liaison or as a representative to coalitions seeking structural change. Alternatively, he may undertake these efforts in his role as a citizen. In either case, he will find helpful guidelines for establishing relationships with decision makers and other change agents, building coalitions, providing constructive resources for policy discussions, communicating effectively, and targeting promising opportunities for change (Mizrahi, 2022).

As a change agent, Vernon should be mindful of the standard that "Social workers should make clear distinctions between statements made and actions engaged in as a private individual and as a representative of the social work profession, a professional social work organization, or the social worker's employing agency" (NASW, 2021, 4.06a).

Even if he becomes an active advocate in efforts to change welfare laws and policies, Vernon may find it difficult to correct flaws in the system or to continue to work in that system. Against such odds, some social workers opt for other careers, and some for other positions or fields of practice where they believe they can best exercise their abilities. The key in such decisions is to have sufficient self-awareness and social support to know when it is no longer possible to be an effective agent of change, and to consider and pursue other opportunities before hopelessness, pessimism, and burnout reveal themselves in practice and erode professionalism. Research might help Vernon and his supervisor evaluate the risks for burnout inherent in his current work role (Dalphon, 2019). His inability to properly assist deserving clients like Angela may have a detrimental effect on his suitability for practice in that setting.

Now it is your turn to practice using the decision-making framework. Box 9.5 presents a case about the complexities of defining professional integrity.

BOX 9.5

A Case for You

Allie and her colleagues are school social workers. They are friends of Tamara, a former coworker, who is getting married soon and leaving the area. The group flew to Winnipeg to celebrate Tamara's bachelorette party. During their stay at a resort, they gambled, went to shows, and enjoyed exotic cocktails. Tamara posted some pictures from the trip on her wedding website. The site is private, with access exclusively for family and friends of the bride and groom.

Today, the groom's uncle called Allie's supervisor to complain about the morals of the school social work staff. He had seen the site and was offended by their "lascivious behavior." "As a taxpayer and a member of the school board, I feel they have no business as role models for the children of our area and I expect you to take action."

Use the decision-making model to consider what you would do if you were the supervisor in this case. What might constitute unprofessional behavior in the photos? The NASW code states, "Social workers should not permit their private conduct to interfere with their ability to fulfill their professional responsibilities" (NASW, 2021, 4.03), and the CASW (2005b) *Guidelines* state, "Social workers take appropriate action where a breach of professional practice and professional ethics occur, conducting themselves in a manner that is consistent with the *Code of Ethics* and *Guidelines for Ethical Practice*, and standards of their regulatory body" (CASW, 2005b, 7.2.1). Workplace policies often expect that employees' personal conduct "not reflect negatively on the organization or their professions." Are Allie and her colleagues in violation of these standards?

What guidance should faculty and supervisors give social workers about professional conduct? What policies should professionals have about their conduct in public (yelling at referees at youth sports, attending a dance club, drinking with friends, protesting about social issues)? How would these policies translate to online behavior?

Conclusion

Social workers often find themselves applying or enforcing policies they know are flawed. At times, they struggle for the flexibility to consider individual circumstances in a one-size-fits-all world. The cumulative result of such no-win situations is often cynicism, burnout, and erosion of the reformist spirit that brought many to the field of social work in the first place. While it is difficult to face pain and suffering and live out one's ideals in a world that may not embrace those ideals, the hallmark of professionalism is the ability to face those challenges with integrity. A wide-ranging concept, integrity embodies the qualities of trustworthiness, fairness, and honesty. Social workers are expected to exercise these qualities in their dealings with clients, colleagues, and the general public. Professionalism doesn't require social workers to maintain a happy facade in the face of troubled individuals or troubling policies. Rather, it sets norms for resolving disputes in a transparent and above-board manner.

Lapses in professionalism have repercussions beyond the individuals involved. Unhealthy organizational norms can develop where problems are not handled in a forthright fashion. The misuse of power and erosion of the public trust can damage an organization's reputation and take decades to repair (Alsan & Wanamaker, 2017; Shepard, 1992). Unprofessional conduct reflects negatively on all members of the profession, as all members pay the price for the actions of a few. People who are treated unprofessionally develop a disdain for experts that may carry over into subsequent helping relationships.

Despite its long history and noble aims, social work is an often misunderstood and poorly regarded profession. All members of the profession must be mindful that their actions speak for their employers and their field, and not only for themselves as individuals. Acting with integrity ensures that social workers are endeavoring to do the right things the right way for the right reasons.

For Continuing Conversation

1. Whether in public behavior or online activity, should social workers and other professionals be held to a higher standard than others?
2. How are meritorious complaints about integrity and professionalism distinguished from frivolous or unfair criticisms?
3. If you refuse to do something dishonest, such as backdate records, yet you know your fellow worker agreed to do it, do you have any responsibilities to act on that knowledge? How can you uphold integrity and professionalism in the actions of others?
4. Banks suggests that integrity is about commitment to the profession's ideals and the individual worker's ongoing character and capacity for reflection (Banks, 2010b). How can faculty, colleagues, and supervisors help encourage these practices?

Key Concepts

Integrity. The quality of being truthful, keeping one's promises, treating colleagues with fairness, and behaving in a trustworthy manner.

Professionalism. The expected characteristics of a professional, including all elements of integrity, as well as a worker's appearance and self-conduct, such that her behavior reflects positively on the individual, agency, or profession.

CHAPTER 10

Nondiscrimination and Cultural Competence

Introduction

> "Viruses don't discriminate. Societies and systems do." (Schalatek, 2020)

In 2020 and 2021, structural inequalities laid bare by the COVID-19 pandemic, graphic deaths of Black Americans at the hands of law enforcement, and the discovery of mass graves of Indigenous children in Canada, combined with other factors, brought renewed attention to systems of oppression and inequality. Social work is a mechanism for structural change and social justice, but it is also embedded and authorized by the discriminatory systems social work would strive to deconstruct.

Social work requirements regarding **nondiscrimination** and **cultural competence** are natural manifestations of principles that emphasize the dignity and worth of all persons and the responsibilities to treat clients fairly and engage in social justice. While always important, these principles are now foregrounded in discussions of professional obligations and competencies, power and **positionality**, and strategies for individual and social change (Finn, 2021). Good intentions for unbiased and culturally competent service delivery are necessary but insufficient to meet the challenge of dismantling oppressive systems and **ethnocentrism** (Bernard & Moriah, 2007; Este, 2007; Newfoundland & Labrador Association of Social Workers, 2016; Weinberg & Fine, 2020). This chapter addresses the ethics of culturally competent, equitable, inclusive, and empowering social work as reflected in current codes of ethics. It builds on those standards with tenets for achieving aspirational goals of significant structural social change.

The CASW *Code of Ethics* begins with a call to action "The social work profession is dedicated to the welfare and self-realization of people . . . and the achievement of social justice for all. The profession has a particular interest in the needs and empowerment of people who are vulnerable, oppressed, and/or living in poverty. Social workers are committed to human rights as enshrined in Canadian law, as well as in international conventions on human rights created or supported by the United Nations. . . . [S]ocial workers respect the distinct systems of beliefs and lifestyles of individuals, families, groups, communities and nations without prejudice" (CASW, 2005a, p. 3).

The NASW advocates for "cultural and linguistic competence at three intersecting levels: the individual, institutional, and societal. Cultural competence requires social workers to examine their own cultural backgrounds and identities while seeking out the necessary knowledge, skills, and values that can enhance the delivery of services to people with varying cultural experiences . . ." (NASW, 2015b, p. 65). Other mental health professions have similarly adopted standards and procedures to define and embrace culturally competent practice. For example, the American Psychiatric Association's Council on Minority Mental Health and Health Disparities "represents and advocates for both minority and underserved populations and psychiatrists from those groups" and is charged with increasing "awareness and understanding of cultural diversity, and to foster the development of attitudes, knowledge, and skills in the areas of cultural competence through consultation, education, and advocacy within both the APA and the field of psychiatry and public policy" (American Psychiatric Association, 2022).

One could argue that cultural competence should be considered a subset of the other areas of professional competence addressed in Chapter 8. An active dialogue exists about whether cultural competence is an achievable, finite destination, rather than a commitment to engage in a lifelong process of reflection and learning. Some suggest that cultural humility is a more appropriate standard, emphasizing learning rather than proficiency (Loya & Peters, 2019). However, cultural competence is inextricably linked to values of justice, dignity and worth, and the centrality of human relationships. It requires self-awareness, intentionality, and action regarding diversity and oppression and thus it intentionally sets a higher standard than humility (Finn, 2021; Murray, 2021). Ignorance and the lack of cultural humility are problematic, but the failure to understand the cultural-political context of social systems poses far greater risk. Without cultural competence and the commitment to nondiscrimination and social justice, social workers may perpetuate the marginalization and othering of those they serve; contribute to harmful social constructions that pathologize human behavior; and fail to be agents of change for interventions with systems at all levels. The list in Box 10.1 enumerates the key components in cultural competence for individuals and organizations.

The NASW *Code of Ethics* (2021) addresses cultural competence by stating that social workers should

- "Demonstrate understanding of culture and its function in human behavior and society, recognizing the strengths that exist in all cultures." (1.05a)
- "Demonstrate knowledge that guides practice with clients of various cultures and be able to demonstrate skills in the provision of culturally informed services that empower marginalized individuals and groups. Social workers must take action against oppression,

BOX 10.1

Elements of Personal and Organizational Cultural Competence

- Awareness of biases and prejudices
- Conscious efforts to prevent **discrimination**, create safe spaces, and redistribute power
- Knowledge about identity, group affiliations, and intersectionality, including language, class, race and ethnicity, religion, gender identity and expression, sexual orientation, ability, age, and other factors
- Viewing historical context, power relations, community and intergenerational dynamics and the interplay of structural forces and cultural processes as factors shaping strengths and struggles (Finn, 2021)
- Fostering behaviors, attitudes, skills, and policies that function effectively across cultures.

racism, discrimination, and inequities, and acknowledge personal privilege." (1.05b)
- "Demonstrate awareness and cultural humility by engaging in critical self-reflection (understanding their own bias and engaging and self-correction), recognizing clients as experts of their own culture, committing to lifelong learning, and holding institutions accountable for advancing cultural humility" (1.05c)
- "Obtain education about and demonstrate understanding of the nature of social diversity and oppression with respect to race, ethnicity, national origin, color, sex, sexual orientation, gender identity or expression, age, marital status, political belief, religion, immigration status, and mental or physical ability." (1.05d)
- "Prevent and eliminate discrimination in the employing organization's work assignments and in its employment policies and practices." (3.09e)
- "Not practice, condone, facilitate, or collaborate with any form of discrimination on the basis of race, ethnicity, national origin, color, sex, sexual orientation, gender identity or expression, age, marital status, political belief, religion, immigration status, or mental or physical ability." (4.02)
- "Promote conditions that encourage respect for cultural and social diversity within the United States and globally. Social workers should promote policies and practices that demonstrate respect for difference, support the expansion of cultural knowledge and resources, advocate for programs and institutions that demonstrate cultural competence, and promote policies that safeguard the rights of and confirm equity and social justice for all people." (6.04c)

The CASW *Guidelines for Ethical Practice* (2005b) addresses cultural competence by stating,

- "Social workers strive to understand culture and its function in human behaviour and society, recognizing the strengths that exist in all cultures." (1.2.1)
- "Social workers acknowledge and respect the impact that their own heritage, values, beliefs and preferences can have on their practice and on clients whose background and values may be different from their own." (1.2.3)

- "Social workers seek a working knowledge and understanding of clients' racial and cultural affiliations, identities, values, beliefs and customs." (1.2.4)

As the standards indicate, cultural competence results from the interaction of knowledge, attitudes, and actions. Professionals cannot be expected to possess knowledge about every aspect of every culture represented by their clients and colleagues. They are, however, expected to pursue continuous growth through rigorous self-reflection and self-understanding and continuous pursuit of knowledge about different cultures and the heterogeneity within cultures (Community Toolbox, 2022; Lum, 2011; NASW, 2015a).

Beyond having an attitude of acceptance and curiosity and a dedication to knowledge acquisition, contemporary ethics standards expect social workers to put those insights into action "to challenge institutional and structural oppression and the accompanying feelings of privilege and internalized oppression" (NASW, 2015a, p. 11). Nondiscrimination means eliminating policies and practices that expressly disadvantage particular groups of people and those that appear neutral but have a disparate impact on members of a particular race, gender, faith, sexual orientation, or any other background (Strom, 2021). It also means accepting an active role in support of social justice. Cultural competence includes action. The case in Box 10.2 describes social work practice that is sensitive to cultural considerations.

The consideration of race in college and graduate school admissions is a highly charged social issue (Hoover & Gluckman, 2022). The arguments in support of racial considerations or quotas cite the historical disadvantages some groups have faced and the importance of advanced degrees for individual and community development. These advocates contend that certain indicators of merit such as standardized test scores reflect institutional biases that will always yield classes that are not racially or socioeconomically diverse (Young, 2003). In 2003 the U.S. Supreme Court "reaffirmed that the educational benefits of diversity were a compelling interest under federal law" (Bell et al., 2005, p. B9) though affirmative action is continually readjudicated.

Similar to the affirmative action and anti-discrimination laws in the U.S., Canadian policy, regulated by the Employment Equity Act of 1995, is designed "to correct the conditions of disadvantage in employment

BOX 10.2

Upholding the Standard

Nelson is a master of social work (MSW) student doing his field placement at a Native American men's center. He is a member of the Mille Lacs Band of Ojibwe and is dedicated to helping to ameliorate the social conditions that have damaged the well-being of so many members of his community. Nelson has applied for entry into a doctoral program in public policy at a university where Sarah, his research professor, is a member of the admissions committee. The application is a multifaceted process requiring the applicant to submit test scores, letters of recommendation, undergraduate and graduate grades, personal statements, and writing samples. The committee strives to select candidates who hold promise for successful graduate study and the capacity to effectively evaluate and influence public policy.

Nelson's portfolio presents a mixed picture. His writing, personal statements, recommendations, and graduate-level grades are superb. His test score and undergraduate grades are significantly below those of other applicants. In an effort to streamline and quantify the selection process, several members of the admissions committee have suggested that test scores and grades be used as the sole criteria for differentiating candidates. Sarah objects vigorously. "There are many ways in which applicants show promise for our program. If these are the only things that count, why do we ask for everything else?"

The chair replies, "You are just trying to advocate for Nelson because of your soft spot for him. Should we loosen the criteria for everyone?"

"I don't see it as weakening the standards. I see it as appropriately using the criteria we have. Nelson, and perhaps some other candidates, overcame significant odds, including a poor preparation for college, to get where he is today. His experience in social services, his grades from graduate school, and his legislative advocacy on policy change all are indicators of his promise. I'm saying we shouldn't discount those qualities for any of the candidates."

Other committee members nod their assent and begin to develop a schema to evaluate all the candidates using all the data in their applications.

experienced by women, Aboriginal peoples, persons with disabilities and members of visible minorities by giving effect to the principle that employment equity means more than treating persons in the same way but also requires special measures and the accommodation of differences" (Government of Canada, 2022c, p. 1). More broadly, the Canadian Human Rights Act, in conjunction with provincial and territorial anti-discrimination laws, protects rights on the basis of national or ethnic origin, color, genetic characteristics, gender identity or expression, certain criminal convictions, and other statuses (Minister of Justice, 2022). As Kuspinar (2016) notes, "[O]ver time, equity programs in the employment sector shifted to the education sector, and . . . educational equity emerged in higher education in Canada" (p. 48). Professional programs, such as law and medical schools, initiated initiatives intended to improve the conditions of disadvantaged groups in society, with special emphasis on the needs of Indigenous persons. As an example, admissions policies can "ensure the provision of a University learning environment that encourages full access, participation and success for Aboriginal students, and enriches all aspects of the intellectual and cultural life of the University of Calgary through full participation of Aboriginal students" (University of Calgary, 2013).

The example of the admissions committee above symbolizes common strategies about evaluating merit, building diversity, and ameliorating histories of racism or disadvantage. The committee's decision to review and weigh a variety of applicant materials reduces the bias and disparate impact associated with prioritizing standardized test scores. It also opens the door for the committee to reevaluate what qualities they want in their doctoral students and in their program. For example, resilience and grit may be predictive of graduate school success and the doctoral program's mission may focus on social policy research. These factors would affect what data the admissions committee reviews and how they weigh different pieces of information. If the goal is to enroll a diverse student body and improved access to higher education for all citizens, there may be proxies for race, ethnicity, or other factors that can be identified and credited in an application. For example, is the applicant the first generation in the family to attend college? What is the quality rating of their high school? Has the applicant overcome personal adversity, such as prejudice, socioeconomic disadvantage, family tragedy, or violent surroundings, in striving for a college or graduate education? A further consideration is the composition of the faculty and the admissions committee. That is, without representation, preparation, and intentionality, a homogeneous group risks becoming a self-replicating organism (Stewart & Valian, 2018).

Sarah's argument that the committee should utilize all the sources of data it seeks from candidates demonstrates several ethical principles, including integrity, nondiscrimination, and cultural competence. Depending on the qualifications of the other applicants, the schema that the committee develops may not necessarily lead to Nelson's admission, but it will ensure that his abilities and experiences are accounted for as the committee determines his promise for doctoral education.

In contrast to Sarah's efforts on behalf of Nelson, the social work student in the case in Box 10.3 demonstrates insensitivity to worker–client difference.

BOX 10.3

Violating the Standard

Jane is a twenty-three-year-old social work student in the first week of her internship at a veterans' hospital. Her clientele is predominantly men over the age of forty who have experienced acute bouts of post-traumatic stress disorder. Mr. Carter, her first client, has just undergone an amputation of his arm following repeated failed surgeries to treat a wound he received on military deployment in a warzone. He has a history of homelessness since his military discharge but no predominant psychiatric problems. Jane's responsibility is to arrange the rehabilitation services and adaptive devices he will need after his discharge.

At their first meeting, Mr. Carter is sullen and resistant to Jane's suggestions. When asked about his arm, he reports that he can still see it there and feels as if it is still attached. He is discouraged that after all the hospitalizations and painful interventions he still lost the arm. Jane replies matter-of-factly, "But the reality of the situation is that you have lost it, so what can we do to get you functioning again?"

Mr. Carter explodes. "Listen, sister, I am functioning! You have no clue what I've seen, what I've been through. WE?! Bullshit! You can't do anything for me."

Jane replies, "Well, that's certainly your choice," and ends the interview.

As she packed up to leave for the day she described Mr. Carter's reaction as explosive anger, saying, "He just went off on me!" In the case record she posited that Mr. Carter's phantom pains were signs of psychosis, and in a meeting with the treatment team she described him as resistant and suggested that "his lack of motivation indicates a poor prognosis for success post-discharge." Jane's colleagues and supervisor accept Jane's analysis at face value without exploring other factors at play in the interview.

The vignette doesn't reveal all the sources of difference between Jane and Mr. Carter, but it does indicate that they differ in age, ability, and gender, and probably in military experience. Bridging such differences to build a trusting helping relationship takes effort, time, and compassion. Successful cross-cultural practice requires a high degree of self-awareness on the part of the worker, a commitment to learn more about others and their cultural experiences, and a willingness to acknowledge mistakes and misunderstandings and work to overcome them. Nondiscrimination and cultural competence mean that clients aren't penalized by the worker's lack of sensitivity, lack of knowledge, or abuse of power (Banks, 2021; Corey et al., 2019; Lieberman & Lester, 2004; NASW, 2015a).

In the interaction with Mr. Carter, Jane appears insensitive to his experience and more focused on her agenda than on the needs of her client. Perhaps their differences exacerbated Mr. Carter's reaction. His presumptions about Jane and the intensity of his response indicate outrage at not being heard or respected, and disbelief in her capacity to help him, given their differences. Rather than ending the session, Jane could have defused the situation by acknowledging her error. "You are right, Mr. Carter. I apologize for focusing on the future instead of on what you'd just told me. Can we start over?" In addition to providing assistance with his immediate needs, she could also use their sessions to learn more about him and his background, establishing the trust necessary for a helping relationship, especially one where the participants come from very different worlds (NASW, 2015b). Beyond helping Mr. Carter, such conversations would help broaden and deepen Jane's cultural awareness.

Instead, Jane ends the interview, and her communications reflect a lack of empathy toward Mr. Carter's position, and poor awareness of her own role in the transaction. Her ignorance of the physical phenomena that accompany amputations results in an inappropriate diagnosis. Her colleagues' passivity or complicity mean that there is no opportunity for Jane to learn from the incident and devise strategies to salvage her work with Mr. Carter. It also means that her flawed treatment notes will stand as written and could take on a life of their own, as the workers on other shifts and those who read them in subsequent admissions or referrals may come to believe her account and respond to Mr. Carter accordingly.

While nondiscrimination and cultural competence are highly valued in social work practice, upholding them is not always clear cut, as the case in Box 10.4 reveals.

BOX 10.4

Resolving Dilemmas in Discrimination and Cultural Competence: The Telltale Office

Mary is a social work supervisor at a multiservice mental health center. Susan is a student intern who began placement at the agency three weeks ago. Yesterday Susan asked to meet with Mary and on doing so expressed her distress and disgust at the office decor of her supervisor, Stan. The agency is located in a large metropolitan area where one of the professional sports teams has an Indigenous nickname and mascot. Like many employees, Stan is an avid fan of the team. His office reflects his interests and is full of memorabilia supporting the team. Susan voiced her objections to the display to Stan, and now to his supervisor, on the grounds that it is derogatory to Indigenous people, perpetuates damaging stereotypes, and violates social work values about human dignity and respect. She finds it offensive and distracting and wonders if clients might not feel the same, though no one has voiced such concerns.

Mary thanks Susan for taking the initiative to share her concerns and promises to take it up with Stan. When she does, he is adamant in his rejection of Susan's request that he remove the sports memorabilia. Stan maintains that the team is a source of civic pride, and that the decorations help clients relax in his office and create a bond with him. Furthermore, he notes that the logo and mascot are fixtures throughout the city on buses, billboards, clothing, and bumper stickers. Removing them from the office, he says, would be "political correctness run amok. And, Mary," he adds, "if you are going to tell me how to decorate my workspace, will you do the same with Alice's religious paraphernalia and slogans, or Joan's incense and New Age posters? Or do only Susan's sensitivities matter here?"

Susan and Stan both feel confident in the correctness of their respective positions, but it is Mary who experiences an ethical dilemma. Susan's questions about the appropriateness of Stan's office decorations raise several issues that Mary must address. She must contend with the relationship between the supervisor and supervisee, which is at risk of rupture given Susan's interpretation of Stan's decorations, his refusal to change them, and his reactions to her complaint. Regardless of what she decides to do about Stan's office, Mary must determine if and how the supervisory relationship can be saved. She must also address the issue sparked by Susan's complaint: Who decides when office decor is offensive or inappropriate? Is the sports decor discriminatory, marginalizing, or culturally insensitive? Moreover, what norms or policies should be in place at the agency to foster a welcoming and inclusive environment? This section focuses primarily on resolving the ethical dilemma embedded in the issue of office decor, though we will also consider the strategy for assisting Susan and Stan.

Applying the Six-Question Model

Who Can Assist Mary in Determining the Ethics of Office Decor?

In deciding how to respond to Susan's original complaint and Stan's rejoinder about others' offices, Mary should consult her own supervisor about agency policies and about the process for addressing the issue. If the agency has a policy, does it clearly resolve the question regarding decorations such as Stan's? Or is it worded in such a general way ("modest and tasteful decorations," for example) that its interpretation is open to dispute?

Whether or not the policy is clear, if it exists and has not been enforced, perhaps Mary's supervisor can explain why and advise her on bringing attention to it. Key questions include who else will be affected if the policy is imposed and what will result if the policy is enforced after it has been dormant for some time. The agency's human resources department may also be helpful in interpreting the policy or crafting a new one. Human resources staff can also describe other agency policies that may relate to Mary's dilemma, such as those on the use of agency property or criteria for what constitutes a hostile work environment under sexual harassment or discrimination provisions.

Mary may want to consult with other supervisors at her agency. Have they experienced similar dilemmas? How do they perceive Stan's office environment? If her colleagues represent diverse backgrounds, it may be useful to hear their perspectives on office environments in general, and on the intentional and unintentional messages that those environments send. Perhaps there is also merit in surveying current and former clients about the agency environment and their perceptions of the cultural competence reflected there.

Social service consumer groups or colleagues in other settings may be additional resources. Given the visibility of the team logo in the city, it is likely many other organizations—corporate, nonprofit, and otherwise— have struggled with similar questions and it will help to benefit from their wisdom on this matter and on the qualities that make an office environment welcoming and inclusive.

Have leaders in Indigenous communities spoken out about the logo and mascot? Have they said that they feel it is insensitive or off-putting? (Canadian Heritage, 2019). If official pronouncements have been made, to what extent do they help with Mary's decision? Tribal leaders in some regions of the United States have approved the use of their names by local teams (for example, the Seminoles at Florida State University). If that is the case with the team in Mary's area, does that mean such decor is acceptable there but not in other regions where tribes have come out against the practice? Do those official sanctions mean the decorations Stan and others use are automatically rendered inoffensive?

Beyond the message sent by the logo, how much latitude do other employers offer staff in decorating their workspaces? How would they handle a dispute when one worker is upset with another's decor? The human resources staff at Mary's agency may be able to take the lead in conducting research on the standards in other organizations.

Mary should also talk further with her own staff about the issue of office decor, moving it away from Susan's complaint about Stan, and explore the following:

- What norms would the group wish to develop to create a welcoming workplace?
- Without personalizing the issue, where would they draw limits in individual choice?
- What are the clinical implications of certain signs and symbols? What are the implications for colleagues?
- If clients are in distress and disempowered when they appear for service, might they feel inhibited about voicing concerns about decorations they find unsettling?
- How can the staff anticipate and honor the views of clients?

Other policies and consultations may serve as resources to Mary as she tries to resolve her dilemma concerning Susan and Stan's supervisory relationship. Since Susan is a student, the social work program that placed her at the agency likely has a contract that specifies how disputes are supposed to be addressed. Typical conflict resolution steps would include the following:

- Have Stan or Susan spoken to the school's field liaison about the friction between them?
- Should Mary meet with Stan and Susan to determine if the issue of office decor is inhibiting a constructive supervisory relationship and help to create a remediation plan if it is?
- Should Mary be in contact with Susan's social work program about the problem?
- Does Susan's background mean that her concerns could constitute a discriminatory environment by law, in which case she should be provided with information about her rights and resources to file a report and seek a remedy.

Beyond the student placement contract, Mary should determine what policies the agency has for addressing supervisory disputes. There may be a grievance process or mediation assistance that either party can access, or there may be a process for reassigning supervisees. Whether or not any of these are called for at this time, Mary should be aware of her options.

What Are Mary's Choices?

Mary must decide whether Stan's office decorations are inappropriate because they are racially insensitive, upsetting to clients or coworkers, or just plain excessive. If she decides that they are inappropriate, she will have to consider whether his is the only office that raises such concerns or whether other offices reflect similar problems. If she decides it is just Stan's office, she should deal with him individually and discuss with him both the office itself and any related concerns about cultural competence.

However, if Stan's office is only one example of insensitive or potentially offensive office decor, Mary must create or enforce a policy and a process that would address his decorations and those of other workers. Finally, if Mary decides Stan's office decor is not inappropriate, she must deal with Susan's feelings and with the effects on her relationship with the agency.

When Has Mary Faced a Similar Dilemma?

In past evaluations of the agency's environment for inclusive employment and service delivery, the leadership team has audited the surroundings and made adjustments to convey a message of cultural competence. Recently the waiting area was redecorated with signs in three languages (English, Spanish, and French) and prints by Asian, Latino, and Black artists to send a welcoming message to the agency's diverse clientele. As part of that team, Mary clearly believes that decor sends a message to clients and that everything—from the selection of reading material in the waiting area to the languages spoken on the voice mail service—should encourage clients of all backgrounds to feel welcome there. If the discussions in the environmental audit addressed individual offices, that information would impinge on her current thinking about Stan's office. Certainly, the agency's attention to the importance of artwork, signage, and the like would indicate that it views decoration as a significant form of communication.

Mary's experiences as a supervisor, and specifically as Stan's supervisor, will aid her in this situation. Specifically, these reflections may uncover helpful precedents.

- How has she handled supervisory disputes in the past?
- What interventions have proved successful?
- At what point does Mary think she must become involved because the two parties can no longer effectively address the issue?
- Which parties and positions in the dispute does Mary most identify with?
- How does Mary experience Stan? To what degree does she believe his office reflects deeper cultural insensitivity or biases?
- Do service statistics and client feedback indicate that he has difficulty connecting with clients of different backgrounds?
- Is he typically resistant or defensive when presented with feedback from Mary or his colleagues?
- Is he respectful of agency policies and willing to follow them even if he doesn't wholeheartedly agree?

This ethical decision also requires Mary to reflect on her own experiences with oppression or discrimination. How do her history and worldview shape her appraisal of the degree to which staff members' offices are offensive? Can she put herself in an outsider's shoes and examine the messages that the surroundings convey? Has she experienced the type of outrage or marginalization Susan felt when her concerns with Stan's sports memorabilia were rebuffed? How did Mary handle those experiences? Can she draw on them in this situation?

Perhaps Mary has had experiences with students whose zeal and moral clarity conflict with the realities of contemporary service delivery. Has Mary's response been to demean or temper the students' good intentions or explain why conditions are, immutably, the way they are? Or has she helped students both to understand the workplace and to be constructive agents of change? In these ways, too, Mary's past provides a basis for her current decisions.

Where Will Ethical and Clinical Guidelines Lead Her?

Rule-based ethics. Three rules are clearly embedded in Mary's choices:

1. "Office decorations should not be offensive to clients or staff."
2. "Office decor should not demean others on the basis of race, gender, or religion."
3. "Employees have a right to decorate their offices any way they want to."

Of these, the last is the most troubling when taken to an extreme. If we chose it to be a universal law, we'd be supporting the office occupant's individual rights over all other considerations, and permitting any deécor that suits that individual's taste. On what basis would we want to support such a rule? Is an individual's control over their workspace compelling enough for the agency to give up its voice in the matter? Is the risk of abuse so slight that the right to free rein is warranted?

The first two rules are probably already reflected in the organization's norms: staff members are expected to treat others with respect, create an affirming environment, and reject offensive characterizations of others' backgrounds. If Stan's decorations were not affiliated with a famous sports team, he would probably view them as inappropriate and demeaning. The fact that they are tied to the sports team may explain why he and others are attracted to the logos and mascots and are inured to their offensive symbolism. This suggests an additional option: Can Stan's office decor reflect his loyalty to the team without using the logos and mascots that Susan and others find distasteful? Whether or not this compromise works, the deontological perspective would encourage Mary to take some action concerning provocative office decor to encourage a nondiscriminatory and respectful work environment.

Outcome-based ethics. Taking a utilitarian perspective, what are the possible consequences of Mary's choices? If the agency develops or enforces a policy about office decor, the result could be more uniformity in the offices and an environment in which the risk of offending or alienating any client is reduced. An unintended result may be a sterile environment where workers and clients feel ill at ease because of the lack of personality and individualism in the clinicians' workspaces. Whether Stan alone is targeted or the policy is directed at all staff, Mary can expect backlash from those who are strongly attached to the work environments they have created. Perhaps there will also be retribution toward Susan as the perceived instigator of the change.

A failure to address concerns about the decor may mean that individual workers' offices are so highly personalized that they prove distracting or upsetting to clients. The offices may be the province of the workers, but they are the property of the agency; the organization has a stake in the decor, particularly given its efforts at inclusive messages in the common agency space. Doing nothing may send the wrong message to the staff about their individual workspaces and about honoring the perspective of people who express discomfort about them. Inaction will also prove a grave disappointment to Susan, who might continue to fight the battle over Stan's decor with her social work program and with human rights agencies outside the placement setting.

Of the consequences of inaction, the most serious for the agency's mission is the potential for clients to be alienated. As such, it seems Mary should at least initiate conversations in the agency about decor and its effect on clinical services and the agencies cultural competence. Hopefully the resulting discussion will lead to norms or policies that balance the employees' interests with those of the people they serve.

Values. A number of values warrant consideration in this case. Clearly Stan and the other workers value the autonomy to create environments in which they are comfortable. Susan, too, wants to be comfortable in the offices she visits at the placement. We might assume as well that the agency's administration and staff value respect for clients and for culturally sensitive approaches to service.

Ethical principles. The NASW ethical principle of justice states, "Social workers pursue social change, particularly with and on behalf of vulnerable and oppressed individuals and groups of people. Social workers' social change efforts are focused primarily on issues of poverty, unemployment, discrimination, and other forms of social injustice. These activities seek to promote sensitivity to and knowledge about oppression and cultural and ethnic diversity. Social workers strive to ensure access to needed information, services, and resources; equality of opportunity; and meaningful participation in decision making for all people" (2021, p. 5).

The value upholding individuals' dignity and worth would also apply to this case, in that the principle behind it states, "Social workers treat each person in a caring and respectful fashion, mindful of individual differences and cultural and ethnic diversity" (NASW, 2021, p. 5).

Sports memorabilia at one nonprofit agency may seem a minor concern when compared to vast historical and contemporary mechanisms of oppression and discrimination. However, if office decorations make clients and coworkers ill at ease about **biases** or stereotypes concerning race, religion, gender, sexual orientation, or other characteristics, overlooking them on any scale would seem inconsistent with social work values. Social work values suggest that Mary should act.

Professional standards. Ethical standards also support action. In addition to those on nondiscrimination and cultural competence stated at the outset of the chapter, the following tenets may be applicable to this case:

- "Social work administrators should take reasonable steps to ensure that the working environment for which they are responsible is consistent with and encourages compliance with the NASW Code of Ethics. Social work administrators should take reasonable steps to eliminate any conditions in their organizations that violate, interfere with, or discourage compliance with the Code." (NASW, 2021, 3.07d)
- "Social workers should not permit their private conduct to interfere with their ability to fulfill their professional responsibilities." (NASW, 2021, 4.03)
- Social workers conduct "themselves in a manner that is consistent with the *Code of Ethics* and *Guidelines for Ethical Practice*, and standards of their regulatory body." (CASW, 2005b, 7.2.1)
- "Social workers acquaint organizational administrators with the ethical responsibilities of social workers. Social workers encourage employers to eliminate workplace factors that prohibit or obstruct adherence ethical practice." (CASW, 2005b, 4.3.1)

The first standard encourages Mary and her superiors to take seriously ethics provisions on respect and nondiscrimination. Several options might constitute reasonable steps to address conflicts with the *Code*, such as holding meetings to craft a policy about office space, discussing strategies to best serve a diverse clientele, offering staff development sessions around cultural competence, and encouraging open communication among paid and non-paid staff about ways to enhance the organizational environment.

The second standard might be relevant to Stan or other workers who consider their offices an extension of themselves and an expression of who they are. The concept of private conduct may go beyond activities on the employee's personal time to include individual expression through one's appearance or surroundings. At its essence the standard asks social workers to give priority to their professional responsibilities when private interests might infringe on those duties. This is in keeping with the value of elevating "service to others above self-interest" (NASW, 2021, p. 5). A worker whose office is laden with family photos, or another who routinely wears jewelry with religious symbols, may be sending a message of "This is who I am." But as professional social workers, they must also be mindful of the message received by the clients they encounter: "I don't belong here," "Can this person understand me?" or "Will this person be able to help me?" Even if only a fraction of the clientele is put off or put down by those messages, is that a worthwhile trade-off for freedom of expression at work?

Ethical principles. Embedded in this tension is the principle of autonomy and the balance between policies that support the workers' rights with those of the clients. In this case, the clients are in a less powerful position, in that they likely have little choice in which workers they see at which agencies, and limited ability to take issue with aspects of service they find disconcerting. Mary's choice should help to maximize the autonomy of all involved, but particularly that of the least powerful members of the transaction—the clients.

Which option represents fidelity and justice? Mary must consider the implicit and explicit promises made to employees, to Susan and other students, and to clients. She must act in a manner that is congruent with stated policies and encourage others to do the same. The process she uses for making and implementing her decision should be transparent and reinforce her trustworthiness. And her decision must meet the standards of fairness. In this she should be particularly careful in singling out Stan and his office for scrutiny. If her rationale for limiting the personalization of offices has to do with unwelcoming messages for clients and colleagues, she should be certain that the rule is applied to all offices. If Mary determines that Stan's office is not out of line, fairness demands that she be certain that no precedents exist where workers in the organization were disciplined for similar issues.

The principles of beneficence and nonmaleficence would aspire to enhance the positive opportunities in the case and minimize the negative effects. While it is good for workers to be happy in and comfortable with their office environments, the greater good is for clients to be comfortable there, and the greater damage occurs when they are not.

How will her decision fit with the principle of publicity? Maybe Stan is right that it "smacks of political correctness and a tendency to allow the sensitivities of a few to dictate the actions of the majority." If this perception is shared by others, Mary's efforts could be met with derision inside the agency and in the professional community. Nevertheless, there is also power in the messages sent by her attempt to enhance cultural competence: We care about what people think, we care about inclusion and belonging, and when in doubt, why not err on the side of sensitivity?

If Stan and the other staff could imagine themselves in their clients' positions, complete with apprehensions about treatment, histories of powerlessness and marginalization, and limited authority at the agency, what option would they choose? Can the principle of reversibility help them appreciate the need to make accommodations for others? Does it reinforce Mary's conviction that she should act for change? As she considers what feels appropriate to her, and what her mentors might do, is she confident in her decision?

Laws and policies. Although the laws about discrimination don't encompass office decorations, numerous statutes and regulations address discrimination in the workplace. In the United States, Title VII of the Civil Rights Act of 1964 prohibits employers from discriminating against or harassing people on the basis of sex, race, color, religion, or national origin (Strom, 2021). Subsequent interpretations of the statute and rulings of the Equal Employment Opportunity Commission have shaped the application of this law in areas such as dress codes, holiday decorations, work schedules, and proselytizing (Atkinson, 2004).

In Canada, the Employment Equity Act (1995) similarly enforces employment protection of women, visible minorities, Indigenous people, and people with disabilities. An understanding of the characteristics of unequal treatment of employees and the unequal impact of ostensibly neutral policies will be essential as Mary and her colleagues respond to this case and craft new organizational guidelines.

Beyond information on nondiscrimination, Mary may also review policy and position statements on Indigenous mascots. For example, a position statement by the U.S. Commission on Civil Rights (2001) states,

> The Commission assumes that when Indian imagery was first adopted for sports mascots it was not to offend Native Americans. However, the use of the imagery and traditions, no matter how popular, should end when they are offensive. We applaud those who have been leading the fight to educate the public and the institutions that

have voluntarily discontinued the use of insulting mascots. Dialogue and education are the roads to understanding. The use of American Indian mascots is not a trivial matter. The Commission has a firm understanding of the problems of poverty, education, housing, and health care that face many Native Americans. The fight to eliminate Indian nicknames and images in sports is only one front of the larger battle to eliminate obstacles that confront American Indians. The elimination of Native American nicknames and images as sports mascots will benefit not only Native Americans, but all Americans. The elimination of stereotypes will make room for education about real Indian people, current Native American issues, and the rich variety of American Indians in our country.

Mary might also reference the American College Personnel Association's (ACPA's) statement on Indigenous mascots, including its 2012 resolution to immediately retire all Indigenous mascots from colleges, universities, and other higher education institutions based on their view that the use of these mascots "is a form of discrimination against Indigenous Peoples that can lead to negative relations between groups" (ACPA, 2012). The resolution further stated, "the ongoing use of American Indian mascots, symbols, images, and personalities on college campuses must be eradicated because their use is harmful to all college students and their positive psychosocial development" (ACPA, 2012).

Similarly, the president of the National Congress of American Indians (n.d.) states, "The National Congress of American Indians strongly condemns the use of sports team mascots that claim to portray Native Americans and Native cultures in a positive light. . . . It is only with Native Americans that this practice continues. It is a national insult and does nothing to honor the Native peoples of this country." Canadian sports teams have experienced similar pressures to change mascots that display unflattering or insulting images of Indigenous people, including a 2013 social media campaign that prompted Ottawa's professional basketball team, formerly the Tomahawks to drop their logo and nickname (National Post Staff, 2013).

Social media has also fueled a movement to change the Redmen mascot of Bedford Road High School in the Saskatoon school district. Advocates for the name change have used a Facebook page to voice their opinions and to post statements from organizations supporting their cause, including the Department of Native Studies at the University of

Saskatchewan, whose statement was posted on the group's home page: "The department recommends that the Saskatoon School Board and the Ministry of Education implement a policy to remove all stereotypical and inaccurate labels of Aboriginal people from school teams, and issue an apology for using these because they contribute to the misunderstanding and perpetuation of stereotypes of Aboriginal people" (Bedford Road "Redmen," 2013).

Statements such as these and decisions to rename some college and professional teams provide support for Susan's complaint and for Mary's efforts to take action on Stan's office (Associated Press, 2012; Axelrod, 2021; De la Fuente & Sterling, 2020; Wetzel 2012). However, these statements don't remedy other forms of offensive décor, nor do they address any underlying concerns about cultural competence.

Might office decorations be considered a form of free speech and thus be protected from intrusions by the employer? While the First Amendment of the Bill of Rights and the Canadian Charter of Rights and Freedoms prohibits the governments of the United States and Canada from abridging free speech, the expressions of that right are continually defined and redefined by laws, court decisions, and social policies (American Civil Liberties Union, n.d.). If the agency is not a governmental entity and the actual office space is the private property of the organization, it seems unlikely that the First Amendment would apply. However, if Mary expanded her efforts to address personal appearance (such as religious insignias on jewelry) the workers' First Amendment protections might apply.

Practice principles. How do practice norms apply to this case? Some clinicians' decisions about their office decorations are dictated by their theoretical orientations, in that some perspectives would encourage more worker self-revelation and others less (Farber, 2006). Some workers are guided by pragmatic considerations—they choose not to reveal very much about themselves in order to reinforce attention to the client, or they share office space and have determined that neutral furnishings are in order. Other workers create a culturally welcoming space by purposefully selecting furnishings to convey a particular message or worldview (Mason et al., 1996). Beyond the norms about decoration, there appears to be scant published information about what decor should not be encouraged or the strategies that supervisors and administrators can use to ensure compliance with agency standards.

Why Is Mary Selecting a Particular Course of Action?

The information we have about the case and the ethical analysis support Mary in taking action about Stan's office and similar offices, not only on the basis of Susan's discomfort, but also because such decor contradicts agency values and may be troubling or distracting to those the agency serves. Her decision is reinforced by a consideration of the various errors in judgment had she made a different decision. For example, choosing to do nothing would certainly be easier for her and would preserve her relationship with her staff, even at the expense of her relationship with the student intern. But it places those relationships above her responsibility to clients and to culturally sensitive practice. It allows her to avoid the search for acceptable compromises and privileges some workers' rights over those of their colleagues and clients.

How Should Mary Carry Out Her Decision?

Mary will need to engage the agency's leadership in this situation. If she finds that the problem involves only Stan's office, she will want to be sure that she has the administration's support and guidance for the actions she takes. If this is a systemic problem, then the administration and other supervisors must be involved to craft a consistent, agency-wide strategy.

The change effort itself is likely to be most successful if it is inclusive of all personnel and if both the rationale for change and the implementation process are fair and transparent. Mary and others must be careful not to make Susan the scapegoat for the change but rather acknowledge that she brought to their attention an issue that is of concern to the organization. Those promoting the change should emphasize that the policy is in the interests of the agency and its workers, in that it makes it a more welcoming and effective workplace. Their change strategy should consider various options that reconcile the interests of the workers and their desire for personalized and unique office space with the need for a culturally sensitive workplace. That may mean limiting the proportion of personal furnishings in an office or requiring workers to convey their interests in an inoffensive way (for example, team memorabilia without the troubling mascot or logo). Whatever strategy they employ, Mary and the leadership should also strive to evaluate the change and document that it had the desired effects. If it does not, they should refine it accordingly.

BOX 10.5

A Case for You

Ed works at a large metropolitan hospital as a social worker on the medical-surgical unit. Most of his tasks involve discharge planning, referrals, and working with the patient and his family to educate them about aftercare and follow-up needs. Ed's field placement was in a small health clinic, so he was prepared for many of the procedures and diseases his hospital patients would encounter and is familiar with many regional resources for rehabilitation. He also learned to work as part of an interdisciplinary team, and he is able, if needed, to address disagreements about proper care for patients. His new position, however, has challenged his cultural competence. The demographics of his caseload reflect the diversity of the city. His patients come from many different socioeconomic, religious, cultural, and racial groups. Some have been in the country for generations, while others are newly arrived, some of these as refugees without proper documentation. Most speak languages that he does not understand.

Ed's master's program prepared him for cross-cultural practice, but advice from that program seems unrealistic in this setting with so much diversity and so little time with patients.

The case in Box 10.5 gives you an opportunity to apply your decision-making skills to a case that considers how to uphold professional obligations for cultural competence.

In some ways, this may seem like an easy scenario. Ed should just study up and do more to improve his cultural competence. However, it is a more complex ethical dilemma involving justice: how to make the best use of limited resources (his time and energy) to properly serve his clientele. In the absence of comprehensive knowledge, is Ed in violation of the professional standards on competence? What role should **cultural humility** play in Ed's development? As you work through the decision-making model, how would you advise Ed (and his colleagues) to address this dilemma?

Conclusion

Ethical standards on nondiscrimination require social workers to treat their clients, employees, students, and colleagues in a fair and unbiased fashion. The commitment to social justice obliges social workers to advocate for improved social conditions and dismantle systems that perpetuate inequality. Cultural competence encourages an array of activities to help workers understand and respond sensitively to various forms of diversity. Effective social work requires an ongoing commitment to engage in self-reflection and self-interrogation, while learning more about others and incorporating that knowledge into practice.

Professionals should be mindful of the messages sent by their dress, surroundings, and behavior. Do those messages foster trust and convey a sense of helpfulness and acceptance of difference? Are they congruent with the agency's mission and the intentions of the professionals involved? While culturally sensitive surroundings are important, office furnishings and decor should be an authentic expression of interests, not window dressing advertising a competence that does not exist.

A healthy organizational environment invites open discussion of differences and concerns and adopts practices benefiting the organization's clientele and workforce. Even in effective agencies, conversations about racism and discrimination can be difficult. So too is reconciling the rights and interests of various parties. However, those efforts can help to strengthen the workplace, improve morale, and develop a culture where diverse perspectives are honored and valued.

For Continuing Conversation

1. History, economic insecurity, ignorance, and contemporary events can lead to societal prejudice against certain groups (e.g., immigrants, Muslims, same-sex couples). When direct practitioners become aware of institutional racism or other large-scale forms of discrimination, how can they create nondiscriminatory practices?

2. The rainbow connotes alliance or identification with LGBTQQ people. Is it aways ethical for social workers to have rainbow decals on their cars, laptops, office doors, or work other spaces?

3. Imagine you are in a meeting with a potential donor to an important social cause when the person uses a bigoted term. How would you handle that situation?

4. When is it appropriate for organizations to restrict their services to certain gender, age, religious, or ethnic groups?
5. How does your power or positionality affect your ability to incorporate the social justice and cultural competence standards into your practice?

Key Concepts

Bias. Preference or prejudice in favor of or against one perspective, individual, or group in comparison with another, typically in an unfair manner.

Cultural competence. "Cultural competence is a set of congruent behaviors, attitudes, and policies that come together in a system or agency or amongst professionals and enable the system, agency, or those professions to work effectively in cross-cultural situations" (National Center for Cultural Competence, n.d., p. 1).

Cultural humility. A lifelong commitment to engage in self-evaluation and self-critique. Being other-oriented, open to learning, and relinquishing the role of expert, accepting the limitations of ever achieving full understanding (Barsky, 2018).

Discrimination. The unjust or prejudicial treatment of different groups of people, especially on the grounds of race, age, ability, gender, sexual orientation, faith, or other marginalized identities.

Ethnocentrism. The evaluation of other peoples or cultures according to the values and standards of one's own culture.

Nondiscrimination. The elimination of policies or personal practices that directly disadvantage particular groups of people, as well as those that appear benign but have a disproportionate impact on individuals of a particular race, age, ability, gender, sexual orientation, faith, or other identity.

Positionality. The ways in which differences in identity and social position affect relative power in a given context (Finn, 2021).

CHAPTER 11

Sustaining Ethical Habits

Introduction

Hopefully this book has given you greater familiarity with ethical decision making and enhanced your confidence in your own decisions. Still, you may be weary of all the considerations, equivocations, and ambiguities involved in determining ethical actions. An old *Far Side* cartoon showed a student in a classroom with hand raised asking, "Can I be excused? My brain is full." Given the complexity and seriousness of social work practice, the settings in which the field is represented, and the roles social workers play, it's easy to understand why some people feel the thoughtful examination of dilemmas is burdensome—or, worse, pointless. While there are endless permutations of the cases you have encountered in this book, the effort you make in carefully and critically resolving dilemmas can be viewed as an investment in the resolution of future dilemmas. As indicated in the 6Q decision-making model, past judgments provide precedents for solving subsequent problems. In short, good decisions should beget better and easier decisions. Educated intuitions help us to make a habit of ethical decision making (Sauer, 2017; Sparrow & Hutchinson, 2013).

The capacity to identify and work through ethical dilemmas constitutes an important foundation of knowledge and skills. However, it will not be enough if the will to act ethically is impeded by cynicism, timidity, or self-interest. This chapter will help you consider the perils to incorporating virtue and ethics into a way of life.

Impediments and Avenues to Ethical Habits

The will and capacity for ethical excellence are often imperiled by a variety of circumstances and considerations, including preoccupation with risk, personal characteristics, environmental factors, and the disuse and misuse of decision-making skills. Let's close by examining each of these threats and some ways to avoid or diminish their destructive effects.

Risk

I've tried to make the case in this text that thoughtful, well-supported decisions can mitigate risk. However, they will never eliminate it. In truth, anyone can take issue at any time with the way professionals conduct their practice. Clients may be dissatisfied with the outcomes of their care, the type of services they received, or the way they were treated. Supervisees may take offense at direction, performance appraisals, or assigned tasks. Administrators may question the rationale for services or the costs. Guilt and blame are often directed at social workers who "can be seen as symbols of state welfare, simultaneously representing two of its much criticized facets: bungling inefficiency and authoritarian repression" (Banks, 2021, p. 78). Risk is baked into the practice of social work. The possibilities are endless. They can also be paralyzing.

Clinicians who practice from a risk-averse stance may limit their clientele to avoid complex cases or people with certain diagnoses. In this instance, overly cautious practice is not about competence: it is fear-driven, leading workers to avoid necessary confrontations with clients or overreact to troubling information. They may set policies that are "safe" but unresponsive to client needs, for example, refusing all gifts, which misses opportunities to acknowledge the client's kindness, demonstrate cultural sensitivity, or explore the intent behind the gift. In the concern for self-protection, risk-driven decision makers may emphasize their security over client needs, in effect, increasing some risks by trying to eliminate others. The worker who feels compelled to clear their conscience by breaching a client's privacy is incurring other harms in exchange for their own peace of mind.

The question, I think, is not how to avoid risk, but rather how to put it in the proper place in our decision making. Here are some suggestions: invite it in, give it a seat at the table, acknowledge it, articulate your fear, and use it as a method to anticipate the specific harms you fear. A former colleague of mine used to say, "That which cannot be put into words cannot be put to rest." Ignoring or denying fear or giving it priority in decision-making limits the opportunity for creative, responsible decisions.

Another way to cope with fear is to appreciate the ways that our humanity and our dedication to the profession are diminished in a risk-avoidance paradigm. Consider the price we pay for defensive, risk-proof practice. What client groups are avoided, what services are withheld, what conversations are not pursued in the interest of a largely false sense of safety? This is not an invitation to be oblivious or reckless. To the contrary, it is an invitation to engage in mindful (versus self-conscious) practice, where carelessness is spurned and prudence is encouraged. It is an appeal to look at our work with a wider lens, appreciating the implications when we choose a defensive posture over an affirming and inclusive one. It is a return to the considerations of virtue and the kinds of practitioners we choose to be.

Wrestling with risk also requires us to confront our willingness to act on principle, to do the right thing rather than simply know the right thing to do. This is not a simple task. It entails hazards and demands courage. Whether we are putting our physical well-being at risk by confronting an abusive parent or our personal comfort at risk by confronting a disrespectful colleague, we are committing acts of courage (Papouli, 2019). Physical and **moral courage** do not mean that a person has no fear but rather that they act in spite of those fears (McCain & Salter, 2004). When we uphold ethical principles, even at the risk of condemnation, litigation, or alienation, we are acting with moral courage. "Ethical courage suggests people should be brave in the face of challenging situations. They should have the strength to consider what is ethically correct even when surrounded by people espousing conflicting thoughts or morality. . . . Acting ethically does not mean you will be the most popular person. In fact, you may face strong opposition particularly when you are defending the rights of a minority. You may also face risks such as losing your job, attracting negative media attention, or even receiving scorn from clients, coworkers, close friends, or relatives . . . Courage requires people to acknowledge and deal with their fears, but they should not act out of excessive fear. At the same time, courage requires people to take risks, but those risks should not be reckless" (Barsky, 2019, p. 289).

Box 11.1 lists the things to consider when distracted by professional risks.

BOX 11.1

Considering Risk

- Acknowledge the inevitable reality of liability and risk in social work practice.
- Realize how preoccupation with avoiding risk will limit creativity and ability to help.
- Develop prudent, confident, attentive, mindful habits of ethical decision making.
- Cultivate the will and skills to act with moral courage.

When we avoid upholding principles in the name of risk avoidance, we must always contend with the possibility that our rationale is moral cowardice in disguise (McCain & Salter, 2004). "Cowardice" is a strong word: the intent is not to shame or bully people into action, but rather to recognize it as a phenomenon with which everyone must contend. I suspect we all can recall times when we have not acted as our best selves, or when we have failed to speak up and regretted the failure later. Sometimes we don't calculate the risk to our conscience in making a risk-avoiding decision. As John McCain put it, "I can recall all too well those times I've avoided the risk of injury or disappointment by overruling the demands of conscience. . . . Remorse is an awful companion. And whatever the unwelcome consequences of courage, they are unlikely to be worse than the discovery that you are less a man than you pretend to be" (McCain & Salter, 2004, pp. 70–71).

Risk is real, and good decision making takes all forms of risk into account. Sometimes ethical action requires that we act in spite of risk, and sometimes ethical action is really *in*action—demonstrating restraint, keeping confidences, allowing due process. Upholding moral and ethical principles despite risks and fears demands courage, but even lapses in courage can serve as a basis for learning and an impetus to do better the next time around.

Personal Characteristics

Risk may lie not in those factors external to us (litigious clients, judgmental media, unsupportive administrators), but within us. Like risk aversion, personal traits can also undermine ethical habits. Workers may have power issues, hubris, and compelling needs (the need to be liked, to be right, to be in control, or be successful, for example) that override the needs of the client or the demands of the professional role. While each of these characteristics can be used in social work to constructive ends, they can also lead to dangerous deviations from accepted practice. For example, insecurity or an aversion to conflict can keep the worker from setting appropriate boundaries, calling out workplace racism, or advocating for social justice. Shame or pride can keep the worker from seeking assistance with cases or personal needs. The desire for control and achievement can result in the practitioner bullying colleagues or rejecting clients with poor prognoses for change.

Another assault on ethical habits comes from poor self-awareness. Practitioners who do not have a good understanding of their own zeal, habits, and personal histories are ill-equipped to use them purposefully when they are called for or rein them in when they have the potential to be destructive. For example, a worker who has been drawn to the field due to personal experience with child abuse, or due to volunteer or work experiences in that area, may have passion for righting wrongs and standing up for this vulnerable population. These experiences may prove beneficial in a variety of ways. They may create a vocal and impassioned advocate in child welfare, someone who is willing to work in a difficult field and who will stay in that career even when the going gets tough. The result may be extraordinary empathy for the survivors of maltreatment and uncommon dedication to social change. However, this profile of experiences also has a downside. It may blind the individual to other perspectives in the case and inhibit the ability to work effectively with other personnel in cases of abuse. The worker's zeal may lead to an ends-justify-the-means outlook and a whatever-it-takes determination, in which rights and processes are sacrificed in service of the worker's perceptions of justice.

The acquisition of self-knowledge and the management of personal characteristics and inclinations are prerequisites for effective practice in the helping professions, including the practice of ethical decision making. The pursuit of self-understanding is a lifelong quest. The attention to self that is so much a part of professional development can become obscured over the course of a career. Our workplaces, personal responsibilities, and achievements can divert attention from ourselves, as we lack the time, impetus, inclination, and opportunities required for reflexivity and self-examination.

Self-understanding goes hand-in-hand with **self-care**. Self-care is so integral to competent and ethical practice that it was added to the NASW Code of Ethics in 2021 (Murray, 2021). Self-care is embedded in the principles of nonmalfeasance and beneficence in that the well-being and resilience of the social worker is considered key to the avoidance of harms and promotion of positive outcomes for clients (Greene & Cummings-Lilly, 2019). When viewed through the lend of systems theory, self-care not only sustains the individual social worker against the occupational hazards of the profession, but "through activated self-care practitioners can change responses and interactions with the organization and other stressors" (Grise-Owens & Miller, 2022).

Perhaps paradoxically, our personal characteristics themselves can undermine self-care and self-examination. Take a trait such as insecurity: People who are insecure in their knowledge or abilities may live in fear that someone will discover those vulnerabilities. Under the influence of **imposter syndrome**, they may fail to seek the very advice or input that could help bolster their capacities and increase their confidence (Weir, 2013). The trait of confidence, too, can lead to the same problematic spiral. The excessively confident worker may not see any need for consultation or may ignore the suggestions of others and refuse to reconsider their own decisions. Driven not by fear but by ego, the person with all the answers forecloses opportunities for growth and change.

How do we overcome our internal barriers to developing ethical habits? Sometimes events will demand reexamination despite inertia or resistance. These events can come in the form of personal crises that call for self-reflection, or organizational or community catastrophes that result in wholesale reviews of personnel and processes. The death, fear, and social disruption caused by the COVID-19 pandemic gave rise to new forms of social work service delivery and reevaluation of personal and professional priorities (Banks et al., 2020; Kaplan, 2021). Regardless of the catalyst for self-examination, the process of honest self-appraisal should not be derailed by quests to assign or avoid blame or to put the crisis quickly to rest and move on. On the contrary, a climate of intentionality, trust, and affirmation creates the safe space in which people can examine their actions, take responsibility, and make plans for change.

It is not necessary to wait for a divorce, demotion, death, pandemic, or public scandal to engage in self-care and critical self-reflection. An honest and involved network of colleagues, friends, and family can make us aware of who we are, who we want to be, and how well our choices are aligning with those aspirations. Our civic involvements and faith communities can perform the same function.

Environmental Factors

Beyond attending to their personal characteristics, people who aspire to ethical action must also contend with their environments. Social services, health care, schools, and other settings must address organizational needs and strategic imperatives to survive and thrive. Some of these systemic factors are evident in cases throughout the book: racist structures, policies that restrict access to care, funding and programming changes that fail to account for staff capabilities, and pressures to meet outcome standards, regardless of the means needed to do so. It is easy to understand how social workers might find themselves torn between the organization's expectations and the needs of the people they serve.

The concept of **moral distress** first arose in the field of nursing, occurring when a worker has decided on a course of action, guided by clinical, moral, and ethical considerations, but cannot pursue it due to external influences (Jameton, 1984; Weinberg, 2009). Some conceive of moral distress as akin to a relational trauma experienced by the professional moral agent in conflict with intransigent socio-political impediments (Musto, Rodney & Vahderheide, 2015). Moral distress manifests itself in an array of physical and emotional symptoms, including guilt, anger, powerlessness, gastrointestinal problems, or loss of sleep or appetite (Oliver, 2013). The cumulative effects of moral distress, referred to as "moral residue," may lead to burnout, apathy, desensitization, and job withdrawal (working strictly to tasks or time or exploiting sick and vacation leave).

In the absence of a clear moral compass and the capacity for independent decision making, workers experiencing moral distress may capitulate to the organization's expectations without critically examining the ethical and personal harms involved. Ethical action requires professionals to be assertive in examining organizational directives, taking steps to address those that are ethically or legally compromised. As indicated in the cases in this book, as agents of change, workers in these positions must strategically utilize their skills and resources. They must be able to articulate the principles on which their concerns rest and manage the tensions inherent in the internal advocate role. They must also be mindful of the short-term and long-term consequences of their activism. The courageous follower who is a successful agent of change will help to make the organization a stronger and more effective service entity (Chaleff, 2009). Even those who are unsuccessful in pressing their case on a particular issue may ultimately be able to effect other positive long-term changes in an organization. But people who find that their ethical concerns are consistently rebuffed may ultimately need to move on to a healthier setting. While all organizations must balance many imperatives to successfully stay in operation, not all workplaces manage those tensions in a way that jeopardizes ethical, legal, and personal standards.

Misuse of Decision-Making Skills

Just as our ethical habits can be enhanced by those around us, so too can they be diminished. Individuals with a firm moral compass and a sound history of decision making may drift from those moorings in a sea of corruption. It's not always easy, though, to perceive this turbulence. The principle of "just noticeable difference," also known as the boiled frog phenomenon, suggests that when the changes around us are subtle and gradual, we adjust to the changing conditions without appreciating the distance we have come or the peril in our current surroundings (Stern & Johnson, 2010). Most individual and corporate scandals are years in the making and follow a rather predictable trajectory from minor, well-rationalized transgressions to increasingly more serious, harmful, and indefensible errors. Individuals who resist being swept up in the tide of wrongdoing typically have mechanisms (friends, interests, creeds) that call their attention to an ethical dilemma and reinforce their commitment to do something about it. That something may involve speaking up or in some other way endeavoring to be an agent of change. It may also involve voting with one's feet and leaving the untenable situation or calling a halt to dishonest personal behavior.

The phenomenon of **groupthink** poses another threat to ethical habits. An artifact of extreme cohesion or conformity bias, groupthink results when individual members of a group are consciously or unconsciously inhibited from introducing contrary opinions. In essence, members are reluctant to rock the boat because of the influence of powerful members or the approbation of their fellow group members. Decisions tainted by groupthink can be recognized by characteristics such as insufficient attention to alternatives, a lack of attention to the risks of the preferred choice, failure to reevaluate initially rejected alternatives, a poorly conducted search for information, and biases in weighing and processing that information (Tropman, 1997).

Catastrophes such as the NASA space shuttle crashes and the abuse of gymnasts by U.S. national team physician Larry Nassar have been attributed to groupthink. Troubling results also occur when the phenomenon plays out on a smaller scale such as workplace teams, nonprofit boards, or social groups. Groupthink can lead to poorly considered decisions, such as the failure of a treatment team to weigh an array of service options, a board's acceptance of a policy that disenfranchises specific racial or ethnic groups, or a fraternity posting pictures online of themselves in blackface. Errors such as these are compounded when attempts to cover up mistakes lead to lies, deceptions, ruined reputations, and violations of trust.

The same intra- and interpersonal resources that help individuals avoid the boiled frog phenomenon can provide support in avoiding groupthink. Changes in organizational and team culture can help too. Groups can develop

- norms that invite and acknowledge dissenting views,
- procedures for soliciting minority positions,
- processes to consider possible hazards in plans,
- culture to avoid silent acquiescence,
- courage to point out messages or behavior that shut down debate, and
- habits to carefully examine issues and options and re-consider previously rejected ideas.

This is probably daunting advice for anyone who spends much time in group or committee meetings. It is easy to dismiss it as unrealistic, inefficient, and problematic. But, in keeping with our discussion of risk, let's be mindful of the costs in time, energy, and reputations if group decisions are superficially supported, poorly considered, and potentially hazardous.

Disuse of Decision-Making Skills

Ethical decision making, like any skill, becomes strengthened through practice and weakened by disuse. The lack of opportunities to practice ethical decision making may be an artifact of our success at it; that is, people become so adept that it no longer requires much effort at all. Think of it as hefting a two-pound barbell when you are ready for a ten-pound weight. Opportunities for ethical decision making may also be limited because we fail to identify new dilemmas when they arise. How should social workers apply understood concepts to new settings, populations, issues, or technologies? Think of this challenge as using the weights on different muscle groups instead of one already-strong area of the body. The proliferation of telehealth due to COVID-19 quarantines is an apt example of the need to apply familiar standards about privacy and access to services in novel conditions (International Federation of Social Workers, 2020).

Keeping our ethical habits from getting rusty does not mean going out in search of dilemmas to solve, at least not literally. However, we can seek opportunities to apply and refine our skills by using them imaginatively in the situations we confront in our daily lives, or as Banks suggests, by "seeing ethics everywhere" (2010a, p. 129).

- We can help others with their ethical dilemmas.
- We can test our judgments against those of the ethics and advice columnists in our daily newspapers.
- We can envision our responses to dilemmas portrayed in novels, films, television, and other media.
- In doing so, we ask, "What would I do in a given circumstance? On what basis did I decide that was a good choice? Where would I turn for assistance? Is this particular decision consistent with others I have made and with my overall framework for ethical action?"

I'm not trying to ruin your free time by making it into an intellectual exercise, to turn recreation into work or every TV plot into a Socratic debate. But having an ethical lens that you can train on dilemmas as they arise (even those of which you are not a part), helps you to use those observations to build on the ethical habits you've already established. In truth, most of us do it anyway. When a therapist on *Law and Order* surrenders client information to detectives, castaways on *Survivor* are lying to and manipulating each other, or Jack Bauer is torturing a suspect on *24*, I think our instinct is to declare those actions right or wrong. Exercising ethical habits just gets us to examine why we think that way and generalize the situation to the times we may be called on to make similar, albeit less dramatic, judgments.

Of course, ethical habits can be enhanced by more direct means, including reading texts on topics such as philosophy, courage, cheating, morality, and decision making. In addition to textbooks, many popular works of fiction and nonfiction raise vexing ethical challenges that are ripe for discussion. For example, *My Sister's Keeper* (Picoult, 2004) discusses the role of siblings as donors for ill family members. *The Immortal Life of Henrietta Lacks* (Skloot, 2010) describes the collection and sale of cells harvested from a marginalized Black woman without her knowledge or consent. *Middlesex* (Eugenides, 2002) examines the complexities of gender reassignment surgery in childhood. I also encourage people to participate in online or email ethics discussion groups, subscribe to free electronic digests, read advice columns, participate in moral communities with other therapists (Doherty, 1995), or view online ethics commentaries through their professional organizations.

Organizations can engage in **ethics audits** that provide practitioners and agencies with a "framework for examining and critiquing the ways in which they address a wide range of ethical issues" (Reamer, 2018, p. 245).

Each of these strategies is an opportunity to evaluate the soundness of our positions, further our knowledge, examine our thinking, articulate our positions, and apply our beliefs to real-life quandaries, including those in other fields. While the specifics of corporate dilemmas, international diplomacy, sports, or politics may differ from those encountered in the helping professions, the essential tensions are often the same: due process versus expedience, honesty versus strategic advantage, the well-being of an individual or group versus that of another, and so on.

The Integrated Self

We are shaped by our decisions. As we grapple with ethical dilemmas, the resulting decisions become part of who we are. Banks discusses continuously cultivating our capacities to do "ethics work" (2010a, p. 129). A play on Hochschild's (1983) concept of emotion work, ethics work requires social workers to be caring, attentive, compassionate, attentive to the moral features of situations, capable of recognizing the political context and professional power in issues, and dedicated to personal and professional integrity.

This book has argued for self-evaluation and decision evaluation in service of the development of ethical habits. It has also argued for moral citizenship and courage, based on the notion that our decisions affect other people and the groups of which we are a part. Decisions have reverberating effects on the organizations in which we serve, and the colleagues, citizens, and clients with whom we interact. Healthy, helpful, and affirming decisions contribute to a better culture, and our resulting actions fulfill the promise and privilege that our professional status provides. Inaction, bad decisions, and unethical conclusions can also have reverberating, and detrimental, effects.

As we engage in the journey of integrating our daily decisions with our individual moral frameworks, let's be mindful not only of the challenges, but also of the possibilities. Some dilemmas and choices will fit seamlessly with our existing value framework, and others will challenge our beliefs, at times changing our belief system and at other times capitulating to it. The tensions in reconciling the two, the effort required to develop ethical habits and arrive at good decisions, and the pressures of the practice environment can all conspire to portray ethics as idealistic, naive, or irrelevant. But I think in our hearts, even the most cynical among us knows better. Our humanity is enhanced or diminished by the decisions we make. Let's take advantage of the tools at our disposal to make the best decisions we can, strive for improvement when we fall short, and use all of these experiences to create strong relationships, professions, and communities.

A Parting Example

Several years ago my late husband, George, and I were waiting in the gate area at an airport. Across from us a teenager fiddled with his phone and the man sitting next to him spoke into a digital voice recorder while referring to a stack of pink papers with white address or identity labels on them. The man appeared to be doing dictations, and in fact George and I could hear the occasional word or diagnostic term such as "primary caregiver" or "cystitis." My husband whispered to me, "Looks like this is a job for Miss Ethics."

"No way!" I replied. "It's my birthday and I am *not* getting involved in this." I then scuttled off to the gift shop and hung out behind the bookshelves until our flight was called.

When we finally lined up for boarding, the man shot us a dirty look and I figured out that my husband had indeed engaged in an act of moral courage. As the saying goes, no good deed goes unpunished.

Evidently George had caught the man's attention and had said, in a neutral tone, "Do you think that's appropriate?"

"I've tested it," the man said, "and no one can hear me."

"Well, I can hear you and there are people closer to you than I am," he said as he gestured to the teen and to the couple sitting behind the man, their seats attached to his.

"I'm a doctor" the man said, evidently by way of explanation or excuse.

To his credit, George did not jump on this juicy opportunity to say something clever or cutting. Either response would have probably escalated the dispute. Instead, he shrugged and said, "It is what it is."

The man huffed and puffed and put away his paperwork. He didn't thank George for rescuing his career from a HIPAA violation. Perhaps he'll just pick up his dictation again the next time he is in a waiting area. But maybe he will think twice the next time. Maybe the teen next to him took a lesson from the conversation. Despite the discomfort of speaking up, my husband did what he believed was right, overcame possible objections, and used what he had learned through his upbringing, faith, and social work training to gently call attention to a wrong in his midst. Both of us rested easier—me because the burden of being the ethics advocate was not on my shoulders alone, and my husband because he was free from replaying the scene over and over in his mind, wishing he had said something when faced with the opportunity to speak up about unethical practice.

Key Concepts

Ethics audit. An investigation into how well (or poorly) an agency conforms to the standards of its profession or society in a wide range of ethical situations and areas.

Groupthink. The practice of approaching problems or making decisions as a group in a way that inhibits individual creativity or responsibility.

Imposter syndrome. A sense of self-doubt. The inability to internalize and accept success, attributing achievements to luck, sympathy, or deception. Fear of being revealed as a fraud.

Moral courage. A commitment to act upon one's moral beliefs despite the risk of negative consequences to oneself or to others.

Moral distress. Physical, spiritual, or psychological reactions triggered by an "individual's inability to judge or manage ethical conflicts—dilemmas related to external or internal constraints" (Papouli, 2019, p. 229).

Self-care. An essential activity crucial to the development of skills and strategies needed to maintain one's professional effectiveness . . ." (Greene & Cummings-Lily, 2019, p. 37).

REFERENCES

Adams, P. (2009). Ethics with character: Virtues and the ethical social worker. *Journal of Sociology & Social Welfare, 36*(5), 83–105.

Adoption.com LLC. (2020). AdoptionPhotolisting.com. https://adoptionphotolisting.com/

Agency for Healthcare Research and Quality. (2018). *Protection of human subjects in research.* https://www.ahrq.gov/funding/process/grant-app-basics/hsubjects.html

Alagoz, O., Hsu, H., Schaefer, A., & Roberts, M. (2010). Markov decision processes: A tool for sequential decision making under uncertainty. *Medical Decision Making, 30,* 474–83.

Ali, R. (2011). *Dear colleague letter.* Washington, D.C.: U.S. Department of Education, Office for Civil Rights.

Allen, A., & Mendieta, E. (Eds.). (2021). *Decolonizing ethics: The critical theory of Enrique Dussel.* Penn State University Press.

American Academy of Pediatrics. (1995). Informed consent, parental permission, and assent in pediatric practice. *Pediatrics, 95*(2), 314–17.

American Civil Liberties Union (ACLU). (n.d.). *Free speech.* https://www.aclu.org/free-speech

American College Personnel Association (ACPA). (2012). *ACPA resolution supporting the immediate retirement of American Indian mascots, symbols, images, and personalities by colleges, universities, collegiate athletics, and affiliated organizations.* http://www2.myacpa.org/native-american-resolution

American Counseling Association (ACA). (2005). *ACA code of ethics.* American Counseling Association.

American Psychiatric Association. (2022). *Council on Minority Mental Health and Health Disparities.* https://www.psychiatry.org/about-apa/meet-our-organization/councils/minority-mental-health-and-health-disparities

American Psychological Association (APA). (2010). *The ethical principles of psychologists and code of conduct*. http://www.apa.org/ethics/code/principles. pdf

American Psychological Association. (2019). *Publication manual of the American Psychological Association* (7th ed.).

Anesthesia Key. (2020). *Ethical aspects of anesthesia care*. https://aneskey.com/ ethical-aspects-of-anesthesia-care/

Associated Press. (2012, April 3). *ND court won't block Fighting Sioux name election*. http://archive.kare11.com/news/news_article.aspx?storyid=970995

Atkinson, W. (2004). Religion in the workplace: Faith vs. liability. *Risk Management Magazine, 15*(12), 18–23.

Axelrod, B. (2021, July 23). *Cleveland Indians announce "Guardians" as new name*. WKYC Studios. https://www.wkyc.com/article/sports/mlb/indians/cleveland-indians-guardians-as-new-name/95-14c1ef96-f71c-48eb-80db-1f70a818e46d

Badawi, J. (2005, December 4). *Taqwa: Between love and fear*. On Islam. http:// www.onislam.net/english/reading-islam/understanding-islam/ethics-and-values/439939.html

Banks, S. (2010a). From professional ethics to ethics in professional life: Reflections on learning and teaching in social work. In D. Zaviršek, B. Rommelspacher, & S. Staub-Bernasconi (Eds.), *Ethical dilemmas in social work: International perspective* (pp. 119–32). University of Ljubljana.

Banks, S. (2010b). Integrity in professional life: Issues of conduct, commitment and capacity. *British Journal of Social Work, 40*, 2168–84.

Banks, S. (2021). *Ethics and values in social work* (5th ed). Bloomsbury.

Banks, S., & Nøhr, K. (Eds.). (2012). *Social work ethics around the world: Cases and commentaries* (1st ed.). Routledge.

Banks, S., Cai, T., De Jonge, E., Shears, J., Shum, M., Sobočan, A. M., Strom, K., Truell, R., Úriz, M. J., & Weinberg, M. (2020). Practising ethically during COVID-19: Social work challenges and responses. *International Social Work, 63*(5), 569–83. https://doi.org/10.1177/0020872820949614

Barsky, A. (2010). *Ethics and values in social work: An integrated approach for a comprehensive curriculum*. Oxford University Press.

Barsky, A. (2018). *Ethics alive! Cultural competence, awareness, sensitivity, humility, and responsiveness: What's the difference?* The New Social Worker. https:// www.socialworker.com/feature-articles/ethics-articles/ethics-alive-cultural-competence-awareness-sensitivity-humility-responsiveness/

Barsky, A. E. (2019). *Ethics and values in social work: An integrated approach for a comprehensive curriculum* (2nd ed). Oxford University Press.

Beauchamp, T.L. & Childress, J.F. (2012). Principles of biomedical ethics (7th ed). Oxford University Press

Beck, L. (2013, February 5). *Uh-oh: OB-GYN complains about patient on Facebook* [Blog post]. Jezebel. http://jezebel.com/5981691/she-made-a-huge-mistake-ob+gyn-complains-about-patient-on-facebook

Bedford Road "Redmen," it's time for a change." (2011, 18 September).Facebook. https://www.facebook.com/ChangeRedmen

Bell, A., Coleman, A. L., & Palmer, S. R. (2005). Race and diversity practices for the post-"Grutter" era. *The Chronicle of Higher Education, 51*(38), B9.

Beres, L., & Fook, J. (2020). *Learning critical reflection: Experiences of the transformative learning process.* Routledge.

Berg, N., & Todd, G. (2010). *New reform strategies and welfare participation in Canada.* IDEAS. http://ideas.repec.org/p/pra/mprapa/26591.html#biblio

Berman-Rossi, T., & Rossi, P. (1990). Confidentiality and informed consent in school social work. *Social Work in Education, 12*(3), 195–207.

Bernard, W. T., & Moriah, J. (2007). Cultural competency: An individual or institutional responsibility? *Canadian Social Work Review, 24*(1), 81–92.

Betteridge, L. (2013). *Practice notes: Meeting professional obligations and protecting clients' privacy: Disclosure of information without consent.* Ontario College of Social Workers. https://www.ocswssw.org/wp-content/uploads/Meeting-Professional-Obligations-and-Protecting-Clients-Privacy-Disclosure-of-Information-Without-Consent-final-revised-20180430.pdf

Blumenthal-Barby, J. S. (2015, September 14). *The age of contractualism in bioethics?* [Blog post]. Bioethics Today. https://www.bioethics.net/2015/09/the-age-of-contractualism-in-bioethics/

Boisen, L. S., & Bosch, L. A. (2005). Dual relationships and rural social work: Is there a rural code? In L. H. Ginsberg (Ed.), *Social work in rural communities* (4th ed., pp. 189–203). Council on Social Work Education.

Boland-Prom, K. W. (2009). Results from a national study of social workers sanctioned by state licensing boards. *Social Work, 54*(4), 351–60.

Brager, G., & Holloway, S. (1983). A process model for changing organizations from within. In R. M. Kramer & H. Specht (Eds.), *Readings in community organization practice* (pp. 198–208). Prentice-Hall.

Brager, G., & Holloway, S. (1992). Assessing prospects for organizational change: The uses of force field analysis. *Administration in Social Work, 16*(3/4), 15–28.

Brager, G., & Holloway, S. (2002). *Changing human service organizations: Politics and practice.* Free Press.

Brannigan, M. C. (2005). *Ethics across cultures: An introductory text with readings.* McGraw Hill.

British Columbia Association of Social Workers. (2011). *Self-care: An ethical imperative.* Perspectives January 2011 vol. 33 no.1

Brownlee, K., Halverson, G., & Chassie, A. (2012). Multiple relationships: Maintaining professional identity in rural social work practice. *Journal of Comparative Social Work, 2012*(1), 1–11.

Brownlee, K., LeBlanc, H., Halverson, G., Piché, T., & Brazeau, J. (2019). Exploring self-reflection in dual relationship decision-making. *Journal of Social Work, 19*(5), 629–641. https://doi.org/10.1177/1468017318766423

Bruscia, K. (2018). *Understanding countertransference: History of definitions.*
    https://www.researchgate.net/publication/325205751_UNDERSTANDING_
    COUNTERTRANSFERENCE_HISTORY_OF_DEFINITIONS

Buchanan, A., Brock, D. W., Daniels, N., & Wikler, D. (2000). Eugenics and its
    shadow. In *From chance to choice: Genetics and justice* (pp. 27–60). Cambridge
    University Press.

Bullis, R. K. (1996). *Spirituality in social work practice.* Taylor & Francis.

Burkemper, E. M. (2005). Ethical mental health social work practice in the small
    community. In L. H. Ginsberg (Ed.), *Social work in rural communities* (4th ed.,
    pp. 175–88). Council on Social Work Education.

Burton, J., & van den Broek, D. V. (2009). Accountable and countable:
    Information management systems and the bureaucratization of social work.
    British Journal of Social Work, 39(7), 1326–42.

Burton, R. V., & Kunce, L. (1995). Behavioral models of moral development:
    A brief history and integration. In W. M. Kurtines & J. L. Gewirtz (Eds.), *Moral
    development: An introduction* (pp. 141–71). Allyn & Bacon.

Canadian Association of Social Workers (CASW). (2005a). *Code of ethics.* https://
    www.casw-acts.ca/files/attachements/casw_code_of_ethics_0.pdf

Canadian Association of Social Workers (CASW). (2005b). *Guidelines for ethical
    practice.* https://www.casw-acts.ca/files/documents/casw_guidelines_for_
    ethical_practice.pdf

Canadian Association of Social Workers (CASW). (2005c). *Social work practice in
    child welfare.* http://www.casw-acts.ca/en/social-work-practice-child-welfare

Canadian Charter of Rights and Freedoms, s 2, Part I of the Constitution Act,
    1982, being Schedule B to the Canada Act 1982 (UK), 1982, c 11.

Canadian Heritage. (2019). *Building a foundation for change: Canada's anti-racism
    strategy 2019–2022.* Her Majesty the Queen in Right of Canada. https://www
    .canada.ca/content/dam/pch/documents/campaigns/anti-racism-engagement/
    ARS-Report-EN-2019-2022.pdf

Canadian Psychological Association. (2000). *Canadian code of ethics for
    psychologists.* https://www.casw-acts.ca/files/attachements/casw_code_of_
    ethics_0.pdf

Canda, E. R., & Furman, L. D. (1999). *Spiritual diversity in social work practice: The
    heart of helping.* Free Press.

Caplan, A. (2000). What's morally wrong with eugenics? In P. Sloan (Ed.),
    Controlling our destinies (pp. 209–28). University of Notre Dame Press.

Carson, V. B., & Arnold, E. N. (1996). *Mental health nursing: The nurse–patient
    journey.* W. B. Saunders.

Caulkins, C. (2019). The psychological autopsy: What, who and why. *The Forensic
    Mental Health Practitioner, 2*(1), 1–10.

Cavanagh, J., Carson, A., Sharpe, M., & Lawrie, S. (2003). Psychological autopsy
    studies of suicide: A systemic review. *Psychological Medicine, 33*(3), 395–405.

Center for Reproductive Rights. (2015). *Universal Periodic Review Fact Sheet. Rights of Women and Girls with Disabilities.* https://reproductiverights. org/universal-periodic-review-fact-sheet-rights-of-women-and-girls-with-disabilities/

Chaleff, I. (2009). *The courageous follower* (3rd ed). Berret-Koehler Publishers, Inc.

Chan, D. (2009). Philosophy, religion and love. *Philosophy in the contemporary world, 15*(2), 82–90.

Chemtob, C. M., Hamada, R. S., Bauer, G., Kinney, B., & Torigoe, R. Y. (1988). Patients' suicides: Frequency and impact on psychiatrists. *American Journal of Psychiatry, 145*(2), 224–28.

Child Welfare Information Gateway. (2012). *Use of advertising and facilitators in adoptive placements.* https://www.childwelfare.gov/systemwide/laws_policies/ statutes/advertising.pdf

Child Welfare League of America (CWLA). (1999). *CWLA standards of excellence for services for abused and neglected children and their families.*

Code of Federal Regulations. (2022). *Title 34.* National Archives. https://www .ecfr.gov/current/title-34/subtitle-B/chapter-I/part-106?toc=1

Cohen, E. D., & Cohen, G. S. (1999). *The virtuous therapist: Ethical practice of counseling and psychotherapy.* Wadsworth.

Cohen, R. (2002). *The good, the bad and the difference: How to tell right from wrong in everyday situations.* Doubleday.

Cohen, R. (2012). *Be good: How to navigate the ethics of everything.* Chronicle Books.

Community Toolbox. (2022). *Section 1. Understanding culture and diversity in building communities.* University of Kansas. https://ctb.ku.edu/en/table-of-contents/culture/cultural-competence/culture-and-diversity/main

Congress, E. P. (1999). *Social work values and ethics.* Cengage.

Cook, S. (2019). Social work ethics and values within the context of South African social work education and practice. In S. M. Marson & R. E. McKinney (Eds.), *The Routledge handbook of social work ethics and values* (1st ed., pp. 75–82). Routledge.

Cooper, C. (1995). Patient suicide and assault: Their impact on psychiatric hospital staff. *Journal of Psychosocial Nursing, 33*(6), 26–29.

Cooper, Z., & Zerden, L. D. (2021). How COVID-19 has impacted integrated care practice: Lessons from the frontlines. *Social Work in Health Care, 60*(2), 146–56. https://doi.org/10.1080/00981389.2021.1904316

Corey, G., Corey, M. S., Corey, C. & Callanan, P. (2014). *Issues and ethics in the helping professions* (9th ed.). Cengage.

Corey, G., Corey, M. S., Corey, C. & Callanan, P. (2019). *Issues and ethics in the helping professions* (10th ed.). Cengage.

Cosh, C. (2020, June 12) The unpopular "automatism" defence is revived. *National Post.* https://nationalpost.com/opinion/colby-cosh-the-unpopular-automatism-defence-is-revived

Coyne, I. (2009). Research with children and young people: The issue of parental (proxy) consent. *Children & Society, 24*(3), 227–37.

D'Aprix, A. S. (2005). Ethical decision-making models: A two phase study. *Dissertation Abstracts International, 66*(05), 1957A. (UMI No. AAT 3177652).

Daley, M. R., & Doughty, M. O. (2006). Ethics complaints in social work practice: A rural—urban comparison. *Journal of Social Work Values and Ethics, 3*(2). https://jswve.org/download/2006-1/7-Ethics-Complaints-in-Social-Work-Practice-A-Rural-Urban-Comparison-JSWVE-3-1-2006.pdf

Dalphon, H. (2019). Self-care techniques for social workers: Achieving an ethical harmony between work and well-being. *Journal of Human Behavior in the Social Environment, 29*(1), 85–95. https://doi.org/10.1080/10911359.2018.1481802

Decker, J. (2012). Facebook can get you fired: Legal guidance for school administrators and employees, Principal Navigator, 7(2), 14-16.

Décoste, R. (2013, November 16). *The most discriminatory laws in Canadian History* [Blog post]. HuffPost Canada. https://www.huffpost.com/archive/ca/entry/most-discriminatory-canadian-laws_b_3932297

De la Fuente, H., & Sterling, W. (2020, July 13). *NFL's Washington Redskins will change name and logo, team says.* CNN. https://www.cnn.com/2020/07/13/us/washington-redskins-nickname-change-spt/index.html

Devettere, R. J. (2000). *Practical decision making in health care ethics: Cases and concepts* (2nd ed.). Georgetown University Press.

Doherty, W. J. (1995). *Soul-searching: When psychotherapy must promote moral responsibility.* Basic Books.

Dolgoff, R., Harrington, D., Loewenberg, F. M. (2022). *Ethical decisions for social work practice* (9th ed.). Brooks Cole.

Ebert, B. W. (1997). Dual-relationship prohibitions: A concept whose time never should have come. *Applied and Preventative Psychology, 6*, 137–56.

Education Amendments Act of 1972, 20 U.S.C. §1681–1688. (2018). https://www.ecfr.gov/current/title-45/subtitle-A/subchapter-A/part-86

Edwards, G. (2012). Tarasoff, duty to warn laws, and suicide. *International Review of Law and Economics, 34*, 1–8.

Employment Equity Act, 1995 S.C. § 44. (1995). http://laws-lois.justice.gc.ca/eng/acts/E-5.401/FullText.html

Epstein, R. S., & Simon, R. I. (1990). The exploitation index: An early warning indicator of boundary violations in psychotherapy. *Bulletin of the Menninger Clinic, 54*(4), 450–465.

Erickson, S. H. (2001). Multiple relationships in rural counseling. *The Family Journal: Counseling and Therapy for Couples and Families, 9*(3), 302–04.

Ermine, W., Sinclair, R., & Browne, M. (2005). *Kwayask itôtamowin: Indigenous research ethics.* Indigenous Peoples' Health Research Centre.

Este, D. (2007). Cultural competency and social work practice in Canada: A retrospective examination. *Canadian Social Work Review, 24*(1), 93–104.

Eugenides, J. (2002). *Middlesex.* Farrar, Straus, and Giroux.

Farber, B. A. (2006). *Self-disclosure in psychotherapy.* Guilford Press.

Farris-Manning, C., & Zandstra, M. (2003). *Children in care in Canada*. Child Welfare League of Canada. https://web.archive.org/web/20160709110312/http://www.nationalchildrensalliance.com/nca/pubs/2003/Children_in_Care_March_2003.pdf

Finn, J. L. (2021). *Just practice: A social justice approach to social work* (4th ed.). Oxford University Press.

Fisher, C. B. (2003). *Decoding the ethics code: A practical guide for psychologists*. Sage.

Fisher, C. D. (2004). Ethical issues in therapy: Therapist self-disclosure of sexual feelings. *Ethics and Behavior, 14*(2), 105–21.

Fisher, R., Ury, W., & Patton, B. (1991). *Getting to yes: Negotiating agreement without giving in*. Penguin Books.

Ford, G. G. (2006). *Ethical reasoning for mental health professionals*. Sage.

Forester-Miller, H., & Davis, T. E. (1996). *A practitioner's guide to ethical decision making*. American Counseling Association.

Franklin, C., & Jordan, C. (2002). Effective family therapy: Guidelines for practice. In A. R. Roberts & G. J. Greene (Eds.), *Social worker's desk reference* (pp. 256–63). Oxford University Press.

Freundlich, M., Gerstenzang, S., & Blair, E. (2004). Lasting Impressions: A guide to photolisting children. Baltimore: Collaboration to AdoptUSKids.

Freundlich, M., Gerstenzang, S., & Blair, E. (n.d.). *Lasting impressions: A guide for photolisting children*. AdoptUSKids. https://web.archive.org/web/20131112202243/http://www.adoptuskids.org/_assets/files/NRCRRFAP/resources/lasting-impressions.pdf

Freundlich, M., Gerstenzang, S., & Holtan, M. (2007). Websites featuring children waiting for adoption: A cross-country review. *Adoption & Fostering, 31*(2), 6–16.

Frey, G. (1990). Framework for promoting organizational change. *Families in Society, 7*(3), 142–147.

Gabbard, G. O. (1996). Lessons to be learned from the study of sexual boundary violations. *American Journal of Psychotherapy, 50*(3), 311–22.

Gallagher, A. (2020). *Slow ethics and the art of care*. Bingley.

Gallagher, A. & Sykes, N. (2008). A little bit of heaven for a few? A case analysis. *Ethics and Social Welfare, 2*(3), 299–307.

Gartrell, N. K., & Sanderson, B. E. (1994). Sexual abuse of women by women in psychotherapy: Counseling and advocacy. *Women & Therapy, 15*(1), 39–54.

George, L., Newton, S., & Legacy, D.-M. (n.d.). *Trauma-informed practice: Working with Indigenous individuals*. Southwest Ontario Aboriginal Health Access Centre. https://www.omssa.com/docs/2.1_Trauma-Informed_Practice_Working_with_Indigenous_Individuals_-_Southwest_Ontario_Aboriginal_Health_Access_Centre.pdf

Gilligan, C. (2016). *In a different voice: Psychological theory and women's development*. Harvard University Press.

Gottlieb, M. C. (1994). Ethical decision making, boundaries, and treatment effectiveness: A reprise. *Ethics and Behavior*, 4(3), 287–93.

Gottlieb, M. C. (1996). Some ethical implications of relational diagnoses. In F. W. Kaslow (Ed.), *Handbook of relational diagnosis and dysfunctional family patterns* (pp. 19–34). Wiley.

Government of Canada. (2022a). *Research ethics board: Consent process*. https://www.canada.ca/en/health-canada/services/science-research/science-advice-decision-making/research-ethics-board/consent-process.html

Government of Canada. (2022b). *Research ethics board: Overview of the Health Canada and Public Health Agency of Canada REB*. https://www.canada.ca/en/health-canada/services/science-research/science-advice-decision-making/research-ethics-board.html

Government of Canada. (2022c, January 24). *Employment Equity Act*. Justice Laws Website. https://laws-lois.justice.gc.ca/eng/acts/e-5.401/page-1.html#h-215135

Graham, G. (2004). *Eight theories of ethics*. Routledge.

Gray, M., Coates, J., & Yellow Bird, M. (Eds.). (2008). Indigenous social work around the world: Towards culturally relevant education and practice. Ashgate.

Greene, D. S., & Cummings-Lilly, K. T. (2019). Social worker self-care: An ethical responsibility. In S. M. Marson & R. E. McKinney (Eds.), *The Routledge handbook of social work ethics and values* (1st ed., pp. 36–43). Routledge.

Gripton, J. & Valentich, M. (2003, May 29–30). *Dealing with non-sexual professional–client dual relationships in rural communities* [Paper presentation]. International Conference on Human Services in Rural Communities, Halifax, Canada.

Grise-Owens, E., & Miller, J. (2022). Self-care for social workers. In L. Rapp-McCall, K. Corcoran, & A. Roberts (Eds.), *Social worker's desk reference* (4th ed., pp. 29–37). Oxford University Press.

Grossmanss, R. (2010). Justice versus care: A dilemma of ethics. In D. Zaviršek, B. Rommelspacher, & S. Staub-Bernasconi (Eds.), *Ethical dilemmas in social work: International perspective* (pp. 25–38). University of Ljubljana.

Gould, J. W., & Martindale, D. A. (2013). Child custody evaluations: Current literature and practical applications. In R. K. Otto & I. B. Weiner (Eds.), *Handbook of psychology: Forensic psychology* (pp. 101–138). John Wiley & Sons, Inc.

Gulfi, A., Dransart, C., Angela, D., Heeb, J., & Gutjahr, E. (2010). The impact of patient suicide on the professional reactions and practices of mental health caregivers and social workers. *Crisis: The Journal of Crisis Intervention and Suicide Prevention*, 31(4), 202–10.

Gumpert, J., & Black, P. N. (2005). Walking the tightrope between cultural competence and ethical practice: The dilemma of the rural practitioner. In L. H. Ginsberg (Ed.), *Social work in rural communities* (4th ed., pp. 157–74). Council on Social Work Education.

Guthiel, T. G., & Brodsky, A. (2011). *Preventing boundary violations in clinical practice*. Guilford Press.

Guzman, T., Pirog, M., & Seefeldt, K. (2013). Social policy: What have we learned? *Policy Studies Journal, 41*(S1), S53–S70.

Halligan, P., & Corcoran, P. (2001). The impact of patient suicide on rural general practitioners. *British Journal of General Practice, 51*, 295–96.

Halverson, G., & Brownlee, K. (2010). Managing ethical considerations around dual relationships in small rural and remote Canadian communities. *International Social Work, 53*(2), 247–60.

Hardcastle, D. A., & Powers, P. R. (2004). Using your agency. In D. A. Hardcastle, P.R. Powers, & S. Wenocur, *Community practice: Theories and skills for social workers* (2nd ed., pp. 244–71). Oxford University Press.

Health Information Technology for Economic and Clinical Health (HITECH) Act. Title XIII of Division A and Title IV of Division B of the American Recovery and Reinvestment Act of 2009 (ARRA), Pub. L. 111–5, 123 Stat. 226, 111 U.S.C. (2009). https://www.govinfo.gov/app/details/PLAW-111publ5

Health Insurance Portability and Accountability Act (HIPAA). 45 C.F.R. § 164. (1996). https://www.govinfo.gov/app/details/PLAW-104publ191

Halverson, R. (1992, July 6). Sears nixes commission pay in light of fraud charges. *Discount Store News*.

Healy, L. M., & Link, R. J. (2011). Models of internationalizing curriculum. In L. M. Healy & R. J. Link (Eds.), *Handbook of international social work: Human rights, development, and the global profession* (pp. 329–336). Oxford University Press.

Hemmelgarn, A. L., Glisson, C. & James, L. R. (2010). Organizational culture and climate: Implications for services and intervention research. In Y. Hasenfeld (Ed.), *Human services as complex organizations* (2nd ed.). Sage.

Hepworth, D. H., Vang, P. D., Blakey, J. M., Schwalbe, C., & Evans, C. (2022). *Direct social work practice: Theory and skills* (11th ed.). Cengage Learning.

Heward, S., Hutchins, C., & Keleher, H. (2007). Organizational change—key to capacity building and effective health promotion. *Health Promotion International, 22*(2), 170–78.

Heyboer, K. (2010, March 26). *Medical students' cadaver photos gets scrutiny after images show up online*. NJ.com. http://www.nj.com/news/index.ssf/2010/03/medical_schools_examine_ethics.html

Heyd, D. (2012). Supererogation. *The Stanford Encyclopedia of Philosophy*. http://plato.stanford.edu/entries/supererogation/

https://www.hhs.gov/guidance/document/professionals-hipaa-privacy-rule

Hochschild, A. R. (1983). *The managed heart: Commercialization of human feeling*. University of California Press.

Hogan, R., & Emler, N. (1995). Personality and moral development. In W. M. Kurtines & J. L. Gewirtz (Eds.), *Moral development: An introduction* (pp. 209–27). Allyn & Bacon.

Holland, K. J., Cortina, L. M., & Freyd, J. J. (2018). Compelled disclosure of college sexual assault. *American Psychologist, 73*(3), 256–68.

Hooker, J. (2018). *Taking ethics seriously*. Taylor & Francis.

Hoover, E., & Gluckman, N. (2022, January 24). *The Supreme Court has upheld race-conscious admissions again and again. Will this time be different?* The Chronicle of Higher Education. https://www.chronicle.com/article/the-supreme-court-has-upheld-race-conscious-admissions-again-and-again-will-this-time-be-different

Houston-Vega, M. K., Nuehring, E. M., & Daguio, E. R. (1997). *Prudent practice: A guide for managing malpractice risk*. NASW Press.

Howard, R. A., & Korver, C. D. (2008). *Ethics for the real world: Creating a personal code to guide decisions in work and life*. Harvard Business Press.

Hugman, R. (2012). *Culture, value and ethics in social work*. Routledge.

Hutchison, E. D. (2015). *Dimensions of human behavior: Person in environment* (5th ed). Sage.

Institute for Global Ethics. (2001). *Leading with values: Ethics training for nonprofits*. Author.

International Federation of Social Workers. (2020). *Practising during pandemic conditions: Ethical guidance for social workers*. https://www.ifsw.org/wp-content/uploads/2020/11/2020-11-10-Ethical-Guidance-COVID-19-FINAL.pdf

Jameton, A. (1984). *Nursing practice: The ethical issues*. Prentice-Hall.

Jansen, B. (2006, July 10). *Welfare changes threaten funding*. Portland Press Herald/Maine Sunday Telegram. https://pressherald.newsbank.com/doc/news/112CB7162E3F85F8?pdate=2006-07-10

Janessen, J. S. (2022). Walking the rope bridge: Responding to clients' divisive language and behavior. *Social Work Today*. https://www.socialworktoday.com/archive/exc_091212.shtml

Jarolmen, J. (2014). *School social work: A direct practice guide*. SAGE Publications, Inc.

Jordan, J. (2008). Bereavement after suicide. *Psychiatric Annals, 38*(10), 1–6.

Jordan, J., & McIntosh, J. (2011). *Grief after suicide: Understanding the consequences and caring for the survivors*. Taylor and Francis Group.

Kaczynski, D. (2005). My brother, the Unabomber: An interview with David Kaczynski. *Free Inquiry, 25*(5), 12.

Kahn, J. & Mastroianni, A. (2009). The implications of public health for bioethics. In Bonnie Steinbock (Ed.), *The Oxford handbook of bioethics*. Oxford University Press.

Kanani, K., & Regehr, C. (2003). Clinical, ethical, and legal issues in e-therapy. *Families in Society: The Journal of Contemporary Human Services, 84*(2), 155–62

Kane, M. N., Houston-Vega, M. K., & Nuehring, E. M. (2002). Documentation in managed care: Challenges for social work education. *Journal of Teaching in Social Work, 22*(1–2), 199–212.

Kaplan, J. (2021, October 2). *The psychologist who coined the phrase "Great Resignation" reveals how he saw it coming and where he sees it going.* Business Insider. https://www.businessinsider.com/why-everyone-is-quitting-great-resignation-psychologist-pandemic-rethink-life-2021-10

Kelly, J. (2002, December 30–January 6). The year of the whistleblowers. *Time, 160*(27), 8.

Kenyon, P. (1999). *What would you do? An ethical case workbook for human service professionals.* Brooks/Cole.

Kidder, R. M. (1995). *How good people make tough choices: Resolving the dilemmas of ethical living.* Simon and Schuster.

Kidder, R. M. (2005). *Moral courage: Taking action when your values are put to the test.* William Morrow.

Kidder, R. M., & Bracy, M. (2001). *Moral courage.* Institute for Global Ethics.

Kitchener, K. S. (1988). Dual relationships: What makes them so problematic? *Journal of Counseling and Development, 67,* 217–21.

Kleepsies, P. M., Penk, W. E., & Forsyth, J. P. (1993). The stress of patient suicidal behavior during clinical training: Incidence, impact, and recovery. *Professional Psychology: Research and Practice, 24*(3), 293–303.

Klinka, K. (2009). It's been a privilege: Advising patients of the Tarasoff Duty and its legal consequences for the federal psychotherapist-patient privilege. *Fordham Law Review, 78*(2), 863–931.

Knapp, S. J., & VandeCreek, L. D. (2006). *Practical ethics for psychologists: A positive approach.* American Psychological Association.

Koenig, T. L., & Spano, R. N. (2003). Sex, supervision, and boundary violations: Pressing challenges and possible solutions. *The Clinical Supervisor, 22*(1), 3–19.

Kohlberg, L. (1984). *The psychology of moral development: The nature and validity of moral stages.* Harper & Row.

Konrad, S. C. (2020). *Child and family practice: A relational perspective* (2nd ed.). Oxford.

Koocher, G. P., & Keith-Spiegel, P. (1990). *Children, ethics, and the law: Professional issues and cases.* University of Nebraska Press.

Koocher, G. P., & Keith-Spiegel, P. (2008). *Ethics in psychology and the mental health professions: Standards and cases* (3rd ed.). Oxford University Press.

Kurtines, W. M., & Gewirtz, J. L. (Eds.). (1995). *Moral development: An introduction.* Allyn & Bacon.

Kuspinar, H. (2016). *Affirmative action and education equity in higher education in the United States and Canada* [Unpublished master's thesis]. McGill University.

Kutchins, H. (1991). The fiduciary relationship: The legal basis for social work responsibilities to clients. *Social Work, 36*(2), 106–13.

Kuther, T. L. (2003). Medical decision-making and minors: Issues of consent and assent. *Adolescence, 38*(150), 343–58.

Lacayo, R., & Ripley, A. (2002, December 30–January 6). Persons of the year: The whistleblowers. *Time, 160*(27), 30–33.

Ladany, N., O'Brien, K. M., Hill, C. E., Melincoff, D. S., Knox, S., & Petersen, D. A. (1997). Sexual attraction toward clients, use of supervision, and prior training: A qualitative study of predoctoral psychology interns. *Journal of Counseling Psychology*, *44*(4), 413–24.

Lazarus, A. (1994). The illusion of the therapist's power and the patient's fragility: My rejoinder. *Ethics and Behavior*, *4*(3), 299–306.

Legal Information Institute. (n.d.). *42 CFR part 2—Confidentiality of substance use disorder patient records*. Cornell Law School. https://www.law.cornell.edu/cfr/text/42/part-2

Levenson, J. (2017). Trauma-informed social work practice. *Social Work*, *62*(2), 105–13. https://doi.org/10.1093/sw/swx001

Lewers, N. (2019, July 1). *Where professional privilege is blurred*. Centre for Innovative Justice, RMIT University. https://cij.org.au/news-and-views/where-professional-privilege-is-blurred/

Library of Congress. (n.d.). *About the law library*. https://www.loc.gov/research-centers/law-library-of-congress/about-this-research-center/

Lieberman, A. A., & Lester, C. B. (2004). *Social work practice with a difference: Stories, essays, cases, and commentaries*. McGraw-Hill.

Linzer, N. (1999). *Resolving ethical dilemmas in social work practice*. Allyn and Bacon.

Loya, M. A., & Peters, K. (2019). Ethical study abroad. In S. M. Marson, & R. E. McKinney (Eds.)., *The Routledge handbook of social work ethics and values* (1st ed., pp. 240–47). Routledge.

Lum, D. (2011). *Culturally competent practice: A framework for understanding diverse groups and justice issues*. Brooks/Cole, Cengage Learning.

Manning, S. S., & Gaul, C. E. (1997). The ethics of informed consent: A critical variable in the self-determination of health and mental health clients. *Social Work in Health Care*, *25*(3), 103–17.

Manning, S. S., & Van Pelt, M. E. (2005). The challenges of dual relationships and the continuum of care in rural mental health. In L. H. Ginsberg (Ed.), *Social work in rural communities* (4th ed., pp. 259–82). Council on Social Work Education.

Mason, J. L., Benjamin, M. P., & Lewis, S. A. (1996). The cultural competence model: Implications for child and family mental health services. In C. A. Heflinger & C. T. Nixion (Eds.), *Families and the mental health system for children and adolescents: Policy, services, and research* (pp. 165–90). Sage.

McAuliffe, D., & Chenoweth, L. (2007). Leave no stone unturned: The inclusive model of ethical decision-making. *Ethics and Social Welfare*, *2*(1), 38–49.

McCain, J., & Salter, M. (2004). *Why courage matters: The way to a braver life*. Random House.

Menninger, W. W. (1991). Patient suicide and its impact on the psychotherapist. *Bulletin of the Menninger Clinic*, *55*(2), 216–27.

Mill, J. S. (1967). *Utilitarianism*. Bobbs-Merrill. (Original work published 1861).

Miller, W. I. (2000). *The mystery of courage*. Harvard University Press.

Milovidov, E. H., & Treitler, V. B. (2014). The commodification and online marketing of children in transnational adoption. In V. B. Treitler (Ed.), *Race in transnational and transracial adoption* (pp. 84–111). Palgrave Macmillan.

Minister of Justice. (2022, January 24). *Canadian Human Rights Act*. https://laws-lois.justice.gc.ca/PDF/H-6.pdf

Ministry of Children and Family Development. (n.d.). *Know your rights: A guide to rights for young people in care*. https://www2.gov.bc.ca/assets/gov/family-and-social-supports/foster-parenting/know_your_rights.pdf

Mizrahi, T. (2022). Community organizing principles and practice guidelines. In L. Rapp-McCall, K. Corcoran, & A. Roberts (Eds.), *Social worker's desk reference* (4th ed., pp. 816–26). Oxford University Press.

Mosby, I., & Millions, E. (2021, August 1). *Canada's residential schools were a horror*. Scientific American. https://www.scientificamerican.com/article/canadas-residential-schools-were-a-horror/

Moulton, J. F. (1924). Law and manners. *Atlantic Monthly, 134,* 1–5.

Murray, A. (2021). *2021 amendments to the NASW Code of Ethics: Self-care and cultural competence*. National Association of Social Workers. https://www.socialworkers.org/LinkClick.aspx?fileticket=UyXb_VQ35QA%3d&portalid=0

Musto, L. C., Rodney, P. A., & Vanderheide, R. (2015). Toward interventions to address moral distress: Navigating structure and agency. *Nursing Ethics, 22*(1), 91–102.

National Association of Social Workers (NASW). (2000). Cultural competence in the social work profession. In *Social work speaks: NASW policy statements* (pp. 59–62).

National Association of Social Workers (NASW). (2003). *NASW standards for the of social work with adolescents*.

National Association of Social Workers (NASW). (2004). *NASW standards for palliative and end of life care*.

National Association of Social Workers (NASW). (2013). *NASW standards for social work practice in child welfare*.

National Association of Social Workers (NASW). (2015a). *NASW standards and indicators for cultural competence in social work practice*.

National Association of Social Workers. (2015b). Cultural and linguistic competence in the social work profession. In *Social work speaks: National Association of Social Workers policy statements, 2015–2017* (10th ed., pp. 62–67). NASW Press.

National Association of Social Workers (NASW). (2021). *Code of ethics*. NASW Press. https://www.socialworkers.org/About/Ethics/Code-of-Ethics/Code-of-Ethics-English

National Association of Social Workers (NASW) National Council on the Practice of Clinical Social Work. (1994). *Guidelines for clinical social work supervision*.

National Center for Cultural Competence. (n.d.). *Definitions of cultural competence*. https://nccc.georgetown.edu/curricula/culturalcompetence.html

National Center for HIV, STD, and TB Prevention. (2005). *The Tuskegee timeline*. Centers for Disease Control and Prevention. http://www.cdc.gov/tuskegee/timeline.htm

National Conference of State Legislatures. (2018). *Mental health professionals' duty to warn*. https://www.ncsl.org/research/health/mental-health-professionals-duty-to-warn.aspx

National Congress of American Indians. (n.d.). *Position statement: Antidefamation and mascots*. http://www.ncai.org/policy-issues/community-and-culture/anti-defamation-mascots

National Institutes of Health. (2021). *Guidelines and policies for the conduct of research in the intramural research program at NIH*. National Institutes of Health, Office of the Director. https://oir.nih.gov/sites/default/files/uploads/sourcebook/documents/ethical_conduct/guidelines-conduct_research.pdf

National Post Staff. (2013, February 27). Ottawa "TomaHawks" basketball team changes name after outcry. *National Post*. https://nationalpost.com/sports/ottawa-tomahawks-basketball-team-quickly-changes-name-after-outcry

Newfoundland & Labrador Association of Social Workers. (2016). *Standards for cultural competence in social work practice*. https://nlcsw.ca/sites/default/files/inline-files/cultural_competency_standards.pdf

Newfoundland & Labrador Association of Social Workers. (2018a). Dual relationships: An ethical reality. *Ethical Compass*, 3. https://nlcsw.ca/sites/default/files/inline-files/dual_relationships.pdf

Newfoundland & Labrador Association of Social Workers. (2018b). *Social work & decision specific capacity enhancements*. https://nlcsw.ca/sites/default/files/inline-files/Social_Work_And_Decision-Specific_Capacity_Assessments_Final.pdf

Newkirk, V.R. II, (2016, June 17). A generation of bad blood. *The Atlantic* https://www.theatlantic.com/politics/archive/2016/06/tuskegee-study-medical-distrust-research/487439/

Nickell, N. J., Hecker, L., Ray, R., & Bercik, J. (1995). Marriage and family therapists' sexual attraction to clients: An exploratory study. *American Journal of Family Therapy*, 23(4), 315–27.

Office for Civil Rights. (2021). *Sex-based harassment*. U.S. Department of Health and Human Services. https://www.hhs.gov/civil-rights/for-individuals/special-topics/harassment/index.html

Office of the Privacy Commissioner of Canada (OPCC). (2013). *Protecting and promoting privacy rights*. http://www.priv.gc.ca/index_e.asp

Office of the Privacy Commissioner of Canada. (2018). *Summary of privacy laws in Canada*. https://www.priv.gc.ca/en/privacy-topics/privacy-laws-in-canada/02_05_d_15/#heading-0-0-2-1

Office of the Privacy Commissioner of Canada. (2020). *Provincial and territorial privacy laws and oversight*. https://www.priv.gc.ca/en/about-the-opc/what-we-do/provincial-and-territorial-collaboration/provincial-and-territorial-privacy-laws-and-oversight/

Oliver, C. (2013). Including moral distress in the new language of social work ethics. *Canadian Social Work Review, 30*(2), 203–16.

Paasche-Orlow, M., Taylor, H., & Brancati, F. (2003). Readability standards for informed-consent forms as compared with actual readability. *New England Journal of Medicine, 348*, 721–26.

Palmer, B. W., & Harmell, A. L. (2016). Assessment of healthcare decision-making capacity. *Archives of Clinical Neuropsychology, 31*(6), 530–40. https://doi.org/10.1093/arclin/acw051

Papouli, E. (2019). Moral courage and moral distress in social work education and practice. In S. M. Marson & R. E. McKinney (Eds.), *The Routledge handbook of social work ethics and values* (1st ed., pp. 223–32). Routledge. https://doi.org/10.4324/9780429438813-29

Park, Y. (2020). *Facilitating injustice: The complicity of social workers in the forced removal and incarceration of Japanese Americans, 1941–1946*. Oxford University Press.

Patterson, K., Grenny, J., McMillan, R., & Switzler, A. (2002). *Crucial conversations: Tools for talking when stakes are high*. McGraw-Hill.

Pearlman, T. (1992). Response to: When a patient commits suicide. *American Journal of Psychiatry, 149*(2), 282–83.

Piaget, J. (1932). *The moral judgement of the child*. Harcourt, Brace Jovanovich.

Piché, T., Brownlee, K., & Halverson, G. (2015). The development of dual and multiple relationships for social workers in rural communities. *Contemporary Rural Social Work Journal, 7*(2), 57–70. https://digitalcommons.murraystate.edu/crsw/vol7/iss2/5

Picoult, J. (2004). *My sister's keeper*. Washington Square Press.

Pimental, D. (2016). Protecting the free-range kid: Recalibrating parents' rights and the best interests of the child. *Cardoza Law Review, 38*(1), 1–57.

Pinals, D. A. (2019). Liability and patient suicide. *Forensic Psychiatry: Focus on Malpractice and Risk Management, 27*(4), 349–54. https://doi.org/10.1176/appi.focus.20190023

Polowy, C., & Gorenberg, C. (2011). *Client confidentiality and privileged communications*. National Association of Social Workers.

Pope, K. S. (n.d.). *Ethical standards & practice guidelines for assessment, therapy, counseling, & forensic practice*. http://kspope.com/ethcodes/

Pope, K. S., & Keith-Spiegel, P. (2008). A practical approach to boundaries in psychotherapy: Making decisions, bypassing blunders, and mending fences. *Journal of Clinical Psychology, 64*(5), 638–52.

Posluns, K., & Gall, T. L. (2020). Dear mental health practitioners, take care of yourselves: A literature review on self-care. *International Journal for the Advancement of Counselling, 42*, 1–20. https://doi.org/10.1007/s10447-019-09382-w

Preston, P. (2013). Parents with disabilities. In J. H. Stone & M. Blouin (Eds.), *International encyclopedia of rehabilitation*. Center for International

Rehabilitation Research and Exchange. https://web.archive.org/web/
20130120113544/http://cirrie.buffalo.edu/encyclopedia/en/article/36/

Psychotherapy Finances. (2003). Legal issues: Child custody and sex claims
trigger more malpractice suits. *Psychotherapy Finances, 29*(9), 1–3. https://
web.archive.org/web/20031217093118/http://www.psychotherapyfinances
.com/articles/090301.htm

Pugh, R. (2007). Dual relationships: Personal and professional boundaries in
rural social work. *The British Journal of Social Work, 37*(8), 1405–23.

Rachels, J. (1980). Can ethics provide the answers? *Hastings Center Report, 10*(3),
32–41.

Rachels, J. (2003). *The elements of moral philosophy* (4th ed.). McGraw-Hill.

Rawls, J. (1999). *Theory of justice* (2th ed). Harvard University Press.

Reamer, F. G. (2001). *Tangled relationships: Managing boundary issues in the human
services*. Columbia University Press.

Reamer, F. G. (2016). *The complexities of client privacy, confidentiality, and privileged
information*. Social Work Today. https://www.socialworktoday.com/news/
eoe_0216.shtml

Reamer, F. G. (2018). *Social work values and ethics* (5th ed.). Columbia University
Press. https://doi.org/10.7312/ream18828

Reamer, F. G. (2019a). Boundary issues and dual relationships in social
work. In S. M. Marson & R. E. McKinney (Eds.), *The Routledge handbook of
social work ethics and values* (1st ed., pp. 157–64). Routledge. https://doi
.org/10.4324/9780429438813-21

Reamer, F. G. (2019b). Ethical theories and social work practice. In S. M. Marson
& R. E. McKinney (Eds.), *The Routledge handbook of social work ethics and values*
(1st ed., pp. 15–21). Routledge. https://doi.org/10.4324/9780429438813-3

Reamer, F.G. (2021a). *Ethics and risk management in online and distance behavioral
health*. Cognella, Inc. https://bookshelf.vitalsource.com/books/832381A

Reamer, F. G. (2021b). Ethical issues in supervision. In K. O'Donoghue
& L. Engelbrecht (Eds.), *The Routledge international handbook of
social work supervision* (1st ed., pp. 294-305). Routledge. https://doi
.org/10.4324/9780429285943

Richards, D. F. (2003). The central role of informed consent in ethical treatment
and research with children. In W. O'Donohue & K. Ferguson (Eds.), *Handbook
of professional ethics for psychologists* (pp. 377–90). Sage.

Roby, J., & White, H. (2010). Adoption activities on the internet: A call for
regulation. *Social Work, 55*(3), 203–12. https://doi.org/10.1093/sw/55.3.203

Rooney, R. H. (Ed.). (2009). *Strategies for work with involuntary clients* (2nd ed.).
Columbia University Press.

Rossiter, A., de Boer, C., Narayan, J., Razack, N., Scollay, V., & Gillette, C. (1998).
Toward an alternative account of feminist practice ethics in mental health.
Affilia: Journal of Women in Social Work, 13, 9–22.

Rowling, J. K. (1997). *Harry Potter and the sorcerer's stone*. Scholastic.

Saint Luke's Health System. (2013). *Sample consent form*. https://web.archive.org/web/20130909183043/http://www.saintlukeshealthsystem.org/sites/default/files/files/Research/IRB%20forms/CONSENT%20Form%20Sample.doc

Samuels, J. (2018). *Adoption in the digital age*. Palgrave Macmillan. https://doi.org/10.1007/978-3-319-70413-5_

Sanders, S., Jacobson, J. M., & Ting, L. (2008). Preparing for the inevitable: Training social workers to cope with client suicide. *Journal of Teaching in Social Work*, *28*(1–2), 1–18.

Sauer, H. (2017). *Moral judgements as educated intuitions*. MIT Press.

Scarth, S. (2004). *Straight talk about photolisting*. Adoption Council of Canada. https://web.archive.org/web/20101116142944/http://www.adoption.ca/news/050101edphoto0403.htm

Schacht, T. E. (1992). Response to: When a patient commits suicide. *American Journal of Psychiatry*, *149*(2), 282.

Schalatek, L. (2020). *The invisible coronavirus makes systemic gender inequalities and injustices visible*. Heinrich-Böll-Stiftung. https://us.boell.org/en/2020/04/30/invisible-coronavirus-makes-systemic-gender-inequalities-and-injustices-visible

Schank, J. A., & Skovholt, T. M. (1997). Dual relationship dilemmas of rural and small-community psychologists. *Professional Psychology: Research and Practice*, *28*(1), 44–49.

Schuerger, K. (2002). *Information packet: Child-specific recruitment*. National Resource Center for Foster Care and Permanency Planning at the Hunter College School of Social Work. http://www.hunter.cuny.edu/socwork/nrcfcpp/downloads/information_packets/child-specific-recruitment-pkt.pdf

Sendor, V. F., & O'Connor, P. M. (1997). *Hospice and palliative care: Questions and answers*. Scarecrow Press.

Simon, R. I. (1999). Therapist–patient sex: from boundary violations to sexual misconduct. *Psychiatric Clinics of North America*, *22*(1), 31–47.

Sinclair, C., Simon, N. P., & Pettifor, J. L. (1996). The history of ethical codes and licensure. In L. J. Bass, S. T. DeMers, J. R. P. Ogloff, C. Peterson, J. L. Pettifor, R. P. Reaves et al. (Eds.), *Professional conduct and discipline in psychology* (pp. 1–15). American Psychological Association & Association of State and Provincial Psychology Boards.

Singh, K. (2021, November 10). *Sikh ethics sees self-centredness as the source of human evil*. Psyche. https://psyche.co/ideas/sikh-ethics-sees-self-centredness-as-the-source-of-human-evil

Skloot, R. (2010). *The immortal life of Henrietta Lacks*. Crown Publishers.

Smith, D. (2003). Ten ways practitioners can avoid frequent ethical pitfalls. *APA Monitor*, *34*(1), 50.

Spandler, H., Burman, E., Goldberg, B., Margison, F., & Amos, T. (2000). A double edged sword: Understanding gifts in psychotherapy. *European Journal of Psychotherapy, Counseling and Health*, *3*(1), 77–101.

Sparrow, T., & Hutchinson, A. (Eds.). (2013). *A history of habit: From Aristotle to Bourdieu*. Lexington Books

Spohn, W. C. (2000). Conscience and moral development. *Theological Studies*, *61*(1), 122–38.

Staller, K. M., & Kirk, S. A. (1997). Unjust freedom: The ethics of client self-determination in runaway youth shelters. *Child & Adolescent Social Work Journal*, *14*(3), 223–42.

Stefan, S. (n.d.). *HIPAA facts: Parent and minor rights*. United Civil Rights Councils of America. http://unitedcivilrights.org/members/HIPAA/HIPAA-parent-info1.pdf

Steinman, S. O., Richardson, N. F., & McEnroe, T. (1998). The ethical decision-making manual for helping professionals. Brooks/Cole.

Stern, M., & Johnson, J. (2010). Just noticeable difference. *Corsini Encyclopedia of Psychology*, 1–2.

Stewart, A. J., & Valian, V. (2018, July 19). *Recruiting diverse and excellent new faculty*. Inside Higher Ed. https://www.insidehighered.com/advice/2018/07/19/advice-deans-department-heads-and-search-committees-recruiting-diverse-faculty

Strom, K. J. (2021). Managing human resources and personnel practices in nonprofit organizations. In R. L. Edwards & P. A. Kurzman (Eds.), *Leading and managing nonprofit organizations* (pp. 99–137). National Association of Social Workers.

Strom-Gottfried, K. J. (1999). Professional boundaries: An analysis of violations by social workers. *Families in Society: The Journal of Contemporary Human Services*, *80*(5), 439–49.

Strom-Gottfried, K. J. (2005). Ethical practice in rural environments. In L. Ginsberg (Ed.), *Social work in rural communities* (4th ed., pp. 141–55). Council on Social Work Education.

Strom-Gottfried, K. J., & Mowbray, N. D. (2006). Who heals the helper? Facilitating the social worker's grief. *Families in Society*, *87*(1), 9–15. https://doi.org/10.1606/1044-3894.3479

Strom-Gottfried, K. J. (2008) *The ethics of practice with minors: High stakes, hard choices*. Lyceum Books.

Strom-Gottfried, K. J. (2019). Ethical action in challenging times. In S. M. Marson & R. E. McKinney (Eds.), *The Routledge handbook of social work ethics and values* (1st ed., pp. 65–72). Routledge. https://doi.org/10.4324/9780429438813-10

Swanson, J. W., Swartz, M. S., Ferron, J., Elbogen, E. B., & Van Dorn, R. A. (2006). Psychiatric advance directives among public mental health consumers in five U.S. cities: Prevalence, demand, and correlates. *Journal of the American Academy of Psychiatry & Law*, *34*(1), 43–57.

Thomas, L. J., & Scharp, K. M. (2017). "A family for every child": Discursive constructions of "ideal" adoptive families in online foster adoption photolistings that promote adoption of children from foster care. *Adoption Quarterly, 20*(1), 44–64. https://doi.org/10.1080/10926755.2016.1263261

Tillman, J. G. (2008). When a patient commits suicide: An empirical study of psychoanalytic clinicians. *The International Journal of Psychoanalysis, 87*(1), 159–77.

Toft, J. (2010). The political act of public talk: How legislators justified welfare reform. *Social Service Review, 84*(2), 563–96.

Tropman, J. (1997). Obstacles to and guidelines for working together in community development. In *Successful community leadership: A skills guide for volunteers and professionals* (pp. 3–13). NASW Press.

TRT World. (2021, June 21). *Explained: Canada's "cultural genocide" of Indigenous people.* https://www.trtworld.com/magazine/explained-canada-s-cultural-genocide-of-indigenous-people-47835

Truog, R. D., Kesselheim, A. S., & Joffe, S. (2012). Paying patients for their tissue: The legacy of Henrietta Lacks. *Science, 337*(6), 37–38.

Tymchuk, A., & Faulds, P. (2004). Serving as an expert witness on intellectual disabilities and parenting in the Alberta Involuntary Sterilization Class Action. *Journal of Intellectual Disability Research, 48,* 461.

U.S. Commission on Civil Rights. (2001, April 13). *Statement of U.S. Commission on the use of Native American images and nicknames as sports symbols.* http://www.usccr.gov/press/archives/2001/041601st.htm

U.S. Department of Health and Human Services (DDHS). (2003a). *HIPAA administrative simplification.* https://www.hhs.gov/sites/default/files/ocr/privacy/hipaa/administrative/combined/hipaa-simplification-201303.pdf

U.S. Department of Health and Human Services (DHHS). (2003b, April 14). *Protecting the privacy of patients' health information.* https://web.archive.org/web/20131202162612/http://www.hhs.gov/ocr/privacy/hipaa/news/2003/privacyfactsapril03.pdf

U.S. Department of Health and Human Services. (2020). For professionals: The HIPAA privacy rule. https://www.hhs.gov/guidance/document/professionals-hipaa-privacy-rule

University of Calgary. (2013). *Aboriginal students.* http://www.ucalgary.ca/admissions/process/aboriginal

Van Hoose, W. H., & Paradise, L. V. (1979). *Ethics in counseling and psychotherapy: Perspectives in issues and decision-making.* Carroll Press.

Veilleux, J. C. (2011). Coping with client death: Using a case study to discuss the effects of accidental, undetermined, and suicidal deaths on therapists. *Professional Psychology: Research and Practice, 42*(3), 222–28

Velasquez, C., Andre, T., Shanks, T., & Meyer, M. (2014). Thinking ethically: A framework for moral decision-making. Markkula Center for Applied Ethics. https://www.scu.edu/mcae/publications/iie/v7n1/thinking

Voce, A., Cecco, L., & Michael, C. (2021, September 6). "Cultural genocide": The shameful history of Canada's residential schools—mapped. *The Guardian.*

https://www.theguardian.com/world/ng-interactive/2021/sep/06/canada-residential-schools-indigenous-children-cultural-genocide-map

Weinberg, M. (2009). Moral distress: A missing but relevant concept for ethics in social work. *Canadian Social Work Review, 26*(2), 139–69.

Weinberg, M., & Fine, M. (2020). Racisms and microaggression in social work: The experience of racialized practitioners in Canada. *Journal of Ethnic & Cultural Diversity in Social Work* 31(2). https://doi.org/10.1080/15313204.2020.1839614

Weir, K. (2013). *Feel like a fraud?* American Psychological Association. https://www.apa.org/gradpsych/2013/11/fraud

Weiss, K. G., & Lasky, N. V. (2017). Mandatory reporting of sexual misconduct at college: A critical perspective. *Journal of School Violence, 16*(3), 259–70. https://doi.org/10.1080/15388220.2017.1318575

Wetzel, D. (2012, April 3). *ND court won't block Fighting Sioux name election.* San Diego Union Tribune. https://www.sandiegouniontribune.com/sdut-nd-court-wont-block-fighting-sioux-name-election-2012apr03-story.html

Wilkins, D. (2017). How is supervision recorded in child and family social work: An analysis of 244 written records of formal supervision. *Child and Family Social Work, 22*(1) 1130–40.

Wurst, F., Mueller, S., Petitjean, S., Euler, S., Thon, N., Wiesbeck, G., & Wolfersdorf, M. (2010). Patient suicide: A survey of therapists' reactions. *Suicide and Life Threatening Behavior, 40*(4), 328–36.

Yale University. (2022). *Break glass procedure: Granting emergency access to critical ePHI systems.* Yale HIPAA Privacy Office. https://hipaa.yale.edu/security/break-glass-procedure-granting-emergency-access-critical-ephi-systems

Yonan, J., Bardick, A. D., & Willment, J.-A. H. (2011). Ethical decision making, therapeutic boundaries, and communicating using online technology and cellular phones. *Canadian Journal of Counselling and Psychotherapy, 45*(4), 307–26. https://files.eric.ed.gov/fulltext/EJ956975.pdf

Young, J. R. (2003). Researchers charge racial bias on the SAT. *The Chronicle of Higher Education, 50*(7), A34.

Zerden, L. D., Cruden, G., Lombardi, B. M., Grove, L. R., Patel, S. V., & Powell, B. J. (2019). The implementation of integrated behavioral health models. In S. Gehlert & T. Browne (Eds.), *Handbook of health social work* (3rd ed., pp. 189–208). https://doi.org/10.1002/9781119420743.ch9

Zerden, L. D., Lombardi, B. M., & Jones, A. (2019). Social workers in integrated health care: Improving care throughout the life course. *Social Work in Health Care, 58*(1), 142–49. https://doi.org/10.1080/00981389.2019.1553934

Zsolnai, L. (1998). Rational choice and the diversity of choices. *Journal of Socio-economics, 27*(5), 613–22.

Zuckerman, E. L. & Keeley, K. (2017). *The paper office for the digital age.* Guilford.

Zur, O. (2013). Subpoenas and how to handle them: Guidelines for psychotherapists and counselors. *The Zur Institute.* http://www.zurinstitute.com/subpoena.html#quash

INDEX